Detroit Lions

Great Teams' Great Years

Detroit Lions

by Jerry Green

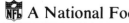 A National Football League Book

Macmillan Publishing Co., Inc.

New York

Collier Macmillan Publishers

London

A National Football League Book
Prepared by Creative Services Division, National Football League Properties, Inc.
Publisher: *David Boss.*
Editor: *John Wiebusch.*
Managing Editor: *Tom Bennett.*
Associate Editors: *Patricia Cross,*
          Doug Kelly.
Art Director: *Bill Von Torne.*
Production Manager: *Patrick McKee.*
Production Staff: *Amy Yutani, Rob Meneilly.*
Executive Director: *Jack Wrobbel.*

Macmillan Publishing Co., Inc., 866 Third Avenue, New
York, N.Y. 10022. Collier-Macmillan Canada Ltd., Toronto,
Ontario

Library of Congress Catalog Card Number: 73-2757
First Printing 1973
Printed in the United States of America

Contents

Introduction

Every club in professional football possesses its own distinctive character, which is immediately recognized by the football public.

The Detroit Lions have always been a team which had character, and characters.

Since their inception in 1934, the Lions have won four NFL championships — in 1935, 1952, 1953 and 1957. The Lions have challenged for the top more often than that, however, placing second 14 times in their first 39 years.

The chief protagonist in the history of the Lions would have to be a blond, swashbuckling Texan with a gutteral voice, an ample stomach and a proclivity for leadership. Bobby Layne was his name. He was the leader, from his arrival in Detroit in 1950 until his exit in 1958.

In those years — the Lions' Great Years — Detroit won three National Football League championships. The Lions had lots of fun winning them. Bobby Layne orchestrated the winning and the laughter. He was a bounder who enjoyed having a good time, and could play the next day with very little sleep.

The Lions became a team when Bobby Layne joined them in 1950. Rookies and rivals feared him, veteran teammates followed him.

Buddy Parker was the dour coach who built the Lions into champions — and then left them at a public banquet during training camp in a moment of pique. It was not an atypical departure of a coach from the Lions. The coaching changes, which happen to every pro team, were a manifestation of the Lions' character. They were noisy and at times acrimonious. Seldom were they routine.

The Lions date back to 1934, when an impoverished franchise in Portsmouth, Ohio, was moved to Detroit. The Lions were headed for a championship that first season — until a late-season collapse. From the start the Lions established the identity that would stick with them through four decades. They were a good second-place team capable of contending for a division title, but usually not good enough to win it. The only times they were good enough were 1935, 1952, 1953, 1954 and 1957. All these teams, except the 1954 club, followed by winning championship games.

Earl (Dutch) Clark was the Lions' first star, and even he was something of a resolute individualist. He became coach and later quit in a dispute with the owner, a flamboyant radio man, G.A. Richards.

The Lions of the 1940s were a dismal team, but they had some superb players — Byron (Whizzer) White, who became a Supreme Court justice, Frank Sinkwich and Bill Dudley. In the 1950s came Layne, Doak Walker and Joe Schmidt, who one day would be head coach.

The '50s were the glory era. Television introduced the sport of pro football to the nation. The game flourished. The Detroit Lions were the epitome of the booming game, and Layne was the sport's most famous character.

Detroit is an industrial town. Automobiles are made there and the auto workers are sports addicts. When the Lions started winning with Layne in the early 1950s, pro football became a blazing success in Detroit after 16 years of inertia. It caught on a little earlier there than in most other cities. Detroiters may have been the nation's first pro football sophisticates.

And they thrived on the controversies stirred up by the Lions, by Layne and Buddy Parker . . . and later by Alex Karras.

The Lions have a rich heritage as one of pro football's old line, establishment teams. They have had great years and they have had great men. And they have not gone unloved.

The Great Years

The Lions traded Bobby Layne away on a Monday, an ironic day for such a banishment. Mondays were the days when Bobby Layne gathered the Lions together for the simple purpose of having fun. He did it through eight football seasons . . . eight seasons which encompassed the team's greatest years.

Rogues and renegades, introspective and independent, Layne assembled them en masse for a Monday afternoon of revelry and camaraderie. It happened every week during the autumns of the 1950s. It was a private team thing . . . in the Stadium Bar, from which other regular patrons would be shooed outside for the duration. Occasionally, the festivities would be transferred to elsewhere.

The athletes would sit around tables and drink some and sing some bawdy ditties. And they would talk with lingering pleasure of their victories on Sunday. Sometimes — and it didn't happen too often — there was a defeat which had to be drowned out and forgotten.

Layne was the spirit leader. It was he who goaded and cajoled them to victory on Sunday with sheer bravado. When he had to, he consoled them in their defeat. Bobby's Monday parties rarely were wakes. He spoke in a low, Texan's drawl — a gravel-voiced demigod who could perform miraculous deeds on a football field. Seldom did he raise the volume of his voice. The men who played with him had faith that he could do anything.

When he came to Detroit in 1950, the Lions ended a long era of defeat and inertia. The beginning of an era of victory — three NFL championships plus a fourth divisional title — coincided with his arrival.

Only once did the Monday event become a wake. On that Monday, two games into the 1958 NFL schedule, the Layne era ended with stark abruptness. Quickly, permanently, cruelly, decisively. The Lions' Great Years ended exactly as they had started — with a trade involving Bobby Layne.

Grown men, his comrades, cursed. Some wept in shock and anguish. Bobby was gone, cashiered, dispatched into exile to the Pittsburgh Steelers. He was traded for the cheap price of a young quarterback, Earl Morrall, and some draft choices.

"I'm sick," said Joe Schmidt, who had joined the Lions as a lesser draft choice and became the greatest middle linebacker and the club's captain during these years. "They traded away the guy who made pro football in Detroit."

Bobby Layne — the dominant quarterback in his colorful age — was gone from Detroit that Monday night on a Pittsburgh-bound airplane.

After the Lions won NFL championships in 1952 and 1953, *Time* magazine featured Bobby Layne on its cover. *Time* correlated the rapid growth in popularity and the increased glamorization of the sport of professional football. with Bobby Layne.

Eulogized *Time* in its staccato prose:

"Of all the pro teams, the best (for the last three seasons) is the Detroit Lions. And the best of all the Lions, the best quarterback in the world, is Robert Lawrence Layne, a blond, bandy-legged Texan with a prairie squint in his narrow blue eyes and an unathletic paunch puffing his ample frame (6 ft. 1 in., 195 lbs.). Layne, a T-formation specialist, led the Lions out of the National Football League's cellar, called the plays and fired the passes that won them the championship in 1952 and 1953."

Throughout the 1940s, Detroit was the NFL's Appalachia. There were two ownership changes — and there was a seemingly constant turnover of head coaches. The Lions, plainly, were a haphazard organization. In 1948, a syndicate of prominent Detroit businessmen and sportsmen purchased the franchise for $165,000. The new owners hired Alvin (Bo)

The man who preceded Buddy Parker as head coach of the Detroit Lions was Alvin (Bo) McMillin (center), shown here with his assistant coaches for the 1949 season, Tim Timerario (left) and George Wilson. Parker joined this staff as backfield coach in 1950 and at the end of the season replaced McMillin as head coach.

McMillin, famed member of Centre College's Prayin' Colonels and then coach at Indiana, as their head coach and general manager. He signed a five-year contract.

That same year, in hopes of ending the Lions' years of travail, a quarterback was drafted. He was Y.A. Tittle, from Louisiana State. Tittle immediately rebuffed the Lions and signed with the Baltimore Colts of the rival All-America Conference.

In the same draft, Pittsburgh selected a young passer-runner from Texas, Bobby Layne. Layne did not care to go to the Steelers, because they still used the obsolescent single wing as their basic offense. So he was traded to the Chicago Bears of George Halas. In Chicago, Layne, the rookie, languished on the bench, a reserve behind Sid Luckman and Johnny Lujack. Halas scanned his payroll and decided $15,000 was much too much to waste on a benchwarmer.

So he peddled Layne to the inept New York Bulldogs, who had no quarterback. The sale price was $50,000 of singer Kate Smith's cash and the Bulldogs' No. 1 draft choices for the 1949 and 1950 seasons.

In New York, Layne became the first string quarterback. He suffered through a 1-10-1 season in 1949 — and swore never to return. Even Broadway lost its lure to Bobby.

"What a nightmare," Layne said. "I weighed 205 pounds when I reported and when the season was over I weighed 176. At the end of 1949 I was ready to give up football."

After the 1949 season, the All-America Conference went under. The Cleveland, San Francisco and Baltimore franchises were absorbed into the NFL with Baltimore, quarterbacked by Tittle, surviving one season before it folded. McMillin hoped to obtain a fresh quarterback from the AAC. But he was foiled. So McMillin turned to the Bulldogs (who were to become the New York Yanks and

eventually the new NFL Baltimore club). He acquired the disenchanted Bobby Layne for Camp Wilson and more than $50,000. When Wilson quit rather than go to New York, the Lions sent Bob Mann there in his place.

The losers' syndrome had been perpetuated under McMillin. His first two seasons, 1948 and 1949, the Lions had a collective 6-18 record. He was cranky and disliked by a number of his players. His 1950 club went 6-6 with its new quarterback. But at the end of the season, in something of a palace coup, McMillin was fired. Two years remained on his lucrative five-year contract. The Lions' owners, dismayed at the unnecessary expense, paid McMillin off. It cost them $60,000. They vowed never again to give a coach a contract for more than one season.

Raymond (Buddy) Parker, McMillin's backfield coach, was the owners' choice as the next head coach. Parker was given a one-year contract for 1951. His elevation was loudly applauded by the players.

But McMillin did provide a legacy for Parker. It was the hard nucleus for a team which in two years would win the NFL championship.

McMillin's coaching legacy was several of the integral members of the club which won the championship in 1952. It was he who traded for Layne. He also traded for Cloyce Box, who caught 15 touchdown passes in the 1952 championship season. Bob Hoernschemeyer, Bob Smith and Lou Creekmur were obtained by McMillin from the pot of players available from the disbanded All-America Conference franchises. In other deals, McMillin acquired John Prchlik from the Bulldogs and Jim Cain from the Chicago Cardinals. He picked up Dick Flanagan, discarded by the Bears. Ollie Cline was obtained from the Giants.

And in 1950, two of McMillin's prize draftees joined the Lions, each a winner of the Heisman, — Doak Walker from Southern Methodist and

Leon Hart from Notre Dame. Another product of that same draft conducted by McMillin was huge Thurman (Fum) McGraw, from Colorado A&M.

These athletes pushed the Lions to their 6-6 record in 1950. It was the first non-losing season in five years. They were players passed on to Parker in 1951 – to become members of championship teams in 1952 and 1953.

Bobby Layne's favorite receiver in the championship year of 1952 was Cloyce Box. Box was a fellow Texan, tall and with speed. He had been a running back and McMillin converted him to a pass receiver. Box joined the Lions in 1948 for the sum of $250. He was pressed onto McMillin by George Preston Marshall, who was not before reputed to be munificent – as owner of the Washington Redskins.

Marshall had phoned McMillin in April of 1948 – three months after the Lions' change-over in management.

"Bo, you need help and we've got a player who'll improve your ball club," said Marshall. "He's a big, tough rookie halfback from West Texas State who's never played anything other than the single wing. We're running from the T so we can't use him. But he'll fit right into your offense.

"Believe me, Bo, the kid's a great prospect and we'll give him to you."

George Preston Marshall hesitated while McMillin had time to reflect, then bite at the baited hook.

"We'll give him to you, Bo, for only $500."

McMillin was a suspicious man – and new to the pros. He nonetheless had heard of the wily George Preston Marshall. He was not about to allow himself to be hornswoggled after three months on his new job.

"George," responded McMillin, "our scouts know Box. He's a powerful kid, but he's awfully clumsy. He needs a lot of polishing.

That $500 figure is way too high. But we might be able to go to $250."

"Sold," blurted Marshall. "You've bought yourself a player."

So Box became the first of the castoffs who would populate the 1952 NFL champions of Buddy Parker.

Parker had been a player himself for the Lions in 1935 when they won their first championship in their second season in Detroit. A fine runner, he scored a touchdown in the Lions' 26-7 championship game conquest of the Giants. Two years later he was traded to the Chicago Cardinals. He became an assistant under Jimmy Conzelman there – and honed his innovative, intelligent football mind. In 1949, Parker was head coach of the Cardinals, a powerful club just starting a steep decline. The Cardinals were humbled 52-21 by the Bears in their '49 finale. In the locker room, Buddy Parker said he was unfit to be a head coach – and then he quit.

"Man for man the Cardinals are a much better team than the Bears," Parker said. "When you have superior personnel and get beat by 31 points, something must be wrong with the coaching. I guess I'm not good enough to be a head coach in this league, so I'm quitting. Right now."

A month later, he met with Edwin J. Anderson, the brewmaster president of the Lions, and McMillin. They hired him as the Lions' backfield coach under McMillin for 1950.

Days after the Lions ended their 1950 season at .500, there was a secret meeting at the Book-Cadillac Hotel in Detroit. One of the owners gathered several players – Layne, Box, Doak Walker and some others. There were printed reports that Layne issued an ultimatum that he would not play another season for McMillin. Layne says this was untrue. But the owner-member of the Lions' board of directors

asked the players what could be done to transform the club into a winning team. The Lions had won only 12 games in three seasons under McMillin. Fan apathy kept attendance low. The players clamored for Parker as their new head coach.

"We can win with him," said Layne.

It was tantamount to a players' uprising. There was considerable resentment against McMillin. McMillin was paid off and Parker became coach. W. Nicholas Kerbawy, the dynamic public relations director of the Lions, was elevated to general manager, assuming that half of McMillin's dual job.

Years before George Allen would become romanticized as a trading genius — a collector of rejected fossil football players — Buddy Parker adopted this rather unorthodox procurement method.

"What this club needs," said Parker upon being elevated to a job that he had called himself unfit to perform in Chicago, "is a good fullback. Some big guy who can make yardage and block for Layne. Trouble is I've been checking the college rookies coming up this fall and nobody on our draft list looks like a real good blocker. Guess we'll have to make a trade with somebody."

So Parker telephoned Paul Brown, coach of the then NFL champion Browns. Parker wanted Emerson Cole, who didn't play much fullback behind Marion Motley in Cleveland. Brown was amenable to trading Cole to the Lions.

"You know, Buddy, your team is a little thin at tackle, too," said Brown. "Suppose we make a deal and give you Cole and one of our first string tackles. You can give us a halfback — say, Doak Walker."

Parker laughed. "We're not interested in trading a layer cake for two doughnuts," he told Brown.

But the fullback problem pestered Parker.

The Lions had finished fourth in the NFL West with material Parker believed could be in contention in 1951.

"The only way we can improve," he told his staff, "is to keep all the good men we've got and pick up some more good men. That means we'll simply have to make trades with next year's players."

So Parker started wheeling and dealing the Lions' draft choices. First, he called Paul Brown back. Parker surrendered the Lions' first choice in the 1952 draft to the Browns for Jim Martin. Martin was a versatile ex-Marine who could play defensive end, linebacker, center and could also placekick.

"Martin can help us right now, in 1951," said Parker, explaining his philosophy. "That draft choice can't help us until next year, if the guy can then. We want to win this year. We need defensive ends and Martin is as good as they come."

Martin was needed to play defensive end since Jim Cain had been called to Army duty.

"The Browns have extra ends and they were willing to trade one outside their division," said Parker. "Naturally we asked for Martin. He had an excellent season for the Browns when they won the championship last fall."

In training camp in 1951 at Michigan Normal College in Ypsilanti, there were two other veterans acquired by Parker. He picked up Vince Banonis, an all-pro when the Cardinals won the championship in 1947, to play center. With Box recalled into the Marines for Korean War duty, Parker obtained Bill Swiacki, the old Columbia hero, from the Giants to catch some of Layne's passes. Three rookies were prominent in camp — Jack Christiansen, Dorne Dibble and LaVern Torgeson.

Three weeks before the opening of the 1951 season, Pat Harder, the old fullback during the Cardinals' championship and Western Division

title seasons of 1947 and 1948, canceled retirement plans. Parker had been with the Cardinals then and was partial to Harder. He envisioned Harder as the solution to Detroit's fullback situation. The fact that Harder's knees were questionable did not dissuade Parker.

"Don't worry about Harder," Parker informed club president Anderson. "I coached Harder with the Cardinals. He's got a watery right knee that swells up every game. He hobbles around almost all week, but he's always out there gaining his yardage on Sunday afternoon. He's the best blocking fullback in pro football. If he stays healthy, we can win the championship."

So Parker telephoned Chicago and made an offer for the unretired old warrior. Curly Lambeau, the Cardinals' coach, believed Harder's chronic knee maladies had finished his career. The Cardinals accepted John Panelli and the Lions' No. 2 draft choice in 1952 for Pat Harder.

Parker had traded away the Lions' first two draft choices for 1952. But he had a complete team, worthy of title contention, for 1951. The Lions' front office — consisting of conventional business people unwise in the vagaries of football personnel roulette — complained mildly of Parker's gambling with the future. He assuaged them by pointing to the strongest running backfield in pro football.

The Lions now had Harder from the Cardinals, Hunchy Hoernschemeyer from the Brooklyn Dodgers of the defunct AAC, and Doak Walker in the same backfield. Harder and Walker had been NFL scoring champions the previous two years. Bobby Layne was ecstatic. A running threat himself, he had the running game necessary to make his passing game more operational. The starting backfield consisted of great talent — 75 percent of which had been cast away by other clubs.

Harder completed the unit in Parker's estimation. He added mainly the quality of toughness Parker felt the Lions had lacked.

"When somebody slugged on the first play of a game, Harder's eyes would light up like he was saying, 'Oh, it's going to be like that,'" Parker said.

When Harder showed up with the 1951 season nearing, he was asked whether he was in fit condition.

"I'll be all right as soon as I get my elbows sharpened up," Harder responded.

A championship was forecast for Detroit by the new coach on the eve of the 1951 season. The prophecy was premature. The Lions were much improved — and so was their *esprit de corps* under Parker. They challenged in the West and were close. Their challenge went into the final game — as it would six times in seven years. But at the end, the Lions were a half-game short. Parker would have to indulge in more trades before the Lions developed genuine championship fiber.

Despite the frustration at the finish, the 1951 season was the most pleasurable for the Lions since the 1930s. It was successful artistically and financially — true foreshadowing of accomplishments to come. Pro football was just starting its colossal boom. Detroit became one of the first boom cities, and the populace accepted pro football on a level equal to professional baseball.

Parker always seemed to have some homilies to drop on his players in the tense moments in pregame locker rooms.

One of these was "Good teams don't lose close games." The Lions heard it moments before they opened their 1951 season at Briggs Stadium, their home field, against the Washington Redskins. The Lions were better than anticipated. They battered the Redskins 35-17 — and it hardly was a close game.

He led the Lions only three years, but Bo McMillin advanced the team to a .500 record in 1950 and left a cadre of talent for his successor, Buddy Parker. Among them were (left to right) two Heisman Trophy winners, Doak Walker and 6-5, 265-pound Leon Hart; Bob Hoernschemeyer, who set a club record when he gained 198 yards rushing in a 1950 game, and Cloyce Box, who would move from halfback to end on his return in 1952 from a year's Marine duty. Others passed on to Parker: Les Bingaman, Lou Creekmur, Thurman McGraw, John Prchlik – and Bobby Layne. To add to all this talent, Parker traded with the Chicago Cardinals for a sturdy fullback, Pat Harder (right).

But all the preseason propaganda about the Lions' championship potential had not yet sunk in to the city. The stadium was half filled.

Next week the score wasn't close again. Layne had a happy hour against the New York Yanks, the amalgam of the old Bulldogs and the old New York Yankees from the AAC. This time the score was 37-10 – and only 24,194 cash customers – more than 3,000 less than the week before – showed up.

But two lopsided victories whetted the civic appetite for the third game, against the fearsome Los Angeles Rams. The Rams had lost to the Browns 30-28 in the 1950 championship game. They had Bob Waterfield, Norm Van Brocklin, Elroy Hirsch, Deacon Dan Towler and Glenn Davis. It was an event worth attending – and 50,567 of the curious did to determine for themselves whether the Lions had genuine mettle. The Lions lost 27-21.

The defeat sent the Lions into a swoon. The Yanks, whom they had clobbered two weeks previous, tied them 24-24. Then the Bears upset the Lions 28-23.

Parker's preseason prophecy seemed faint now. The Lions were 2-2-1, dragging, trying to hold onto third while the Bears were first and the Rams second.

It was then that Parker, Layne, Harder, Hoernschemeyer and Co. rallied the Lions to a four-game winning streak. They beat the Packers 24-17, then the first-place Bears 41-28, then the Philadelphia Eagles 28-10. On Thanksgiving, when tradition prescribed a pro game in Detroit before the carving of the turkey, the Lions beat the Packers again 52-35.

Quite unexpectedly, the Lions were in first place in the West. They had been in a triple tie with the Bears and Rams until Thanksgiving noontime. The following Sunday the Lions received help from two outside sources. The Redskins beat the Rams and the Browns

stopped the Bears. With a 6-2-1 record, the Lions were a half-game ahead of the Rams and Bears, both with 6-3 records.

The final home game was against San Francisco before 45,757. It was a miserable day and the Lions fell from first place with a 20-10 loss.

The Rams were now their only opposition, though, since the Bears also collapsed. The Lions could win the division by beating the Rams and 49ers in their last two games on the West Coast. They had lost 12 successive games to the Rams. Their last victory had been in 1944, when the Rams played in Cleveland.

In 1951, the Rams would win their third straight Western title if they defeated the tormented Lions in the Coliseum on December 9.

It was a dramatic, inspired football game played before 67,892 fans, the largest crowd ever to see the Lions.

It was Bobby Layne, still a novice quarterback at 24, vs. Bob Waterfield, veteran of four NFL championship games. The Lions and the Rams exchanged the game lead seven times.

"This is a man's game," said Layne. "You have to grow into a man to play it right. A quarterback takes about three years before he knows halfway what's going on. You never really learn this damn game."

This was the day of the first episode in the legend of Bobby Layne, who could march his team downfield against the expiring clock, advancing the football with élan.

The Lions' drive started with the Rams in front 22-17 after Waterfield's record fifth field goal. Only four minutes remained when Woodley Lewis kicked off to the Lions' Don Doll. Doll returned the ball to the 21. With the insouciance of a considerably more mature quarterback, Layne mustered his team deep in its own end of the field.

"Lotsa time," said Layne in that gravelly,

Chapter one of the Bobby Layne story in Detroit was written in the 11th week of the 1951 season at the Los Angeles Coliseum. There he first demonstrated his remarkable capacity for beating both the opposition and the clock. The Rams and Bob Waterfield (right) could win the conference title for the third year in a row with a victory over Detroit. Four minutes remained in the game and the Rams led 22-17 after five field goals by Waterfield. Layne, however, directed the Lions 79 yards and Walker passed to Hart for the winning touchdown, 24-22. Los Angeles won the title, anyway, when a week later the Lions fell victim to a Layne-style drive at San Francisco by Y.A. Tittle (far right).

commanding voice of his. "We're gonna win it."

As if to taunt the Rams, to notify them that the Lions could travel the necessary 79 yards with ease, Layne started the drive with a simple quarterback sneak. The Rams' defense ganged up on him after one yard.

"See, what's the use of hurryin'," said Layne. "Now they expect us to take our time. Now we'll try a pass."

On second down, Layne dropped back, his stomach hanging slightly over his belt line, and passed a wobbler to Bill Swiacki, the end Parker acquired for this very purpose. The gain was 10 yards, to the 32, a first down.

Next Layne tried a little swing pass to Hoernschemeyer, who got hemmed in and trapped after a mere gain of a yard. Imperturbed, Layne called his third passing play in a row.

It was second down again as he dropped back and this time connected with the sprinting Doak Walker to the Rams' 47. In the open field, Doak was the most dangerous athlete in pro football. The gain was 20 yards — and less than three minutes remained.

"We'll make it look like I'm gonna pass again," said Layne in the huddle. "'Cept I'll run. You just block like it's a pass."

With legerdemain, Layne fooled the Rams' defense. He faked a pass, then bootlegged to his left. He was around left end, chugging 25 yards to the Rams' 22. The clock at the deep end of the Coliseum read 2:05.

"Now Doak, Leon, the play we talked about," said Layne in total command in the huddle. "Make it look good."

Walker took Layne's handoff and started his run. Leon Hart moved downfield, as if to throw a block to clear the route for Walker. Suddenly Walker stopped, brought his arm back . . . Hart was still running. The Rams had been slickered. Walker threw the ball and it reached the end zone at the same time as Hart. He caught it. Walker kicked the extra point.

The Lions had beaten the Rams for the first time in the memory of all the victors. The score was 24-22 — in the lexicon of Parker, a close game, the kind good teams don't lose.

So the Lions were again first in the West, with their half-game lead over the Rams. A victory at San Francisco on the final Sunday would do it.

"I figure we can make it now," said Parker in the Coliseum locker room. "Sure, the 49ers beat us last week but we were having our worst day of the season. I don't think they can do it again. This game with the Rams was the big one. The boys, particularly the defense, really dug in to win it. Any time you hold a team like the Rams to one touchdown you've done something."

Waterfield had his five field goals — the most ever kicked by a player in one game at the time. The lead had changed seven times. But in the end it was the Lions and Layne who prevailed.

"That puts us in the driver's seat again," said Vince Banonis, the veteran center Parker had brought over from the Cardinals.

"We still have to beat San Francisco," insisted Les Bingaman, the 300-pound middle guard. "And after that we have to lick Cleveland in the playoff. We'll do our celebrating two weeks from now."

On Monday, Buddy Parker took the Lions north to San Francisco to spend the week in preparation for the game with the 49ers. To keep the concentration on football, Parker billeted the Lions 23 miles north of the city. They stayed in cottages at El Rancho Rafael. Their meals were served commune style, in a team group. Their practices were on an isolated field at Hamilton Air Force Base.

"This is camp at Ypsilanti all over again," said Layne, "except that we don't have to work so hard."

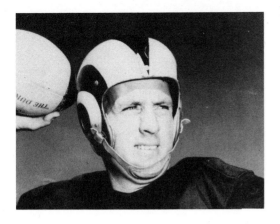 

"It's always good to have the gang living together," said Parker. "That's the reason we'll beat the 49ers."

The Lions had lost three times during the season and all three losses — to the Rams, Bears and 49ers — were home at Briggs Stadium. Their one tie — against the Yankees — also had been at home.

Parker was bound by superstitions and he didn't deny it. He was in a jocular mood one night at El Rancho Rafael and he told Sam Greene of the *Detroit News* a story. It dealt with Parker's belief in the luck of the Irish, specifically in the magical powers of one John Patrick Burke, a moustachioed florist from Beverly Hills. Parker felt Burke was as responsible for the victory over the Rams as Layne, Harder and Walker.

"I first met Burke in 1949 when I was coaching the Cardinals," Parker said. "We were in Los Angeles to play the Rams and Ed Prell of the *Chicago Tribune* was with us. He introduced me to Burke, an old schoolmate of his in Pittsburg, Kansas.

"Since Burke had not bought a ticket for the game I asked him how he would like to sit with the team. He thought it would be quite a thrill. With Burke on the bench, we beat the Rams. On the last play of the game Paul Christman threw a pass to Billy Dewell for a touchdown that pulled us ahead 31-27.

"Last week in Los Angeles I thought of Burke and checked to see if he was still in Beverly Hills. He was and I invited him to sit with us on the bench again. Then Doak passed to Hart to win the game."

Parker reflected and then went on:

"I've invited him to come to San Francisco. But he said he couldn't get away from the flower shop. Maybe we can win this one without him."

On Sunday the Lions needed more than a florist. On Parker's 38th birthday the Lions' season ended in Kezar Stadium.

"We played a good game," Parker said afterwards. "One of our best. It just wasn't good enough. What finally beat us was that runback."

The Lions were within five minutes of beating the 49ers and advancing to the championship game. They led 17-14. But the Lions were forced to punt the ball away. Bob Smith got off a decent punt from behind the Lions' 30. It drove Joe Arenas, the deep return man, into retreat to the 49ers' 27.

Arenas slipped away from the first wave of tacklers, left Lions strewn all around and dashed 55 yards to the Detroit 18 before he was caught from behind.

Y.A. Tittle, the quarterback the Lions had once drafted and lost, huddled the 49ers. Tittle had replaced the veteran Frankie Albert. Tittle sent Joe Perry into the line for four yards. Then he threw for the end zone and the ball struck the goalposts. So he threw deep again and Gordy Soltau caught the ball at the Lions' one-yard line. The defensive line stopped a plunge at the middle.

So on the next play, Tittle bootlegged the ball around end to score. Soltau's conversion put the 49ers in front 21-17 with 3:25 to play.

It was the time when Bobby Layne played with the greatest gusto — his team behind, the clock ticking away.

Layne started from the Lions' 16 on a pass to Leon Hart. Leon lateralled to Jim Martin on a flea-flicker and the play gained 23 yards. The Lions were moving.

Then Layne miscalculated. He hoped to catch the 49ers unprepared for the long pass. It failed. Verl Lillywhite intercepted the bomb — and Tittle ran out the clock.

The Lions lost 21-17 and, in Los Angeles, the Rams won — and edged the Lions for the

divisional crown by a half game, 8-4 to 7-4-1.

The finish was heartbreaking, but the record was the Lions' best since 1945.

The defeat had a sobering effect on the players who moped about the locker room in despair. At last Pat Harder jumped onto a bench and waved a towel. "We'll be back next year to lick the stuffing out of somebody," he yelled.

The party the players had planned to celebrate their title and Parker's birthday was canceled. The chef at the St. Francis had baked a huge birthday cake for the festivities.

One other matter remained. In Detroit, Maurie Schubot, the Lions' ticket manager since the 1930s, made arrangements to open the box office to refund money received for the aborted championship game with the Browns. The Browns were going to Los Angeles to play the Rams instead. And for the first time in their six-year existence, they would lose a championship game the next Sunday 24-17.

After returning from San Francisco, Buddy Parker received plaudits for the marked improvement of the Lions. The acquisition of Harder was hailed as the move which turned the Lions. Harder, it was written, inflamed the Lions with a winning spirit and championship air which became infectious.

Wrote Sam Greene, who was assigned to the Lions for the *Detroit News*:

"Parker promoted harmony on the coaching staff and among the players. If it were left to the Walkers, the Laynes, the Bingamans, the Martins and the Dibbles, they would vote Parker coach of the year.

"Criticism was leveled at Parker, too. From time to time he heard it from the public; less often from the directors with whom Bo McMillin was in frequent disagreement."

And 1951 was the year that the Lions finally gained public acceptance in Detroit. In 1951,

paid attendance jumped more than 100,000 — from 133,331 to 237,161. And when the directors checked the revenue ledgers they found a profit.

Parker's reward was a raise, a continuance of his profit-sharing agreement — and another one-year contract for 1952. He took it, although he would have preferred a longer term. But the directors, after their experience with McMillin, were adamant about their one-year stricture on all coaching contracts. Parker had earned $24,000 in 1951 — half on base pay, the other half from the profit-sharing deal.

Most football coaches would have cautiously decided to maintain a status quo. Parker was radical in this respect. He had no intention of remaining static with a near-title team that could improve within its own natural aging process.

Parker had traded away his top two draft choices for 1952 in the unsuccessful attempt to win the championship in 1951. But he believed a club must also regenerate itself every year with young players.

Despite the vacuum in the first two rounds, and despite the Lions' low position in the draft rotation, Parker drafted exceedingly well in 1952. When he finally had a chance to select on the third round, Parker picked Yale Lary from Texas A&M. The draft went into the 22nd round and Parker picked a tough defensive back named Jim David from Colorado A&M.

And as in the year before, Parker filled in by making trades for veterans. He wanted a reliable backup quarterback for Layne. So he went back to the Cardinals and picked up Jim Hardy for two expendable young players.

On Friday, June 13, there was bad news from Dallas. Doak Walker had gashed his right arm on a jagged car window while attending the U.S. Open golf tournament. Doak would be all right, said the doctors who stitched up his arm,

With the signing of Yale Lary (left) and Jim David in 1952, and the continued good play of Bob Smith (third from left), "Chris' Crew" had been assembled. This was the extraordinary defensive backfield led by Jack Christiansen (right). Lary was the team's third draft choice in 1952; David was the 22nd. Each became a solid regular as a rookie. Smith returned an interception 102 yards for a touchdown against the Chicago Bears in 1949. In addition to being a league leader in interceptions, Christiansen was a devastating punt returner, averaging 21 yards a return in 1952.

but he would miss most of the preseason games.

Parker started looking for another running back to take Walker's place.

Earl (Jug) Girard was discontented playing defensive back for the Packers, despite five pass interceptions in 1951. There was some bickering with Gene Ronzani, the Packers' coach. Jug wanted to be transferred to offense. So Parker offered another obscure player for Girard. The deal was consummated just before the Lions assembled at their 1952 camp in Ypsilanti. Girard would play offense as insurance behind Walker.

There was one other bit of bartering. General manager Kerbawy was in Chicago to make arrangements with the Cardinals for a preseason game in Amarillo, Texas. The details were firmed between Kerbawy and Walter Wolfner, the Cardinals' owner. There was some time for conversation before the group went off to the race track. Kerbawy turned to Joe Kuharich, who had become the Cardinals' coach.

"Joe, let's shake the league up," said Kerbawy. "I'll trade you halfback Jerry Krall for Buster Ramsey."

"OK," said Kuharich, and the deal was made.

"What we really did was trade them a free agent for Buster Ramsey," Kerbawy confessed years later, laughing about his coup. "Buster Ramsey was a player-coach with the Cardinals and Buddy wanted him to coach defense in Detroit.

"So while we were waiting to go to the track we made the trade and signed the papers right there in the Cardinals' offices. Since the trade was made, I figured I had to hustle back to Detroit and stayed only a couple of races and left.

"I called Buddy as soon as I got back to Detroit. 'You now have Buster Ramsey,' I told him. 'We gave the Cardinals Jerry Krall for him.'

" 'What do you mean?' Parker said to me. 'You can't trade them Krall. He's a free agent, we don't own him.'

" 'He won't be a free agent in an hour,' I said."

"What I did," said Kerbawy in relating the anecdote many years after the trade, "was drive down to Toledo and sign Krall. Then I sent the contract in to Bert Bell at the league office, predated. That's how we got Buster Ramsey in a trade for a free agent.

"Krall had played with the Lions in 1950 and then we cut him. He was working down in Toledo.

"And getting Ramsey was the key for the coaching staff. Buster was a great defensive coach. Buddy had wanted him. He said Buster had one of the greatest defensive minds in the league. But at the time Parker was piqued about something and said, 'I'm not talking to the Cardinals.' "

Parker's staff was increased from three to four for 1952. George Wilson and Aldo Forte were rehired. Ramsey took over the tutoring of the defense. Added, to scout upcoming opponents primarily, was Russ Thomas. He was a former tackle whose career with the Lions had been curtailed by a knee injury.

At training camp, Parker's main task was recreating his offensive line. Cloyce Box was back from his year in the Marines. But Dorne Dibble had been called up by the military. No problem there. Box replaced Dibble at left end. Leon Hart, with Swiacki behind him, remained at right end. Parker moved Lou Creekmur from guard to left tackle. Gus Cifelli, a young veteran, gained the assignment at right tackle. Vince Banonis remained the center. Two new rookies, Dick Stanfel and Bob Miller, were stationed at guard.

In camp, much interest centered on Pat Harder's campaign to run for sheriff in Milwaukee in the 1952 election. Bobby Layne pinned a 10-cent toy badge on Harder one day for the benefit of the press photographers. The players began calling Harder "Sheriff."

When Parker cut down his squad to the 33-man limit to open the regular schedule, fully one-third of the team consisted of players added since the near-miss of 1951.

"In making our changes, we've tried to improve our reserve strength," said Parker.

In line with his philosophy of invigorating the club with youth, eight of Parker's newcomers were rookies. They were Lary and David for the defensive backfield; Stanfel and Miller for the offensive line; Pat Summerall and Blaine Earon for the defensive line; Tom Dublinski as the third quarterback; and Keith Flowers for the linebacking unit.

The other three additions were veterans: Box, Hardy and Girard.

The early schedule was most difficult. It would start with the annual odyssey to the West Coast. The first game was at San Francisco, the second the following Friday night in Los Angeles. And the season's third and fourth games also were scheduled against the 49ers and Rams, in Briggs Stadium.

Despite the degree of difficulty of the early schedule, the Lions broke camp in late September with the greatest expectations.

They were immediately chastened in their opener at Kezar. The 49ers, who had ruined them in 1951, delivered another sobering blow. The Lions were thrashed 17-3. There were fumbles by Layne and Walker, and a series of dropped passes.

The Lions flew south to Los Angeles for their second game. The Rams were reigning NFL champions, but they also were in the middle of a violent factional hassle involving owners and coaches. Coach Joe Stydahar had his backers; assistant coach Hamp Pool had a different cadre

of supporters among the Rams' owners. After losing their opener to the Browns in the rematch of the '51 championship game, Stydahar was dropped as head coach. Pool was promoted to head coach.

Playing under a new coach gave the Rams a psychological edge. Parker resorted to a gambit of his own. He announced the benching of Bobby Layne in favor of Jim Hardy.

"Any time you hold a team to 17 points in this league," said Parker, still grousing about San Francisco, "you should win."

Parker's ploy worked. Bobby Layne starred on Friday night against the Rams. The defense was even better, holding the world champions to two touchdowns. The Lions won 17-14. The victory was saved when defensive end Jim Doran crashed in on Norm Van Brocklin, the Rams' quarterback, and caused a fumble. Les Bingaman recovered it for the Lions.

A split on the Coast seemed to be standard — and the Lions returned home to play the 49ers and Rams on successive weekends again.

In the home opener at Briggs Stadium, the capricious Detroit fans booed their team. The Lions were terribly inept, especially on offense. The 49ers routed them, 28-0, for their third straight victory. It put them two games ahead of the 1-2 Lions.

Parker was frantic. After Layne was booed by the fans and smeared by the 49ers' Leo Nomellini, he benched him. He then benched Hardy, who also was smeared by the pass rush. Young Dublinski was next; he was thrown to the 49ers in the fourth quarter.

The Lions managed just four first downs and a total offense of 65 yards against San Francisco.

"The worst offensive club I ever saw," said Parker. "In two games with the 49ers we've scored three points."

"What Buddy should do is crack the whip,"

Three weeks into a season that would end with them winning the world's championship, the Lions were 1-2 and had been humiliated 28-0 by the San Francisco 49ers. The offense played miserably and Bobby Layne (left) was benched. Yet, a week later, Detroit defeated the defending champion Los Angeles Rams for the first of nine victories in the final 10 games of the season. The great turnaround by the Lions grew out of a meeting between Parker and Layne. The quarterback told his coach, "I'm going to be your quarterback and this team will straighten out in a hurry."

said Cloyce Box. "We're letting him down. He ought to make us scrimmage an hour on Monday to wake us up."

"Honestly, I don't know what to do," said Parker. "The only thing I'm sure of is there'll be no work Monday. It's always an off-day."

Roy (Friday) Macklem, the Lions' equipment custodian, raconteur, cynic and club employee since 1935, reflected back over years of pitiful performances seen on the sidelines.

"We never looked worse," Macklem decided. "Even in '42, the year we blew 11 straight."

Parker skipped the club's weekly postgame buffet to reevaluate the sorrowful situation at his suburban home in Dearborn.

"Home is the only place to go after you get licked like we did," said Parker. "And I felt I'd never sent a team better prepared into a game."

At his home, Parker had a visitor.

"After the game, Bobby Layne came to my house," Parker related. "I'd used Hardy and Dublinski as replacements for him and he knew his job was in jeopardy. But Bobby made the trip to see me to say, 'I'm going to be your quarterback and this team will straighten out in a hurry.' "

On Tuesday morning, when the Lions reassembled following their day off, a team meeting was called. The players met in secret for 45 minutes with coaches not admitted. They debated the situation, let their feelings run, and emerged, unified, onto the practice field.

Parker had made arrangements to allow the score from Sunday's disaster to linger on the scoreboard. It was still there — SF 28, DET 0 — as the Lions started their workout.

"I thought that might help to wake them up," said Parker. "It did."

The Detroit newspapers talked of pampered Lions, too fat to block and tackle. But the Rams' situation was equally serious. Their advance man in Detroit talked with gravity about the problems besetting the champion Rams. The advance public relations man from Los Angeles was a tall, articulate young fellow with considerable personality. His name, Pete Rozelle.

"That was the same stuff I was hearing and reading in connection with the Rams before I left Los Angeles," said Rozelle, scanning the Detroit critiques. "We were accused of every crime in the book when we got off to a bad start after winning the championship last year. When we lost to the Lions the Rams were described as too swell-headed to get up to the line of scrimmage."

It was a busy week of preparation for the Lions. Parker summoned Ollie Cline out of retirement to help in the backfield. He obtained Sonny Gandee, who had been waived from the Lions' roster during summer camp, from the new Dallas Texans.

Doak Walker was a casualty from the game with the 49ers. Then he aggravated the injury one night when he got up to turn on the television set and pulled a leg muscle.

Jug Girard was ready. Parker started the rematch with the Rams with a makeshift backfield of Girard and Bob Smith at the halfbacks and Bob Hoernschemeyer moved from halfback to fullback. Pat Harder's knees were kicking up.

The Lions started atrociously and boos cascaded onto the field. The Rams opened a 13-0 lead and had another touchdown nullified by a penalty.

In the second quarter, Harder could stand no more. He sidled up to Parker.

"I can't sit on the bench any longer, knee or no knee," said Harder. "Put me in."

Parker sent Harder in and moved Hunchy back to halfback with Girard.

"Okay," said Layne in the huddle shortly before the end of the second quarter.

The season of 1952 was the year of Cloyce Box (left) in Detroit. Rejoining the club from military service, he teamed up with Layne to become what George Halas called "one of the best pass combinations pro football has seen." Box caught two touchdown passes in the triumph over Los Angeles which started the drive to the championship. Linebacker LaVern Torgeson (right, leaving the field with Lou Creekmur) returned an interception for a touchdown in the Rams game. Jug Girard, acquired from Green Bay in a trade and a regular because of an injury to Doak Walker, caught two TD passes (far right) in a 52-17 victory over his old Packers' team.

"Let's break one, Cloyce." And so they did.

Layne fired a pass to Box between two safetymen. Box caught the ball over his shoulder, broke free and sprinted to the touchdown, a 64-yard play.

Later, Lavern Torgeson dropped back from linebacker and intercepted a pass. He trundled 31 yards to the second touchdown and the extra point put the Lions in front 14-13. The noises had changed and the fans were cheering wildly. But the Rams got a field goal to take a 16-14 lead.

Layne had a trick. He handed off to Hoernschemeyer, who worked the old halfback pass to Box. Box caught the ball in the end zone, diving. In the fourth quarter, Harder made matters secure with a 26-yard field goal. The Lions won 24-16. It had been a physical game. John Prchlik, the Lions' defensive captain, was ejected for fighting.

The next Sunday the Lions' offense scored seven touchdowns in a 52-17 whipping of the Packers. Jug Girard remained at halfback while Walker's leg healed. Girard, playing offense as he had wanted, scored two touchdowns against his old club.

But the Lions still had some chasing to do. The 49ers remained unbeaten at 5-0 and the Lions were still two games behind at 3-2. The Rams were struggling at 2-3.

In the sixth week of the season, the Lions played the Browns, the Eastern titlists. The Lions' defense was awesome. It held the Browns to two field goals by Lou Groza. Otto Graham, the sport's leading passer, was under a constant assault by the defense. Jim Doran, the young defensive end, nailed Graham four times personally for 45 yards in losses. Doran was assisted in his pass pressure by Fum McGraw.

Layne pitched for two touchdowns to Leon Hart and Harder kicked a field goal. The Lions were held to 17 points, but they beat the

Browns with ease 17-6. And the 49ers finally lost, 20-17 victims of the Bears. Halfway through the schedule, the Lions were 4-2, the 49ers 5-1. The Rams were 3-3.

A week later the Lions were tied for the top in the West. Their fourth straight victory was a 31-6 rout of the Steelers. Box caught a 46-yard touchdown pass from Layne; Hoernschemeyer ran for 107 yards; Harder played hurt for three quarters; the offense managed 25 first downs; the defense held the Steelers to minus three yards rushing. And the 49ers were upset by the New York Giants.

The next opponent was the Dallas Texans, who followed in the lineage of the Boston Yanks, the New York Bulldogs and the New York Yankees. They were new to the NFL in 1952 and before their first season ended they were an orphan club. The Texans were the Lions' fifth straight victim, 43-13. Harder scored 17 points on a touchdown, five extra points and two field goals.

The standings showed the Lions and 49ers tied at the top at 6-2. The Rams and Packers were a game behind at 5-3.

A week later the race got tighter. After the Lions lost to the Bears 24-23 on a bad center-snap, there was a four-way jam at the top of the standings. The Lions' five-game winning streak ended because of a heroic finish staged by the Bears' young George Blanda.

The Bears had led most of the day. But with two minutes left the Lions took a 23-17 lead on Jack Christiansen's twisting 79-yard punt return. Blanda fired three passes with precision. They moved the Bears 68 yards. The third pass, caught by Ed Sprinkle with 17 seconds left, was for a touchdown. Blanda's conversion provided the one-point margin.

Earlier, the Lions proved that the extra point wasn't a 100 percent certainty. Pat Harder had been perfect on his conversions all season until

this late November day. But after a touchdown in the second quarter, Vince Banonis fouled up the center-snap on the extra point try.

Out West, the Rams defeated the fading 49ers. The Packers defeated the Texans. The Lions, Rams, 49ers and Packers all showed 6-3 in the standings.

The Packers didn't belong in such select company. On Thanksgiving, the Lions removed them from their share of first place in the annual holiday affair at Briggs Stadium 48-24. The Lions scored five times on passes. Box caught three of the touchdown passes and Hart the other two. Layne threw three of them. Box's touchdown catches were for five and 33 yards from Layne and for four yards on the halfback pass from Hoernschemeyer.

The Lions then took their Thanksgiving weekend recess while the Rams and 49ers played again out in California. The Rams, rushing through a winning streak, won 34-21 with Norm Van Brocklin now entrenched as the No. 1 quarterback over Bob Waterfield.

December arrived with the Lions tied with the Rams at 7-3. The following Sunday against the Bears, Bobby Layne threw touchdown passes of 29, 28 and 25 yards to Cloyce Box. All three were in the first 21 minutes — and the Lions crushed the Bears 45-21. It was Box's second consecutive three-touchdown day.

"Detroit is a powerful team with one of the best pass combinations pro football has seen — Layne to Box," said the esteemed pioneer of the sport, George Halas.

Layne enjoyed his finest performance of the season in this next-to-last game of the schedule. He completed 22 of his 35 pass attempts. Layne had to pass often. The running corps was depleted. Girard hurt his knee and was lost for the remainder of the season. Hoernschemeyer suffered injured ribs.

At least Walker was ready for the first time in

two months — but Parker was being very careful not to use him too much.

"If we get to the playoffs, we'll need Doak," said Parker in a statement tinged with more than clairvoyance.

In the emergency, Parker switched Christiansen to running back for the first time. Chris led the ball carriers with 54 yards. He scored one touchdown on an 18-yard run from scrimmage. He set up another touchdown when he returned a punt 56 yards.

With the final games upcoming, the title race was down to two teams. While the Lions beat the Bears, the Rams won their seventh straight over Green Bay. The leaders were 8-3. But the Packers were eliminated. So were the 49ers with their fifth loss in six weeks, this time to the lowly Steelers.

The final weekend could be decisive — and the Lions could be optimistic. Their last opponent was the woeful Texans, who retained that identity although they long before had become wanderers. They left Dallas because of nonsupport and bankruptcy and became a road team, financed by the league treasury. Their only victory in 11 games had been over the Bears in a game played in Akron, Ohio. It drew 3,000 curious spectators. The Texans moved to Hershey, Pa., to practice. Their final game was transferred from Dallas to Detroit on Saturday December 13.

The Lions won with 41-6 ease and their 9-3 record was their finest since 1934, the first year in Detroit. They were assured of at least a tie for the title. The Rams would not play until Sunday, the following day.

There was a momentary scare in the second quarter against the Texans. Bobby Layne rolled over in agony. His injury was diagnosed as stretched ligaments in his left leg.

"I'll be all right," insisted Layne, who watched the second half from a jury-rigged seat in the dugout. The doctors agreed, Layne would be available for the next game — which would be either a playoff with the Rams or a championship game with the Browns.

Before he was knocked out of the game, Layne threw 77 yards to Box for a touchdown. Jim Hardy replaced Layne and threw two more touchdown passes — 40 and 41 yards — to Box. It was the third straight game in which Box had caught three touchdown passes — a remarkable record. He had 15 touchdown catches for the year to lead the league. More than a third of his 42 catches were for touchdowns.

Christiansen again filled in nobly with the offense. He ran 65 yards from scrimmage for a touchdown.

The Lions finished their best regular season in 18 years before 12,252, their smallest attendance at home in 10 years. The change of venue from Dallas, causing a hasty over-the-counter ticket sale, was cited as the reason.

The next afternoon Buddy Parker sat by the radio in Dearborn and listened to the play-by-play of the Rams' 28-14 victory over the Steelers. It was Los Angeles' eighth straight victory. They hadn't lost since the Lions beat them in Detroit in October. Now the Rams and Lions would play again in the Western title playoff in Detroit, with the winner advancing to the championship game in Cleveland.

"Well, that's it," said Parker, snapping off his radio. "We'll be ready for them. Layne will be all right. Hoernschemeyer will be back, but we'll be without Girard. And we'll have Doak Walker ready to start."

Walker had not been available to start for the last 10 games.

Parker analyzed the Lions' season, searching for a turning point. He decided there had been two. One was the night after the crushing second loss to the 49ers, the 28-0 beating which left him so disillusioned. It was the night Layne

appeared at his home with reassurances about his quarterbacking talents. The second occurred the next week when the Lions were behind the Rams by a score of 13-0.

"Bobby proved a real prophet when he said he would be our quarterback and the team would straighten out," said Parker. "And no one had a bigger hand in straightening us out than he did.

"Then I figure the touchdown called back on the Rams provided the real turning point of the season. We won that game, but if their touchdown had counted our lot would have been tougher."

In the playoff game, the Lions had to contend with a team on an eight-game winning streak. Norm Van Brocklin was the catalyst in the Rams' surge. He had led the league in passing efficiency with outstanding receivers in Elroy (Crazylegs) Hirsch and Tom Fears. The only concern of Hamp Pool was the availability of ailing rookie Dick (Night Train) Lane, who had set the interception record of 14. Pool wanted Lane to cover Box, if possible.

It was foggy and the field was spongy on the Sunday of the 1952 National Conference playoff at Briggs Stadium.

The duel between Box and Lane never materialized. Pool put two defenders on Box — as the Lions had anticipated. They put two more on Doak Walker, coming out of the backfield in his first start in so long. They neglected to cover Leon Hart, the giant right end, who roamed freely over the middle. Hart caught five passes, including efforts of 22 and 13 yards on the Lions' first series. Pat Harder took a pitchout from Layne and circled end to score the first touchdown.

In the second quarter, Harder scored again. The Lions had a 14-0 lead and Harder had scored all 14 points. Just before the half, the Rams scored on Van Brocklin's 15-yard pass

The indomitable Pat Harder scored 19 points as the Lions won a playoff with the Los Angeles Rams for the conference championship of 1952. Others in the photo are Jack Dwyer (29) of Los Angeles and Leon Hart (82) of Detroit.

to Fears, half of his preeminent receiver duo.

But in the third quarter, the Lions' pet halfback pass clicked again. Doak Walker passed 22 yards to Hart in the end zone. Five minutes later Harder kicked a 43-yard field goal. The Lions were in front 24-7.

Only then did the Lions' defense — which had been spearheaded by McGraw, Prchlik, Torgeson, Doran, Don Doll, and Jim David — relax momentarily. Veteran Bob Waterfield came in to generate some offense. The Rams scored one touchdown midway through the fourth period on Deacon Dan Towler's five-yard run. The Lions had to punt and Vitamin T. Smith returned the ball through them for 57 yards and another touchdown. Suddenly, the Lions were in peril. Their commanding lead had been slashed to 24-21.

In the last minute, the Rams had the ball again. Waterfield dropped back from the Rams' 11 and passed toward Elroy Hirsch. LaVern Torgeson cut in front and intercepted the pass. With 30 seconds left, Hoernschemeyer hit left guard and ran nine yards for the Lions' fourth touchdown. Harder converted for his 19th point of the day.

It was over, 31-21 Detroit, and the Lions were headed for the championship game for the first time since 1935. They had defeated the 1951 champions, the Rams, three times during the season. It was an hysterical occasion. Little Jim David, who had been Parker's 22nd round draft choice, relished the moment.

"I wonder what excuse the Rams will find this time," said David. "When we beat them in L.A., all we heard was that they had changed coaches and hadn't had time to reorganize. When we licked them again here in October, they blamed an injury to one guy, Hirsch. Well, they came back with Hirsch in shape and a coach who'd won eight straight. I guess we showed 'em." That the Lions did.

Layne had ignited the offense again. Nine pass completions in 21 attempts for 144 yards; six carries for 20 more yards. It hadn't been spectacular, but he had made the big play.

The Lions had beaten the Browns twice, by a point in a preseason game and by 11 points in a game that counted in November. The Lions were made three-point favorites, although the Browns would be at home on the lakefront . . . and although the Browns were experienced in the pressure of playing championship games. This would be the seventh in seven years for the Browns. Nine of the Browns had been with the club from its inception and had played in every championship game.

The Lions lacked this kind of background. Only Harder and Banonis had been in a championship game before, in 1947 and 1948 when they played with the Cardinals.

"We can win the big one over there if we don't get too cocky," said Harder. "You have to keep after these kids. They don't realize yet how damaging a letdown can be. Sure we licked the Browns a couple of times. But what happened in September and November doesn't mean anything now."

The Lions were favored because of their early victories over the Browns but, more significantly, because Paul Brown's team would be without Mac Speedie and Dub Jones.

The 1952 season had been a long, personal one for Doak Walker, who had been pro football's leading scorer as a rookie in 1950 with 128 points. But in 1952 there had been a succession of agonies. First he had gashed his arm at the National Open. Then he had been hobbled with a leg injury. But on December 28, 1952, Doak was at peak health.

He had gone to high school in Dallas with Bobby Layne. They had entered the Merchant Marine together during the war. But then Layne went to Texas and Walker to So. Methodist, and now for three years they were rivals. They were reunited as comrades on the Lions' team in 1950. And on this day they were in the same backfield again. Doak entered the game with only 106 yards rushing for the 1952 season. After scoring 128 points one season and 97 the next, he had scored zero in 1952.

There was a touch of irony to Walker being in the Lions' backfield this championship day. He could have been playing for the Browns against the Lions. Before the All-America Conference folded, the Browns had the draft rights to Walker in their league. The Lions owned the NFL rights, obtained by trading Johnny Rauch to the Bulldogs. Under the terms of the agreement by which the Browns and 49ers entered the NFL, all conflicting draft claims would be settled by a coin flip. But Paul Brown met with Bo McMillin and amicably settled the disposition of the 1948 Heisman Trophy winner. McMillin gave the Lions' second draft choice to the Browns for clear rights to the little guy (at 5-10 and 170 pounds, he was one of pro football's smallest players).

In the second period of the 0-0 championship game in Cleveland, Layne assembled the Lions' offense at midfield. "Doak," said Layne, "you rested up all year, you should be ready."

He then called on Walker to run the ball, and Doak streaked to the Browns' 12. Then Layne passed to Bill Swiacki at the Browns' 3. The Lions were penalized back to the 8, but Layne again handed off to Walker, and Doak turned around end and dashed to the 2. Layne's quarterback sneak produced the Lions' touchdown, and Harder's kick made it 7-0.

That was the score at halftime.

In the third quarter, the Lions began from their 33. All week Paul Brown had told his defense about the Lions' halfback pass, which had suckered so many opponents in the past. The Browns were ready for it.

Cloyce Box broke from the line and headed deep. There was the usual double coverage. Bert Rechichar and Tommy James dashed after Box and hung with him as he maneuvered on his pattern. Back behind the line of scrimmage at the 33, Layne handed off to Walker. Walker did not throw the ball. He hit the gap between tackle and end and veered to his left, into the open. Downfield, Box quickly snapped at the two men covering him. He wiped out Rechichar and James with a single block, and Walker dashed 67 yards for the Lions' second touchdown. It was his first touchdown of the season.

Harry (Chick) Jagade scored four minutes later for the Browns to cut the lead to 14-7, and Otto Graham brought the Browns back toward the Lions' goal again. Marion Motley, the freight-train fullback, broke open and steamed 42 yards to give the Browns first down and goal at the Lions' 5.

On the Browns' next play, Don Doll tore in from defensive back and crashed into Motley just as he took Graham's handoff. Doll spilled Motley for a five-yard loss at the 10. Graham had to pass now. But Jim Doran and Fum McGraw were all over him. Graham never launched the pass. He lost 13 yards to the 23. On the next play, the Lions stopped Graham after a yard gain. Brown shunned the field goal by Lou Groza — and it was a mistake. Graham went for the end zone, as he had to, on fourth down, but Dick Flanagan batted the pass down.

In the fourth quarter, Harder kicked a 36-yard field goal to put the Lions ahead 17-7. As time neared an end, the Browns drove to the Lions' 8. But the drive fizzled again.

The Lions were champions for the first time in 17 seasons.

The Lions' owners were ecstatic. They had won the championship five years after their syndicate had purchased the team. But they remained leery of coaching contracts longer

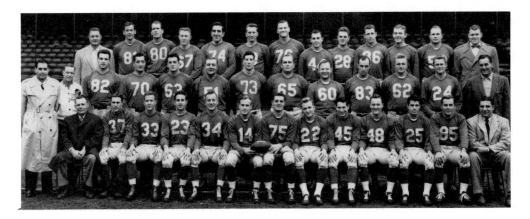

than one year. Parker's reward for coaching the Lions to the championship was a new one-year contract for 1953. He signed it, reluctantly.

Pro football had achieved total acceptance in Detroit. The home attendance was 262,675, another record for the Lions.

As defending champions, the Lions had the honor of opening the football year with the annual game against the College All-Stars in Chicago's Soldier Field. Parker opened the 1953 training camp early in Ypsilanti.

"We're going to make changes," promised Parker. "We don't intend to stand pat. We should be better this year."

He had won the championship with a cadre of castoffs from other clubs — Layne, Box, Hoernschemeyer, Harder, Banonis, Flanagan, Swiacki, Prchlik, Martin, Smith, Cline, Hardy. He had won by fitting rookies in with the veterans to make the whole.

Again Parker had a bountiful draft in 1953. For the first time in three years, the Lions had a first-round draft pick. Parker used it for a blocking guard, Harley Sewell from Texas. There were 23 rookies in camp including Sewell, Gene Gedman, Charley Ane, Lew Carpenter, Oliver Spencer, Carl Karilivacz and a quiet rookie from Pitt named Joe Schmidt. The seven rookies all made the 33-man team. A rookie who had to be cut, although Parker liked him, was a fellow named Pete Retzlaff. Retzlaff drifted to Philadelphia and became a star with the Eagles in later years.

But it was not a joyful camp in 1953. For one thing, Parker was miffed because Les Bingaman, the all-pro middle guard, reported overweight. "Les must be 350 pounds," said Parker. Bing finally shrank to 328.

Parker complained that the Lions were flat in practice, that the blocking was ineffectual and that Layne was throwing scatter-armed.

Jim Hardy sent word from California that he was retiring, but Parker got a reprieve on the one major trade he had conducted. Tom Dublinski, the No. 3 quarterback in '52, had been dealt to the Colts. The player the Lions were to receive refused to report, however. The deal was canceled and Dublinski returned to Detroit. Jim Cain and Dorne Dibble also returned, released by the Army.

Schmidt was the most impressive rookie in camp. So Parker one night called in Dick Flanagan, popular with his teammates, and told him he had been traded to Pittsburgh. Schmidt, a rookie taking the place of a team favorite, was ostracized by Layne and his veteran teammates. But Joe didn't talk much in those days anyway; he preferred to be a loner. He made the club as the starting left linebacker.

Parker was upset over another matter. Jim David was hurt. He had broken his ankle in a sandlot baseball game in Colorado.

Again, Parker's aim was to reconstruct the offensive line. It was the reason he had drafted Sewell first, and later Ane and Spencer. Sewell and Ane made the club as starters.

Parker was somewhat placated when the Lions beat the All-Stars 24-10. Then the Lions won all five exhibition games. Included was a 56-31 rout of the Browns in the championship game rematch. It gave Parker a personal 5-0 record over Paul Brown.

When the season started, some veterans were gone. Hardy had retired. Cifelli, Byron Bailey, Swiacki, Flanagan and Doll had been either traded or cut. Pat Harder was hurting so much he had to be placed on the inactive list while his injuries healed.

The rookies were prominent from the beginning of the regular season. Lew Carpenter scored a touchdown on a punt return of 73 yards the first time he touched the ball in a pro game. Not to be outdone, Gene Gedman scored a one-yard touchdown the first time he touched

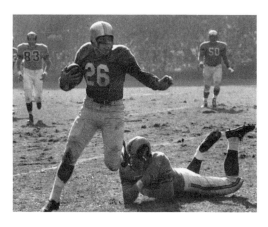

the ball. The veterans would not be shown up. Layne passed 43 yards to Leon Hart for a touchdown and 19 yards to Hoernschemeyer for another. He clicked on passes of 61 and 48 yards to Box, his old favorite. Layne's passing was worth 364 yards. Doak Walker scored a touchdown, a field goal and five extra points for 14 points. It added up to a 38-21 opening game victory over the Steelers.

During Bobby Layne's early days in Detroit his popularity was disputed by a dissident faction of fans. "We want Enke, we want Enke," they would chant on football Sundays. Fred Enke had been the No. 1 quarterback before Layne arrived in Detroit. Occasionally, Buddy Parker received petitions demanding he play Enke and bench Layne. Detroit fans never really have developed patience for a quarterback suffering a bad day. Parker solved his dilemma with Enke, the former starter, by trading him to Philadelphia. He emigrated to Baltimore, where the Colts were starting with a fresh organization.

In the second week of the season, Fred Enke returned to Detroit with his new club and scared Buddy Parker and the Lions. As his old fans roared, Enke got the Colts off to a 17-10 lead over the world champions. Then the Lions rallied to beat the Colts 27-17. Hoernschemeyer scored two touchdowns, Yale Lary contributed a 74-yard punt return and Walker kicked two field goals.

After two weeks, only two clubs in the West remained undefeated. They were the Lions and their old tormentors, the usually fast-accelerating 49ers. They were tied at 2-0 — and on October 11 they met at Briggs Stadium. Through two years of excellence, the Lions had not been able to conquer San Francisco. The 49ers were responsible for preventing the Lions from winning the division in 1951. They beat the 1952 champions twice in two tries. The

49ers had won five games in a row from Detroit.

The game attracted 58,079, the largest home crowd in the Lions' history at the time. They stood on soapboxes in the passageways and made places for themselves on the steps of the grandstands. And they cheered wildly.

Buddy Parker made some special preparations. Swaggering Bobby Layne made a prediction to his comrades.

"We'll score on them in two plays," said Layne.

Bobby was wrong. It took him three plays to get the Lions' first touchdown. The drive consumed 72 yards with Walker passing to Box for the touchdown off the old halfback pass on the third play.

In secret, Parker had come up with a new formation. It placed Walker at right end, Leon Hart at left end and Box at halfback. The Lions were in that formation when Layne passed 49 yards to Hart for a touchdown.

The Lions' defenses were stacked to stop the running of Joe Perry and Hugh McElhenny. It worked. Y.A. Tittle, who had damaged the Lions so many times, finally decided he had to run himself. He tried the old bootleg that had been successful for the touchdown which destroyed the Lions' title dream in 1951.

The bootleg worked again and Tittle made it to the goal line. As he crossed the line, he was hit by half the Lions' defensive backfield. First Christiansen hit Tittle, then David went into the pile. Tittle had scored. But he didn't get up. He was unconscious.

X-rays revealed Tittle had a triple fracture of the jawbone. David was immediately found guilty by the 49ers' kangaroo court and declared a villain.

The Lions won 24-21 — breaking the drought against San Francisco. They were 3-0, the only perfect team in the West.

As usual, the Detroit fans did not savor the

victory or the heroics of Bobby Layne for any length of time. The next week they were unmerciful in their booing of Layne as the Lions lost to the Rams. Though he didn't complain, Layne obviously was irritated at the harsh treatment of the fair-weather customers. Parker was irritated by something else — the Lions' downfield coverage on punts.

After the Rams had administered the Lions' first 1953 defeat, 31-19, a West Coast journalist asked Parker if anything in the game had surprised him. "Sure," said Buddy sardonically, "when the Rams took that punt and ran down the sidelines and no one on our team touched the fellow."

Woodley Lewis had turned the game for the Rams with a 77-yard return of one of Bob Smith's punts.

The loss threw the Western race into a three-way tie. The Lions Rams and 49ers all were locked at 3-1. But the Rams and 49ers were headed home to friendly territory. The Lions were headed for the treacherous two-game visit to the West Coast. The Rams' Tom Fears had a vertebra cracked in the victory over the Lions. David was a villain in Los Angeles as well as San Francisco.

Parker was a cerebral coach, always concocting fresh methods of surprising the opposition. The halfback pass — with its counter, the fake pass — always had the opposition leery. The new formation with Walker aligned at right end had been effective. Now the Lions' failure to stop a punt return caused Parker to alter the Lions' punting formation. He widened the interval of the men who would have to dash downfield in hopes of making the tackle on the return man. And he changed punters, switching to Yale Lary from Bob Smith.

At San Francisco, the Lions promptly fell behind 10-0. Then it was 10-7. The Lions were halted at the 49ers' 45. Lary dropped back into punt formation. He took the snap . . . but he didn't punt. He ran. It was fourth and six and a dangerous ploy. Parker, at the sidelines, recoiled with astonishment. But Lary made the needed six for the first down and kept running. Finally, the 49ers caught him at their 24 after a 21-yard gain. Then Layne passed to Ollie Cline for the touchdown that made the Lions 14-10 winners. Twice in three games they had beaten the 49ers, 24-21 and 14-10.

With the victory, the Lions remained tied with the Rams at 4-1.

It had been a stormy visit to San Francisco. One night Smith, Hoernschemeyer and Layne went out for dinner. Some local fans started giving them trouble. The group went outside to the parking lot. The words became nastier and, according to the reports, the fans started to assail the Lions. Hoernschemeyer and Smith each dropped a fan and it was over. Nobody bothered to file a complaint with police.

In Los Angeles, the Lions were welcomed with newspaper charges that they played dirty football. Parker was furious.

"This has gotten so bad, it's ruining David," said Parker. "I understand that Elroy Hirsch said the Lions have a dirty secondary. There's a league rule that members of one team may not make such allegations against another team. If this had happened back East, Bert Bell would have heard of it, but apparently he doesn't know what's going on out here."

The printed charges against David ignited the Los Angeles fans. Eager to see what would happen, 93,751 came to the Coliseum. They hooted and jeered at David and the Lions.

"We have never worked harder for a game," said Parker during the week. "We can't count on anybody beating the Rams for us to break this tie. We have to do it ourselves."

Layne got the Lions an early 10-0 lead, then a 17-9 edge. But Van Brocklin brought the Rams back. Layne suddenly was off target. Don Paul, the Rams' co-captain and a villain to Detroit fans, intercepted a pass. He ran back 10 yards, lateraled to Lewis, who ran for a touchdown. The 45-yard play sent the Rams ahead.

In the fourth quarter, there was wild whooping as David and Bob Boyd, who was playing in place of the injured Fears, got into a slugging match. David was ejected – and the fans hooted in derision. When the Lions crossed the field to go to the locker room, a spare jersey with a different number was slipped over David's regular jersey.

The Lions lost 37-24 – and they were angry. The loss had dumped them out of the tie for first, leaving the Rams there alone at 5-1. Detroit slipped to a second-place tie with the Colts at 4-2. Parker openly predicted the Rams would not win because to do so they'd have to win all their remaining games. He meant the Lions would not lose again. Buster Ramsey, the defensive assistant, claimed David was thrown out of the game because the officials were intimidated by the crowd's screams for the defensive back's head.

Parker's vow that the Lions would not lose again was delivered in an impassioned moment. The Lions had just been beaten and were out of first place. They had six games remaining, and it seemed unlikely that they would win all six. They were reigning champions – but they just weren't that dominant in the competitive Western Division. No team was dominant.

But Parker's boast turned out to be correct. Two games later the Lions were back in first place. The Lions beat the Colts 17-7 in their seventh game. The Rams lost – as Parker had prophesied – to the 49ers 31-27. Another triple tie was created among the Lions, Rams and 49ers. It remained one week. Then the Lions beat the Packers 14-7 as Yale Lary intercepted three passes. The Rams were held

to a 24-24 tie by the Cardinals. And the Browns helped the Lions by dumping the 49ers 23-21. At 6-2 the Lions ruled the division. They finished the schedule with four more victories to extend their winning streak to six games. The Lions edged the Bears 20-16, trounced the Packers 34-15, intercepted five passes to beat the Bears again 13-7, then they clinched their second consecutive Western title with a 27-16 victory at New York. The 10-2 record was the finest in the club's history.

Bobby Layne and a healthy Walker had supplied much of the impetus to the offense. Pat Harder had missed all but one game with a leg injury. He had had a reprieve of two years – two excellent years in which he aided in the Lions' growth. Now he retired again, this time permanently– as a player. He returned later as an official. Cloyce Box endured a miserable year with merely two touchdown catches. But the 1953 Lions returned to the championship game primarily because of their defense. Jack Christiansen and colleagues – Chris' Crew – intercepted 38 enemy passes in the 12 games. The total led the league. The runnerup had nine fewer interceptions.

Sunday after Sunday down the winning stretch, pass interceptions turned games to the Lions' favor. Christiansen alone intercepted 12 passes. He was the league leader.

Now the Lions would meet the Browns again in the championship game. After their defeat by the Lions in the 1952 championship game, the Browns were near perfection in 1953. Otto Graham led the league with a 64.7 pass completion percentage. By comparison, Bobby Layne completed only 45.8 percent of his passes. But while Graham had thrown only 11 passes for touchdowns, Layne had thrown 16.

The 1953 championship game at Briggs Stadium would basically be a clash between the two quarterbacks and the systems they repre-

A reserve end, Jim Doran, caught a 33-yard pass from Bobby Layne and Doak Walker kicked the extra point to give Detroit a 17-16 victory over Cleveland for its second straight NFL championship. Carl Karilivacz, newest addition to Chris' Crew, intercepted a last-minute desperation pass by the Browns' Otto Graham. Bob Hoernschemeyer gains yardage in the title game (right). No. 87 is end Dorne Dibble.

sented. The Browns were more disciplined. Paul Brown called the plays with his messenger guards. Layne free-lanced.

Both methods were eminently successful for the team utilizing them. While the Lions were in danger every Sunday of the title race, the Browns were trouble free in the East. They were 11-0 entering their final game. Their title was clinched. Their goal of absolute perfection was shattered in the last game when the Eagles beat them 42-27. But the defeat was hardly disastrous. The upcoming championship game in Detroit was the one that counted.

It was the Browns' eighth championship game in eight years. But since entering the NFL they had been beaten in two of three of those championship games.

The Lions were concerned about Leon Hart's leg injuries. In reserve was Jim Doran, the team's most valuable player a year earlier as a defensive end. Sure enough, Hart went out of the championship game early, and Doran took his place in the lineup.

With 4:10 to play, the Lions trailed the Browns 16-10. A 10-0 Detroit lead had been eclipsed by Lou Groza's three field goals and Chick Jagade's touchdown.

In every football game there is the subplot of individual matchups, the subtle one-on-one confrontations. Jim Doran was against Warren Lahr in the Browns' secondary. Layne passed 17 yards to Doran. Then two passes misfired and it was third and 10. Another incomplete pass and the Lions would be forced to punt. Layne tried Doran again and he caught the ball and advanced it 18 yards to the Browns' 45. The drive still viable, Layne passed nine more yards to Box. A run failed and it was third down again. Layne gained the necessary yardage with a quarterback sneak for three yards to the Browns' 33.

Layne went to the bench and conferred with

Parker. He returned with the advice to try a screen pass. In the huddle, Doran conferred with Layne. He told Layne he could beat Lahr in a footrace toward the end zone. Layne gambled on the footrace and on Doran winning it. Bobby was the winner again. Doran outstepped Lahr, and Layne was perfect on his throw. Doak Walker kicked the extra point and the Lions were in front 17-16. The victory was assured moments later when Carl Karilivacz, a 23rd-round draft choice, employed the Lions' most effective weapon of 1953. He intercepted Graham's desperation pass.

Otto Graham, the NFL's champion passer, was limited to just two completions in 15 pass attempts. In the money game, Bobby Layne completed 12 of 25 passes. Doran, the converted defensive end, caught four of them for 95 yards. Three of the catches were on the final drive.

For the second year in a row, Layne prevailed and the Lions were champions. Again they set an attendance record, 315,549 customers for six home games. Never before in the history of professional football had a club attracted so many spectators in a season.

Buddy Parker believed he had earned a contract longer than one more year and he said so publicly. The Lions' management was unswayed, and again Parker relented, signing for 1954 only, his fourth contract of only one year's duration.

"I felt our 1953 team was better, considering everything, than our 1952 championship team," said Parker. "And our team will be better still in 1954."

Since the NFL invoked the divisional system with a championship game between the two winners in 1933, no team had won three NFL titles in a row. The Bears had won the championship consecutively in 1940 and 1941. The Eagles had matched this accomplishment in

1948 and 1949. Now the Lions of 1952 and 1953 had won two consecutively.

The city was rabid about the Lions. In the ballroom of a downtown hotel, the Meet the Champions banquet was a gala affair. It broke up the regimentation of training camp for the Lions. Adoring fans clustered around the gridiron heroes.

"We've got the heart to become the first team to win it three years in a row," Edwin J. Anderson, the bushy-browed president of the Lions, told the assemblage.

The 1954 training camp at Ypsilanti was not harmonious. Even with veterans who would pay little attention to training rules, Parker was lenient about regulations. But one night Hunchy Hoernschemeyer went over to nearby Ann Arbor for an evening. Hoernschemeyer got into a fight there and lost a tooth in the melee. Angry, Parker slapped an 11:30 p.m. curfew on the Lions during training camp. Then he ruled that Ann Arbor was off limits for all player personnel.

But as always there was time for frolic and frivolity. There was a great training camp mystery, an annual occurrence, about the actual weight of Les Bingaman. Again in 1954, the peerless middle guard reported to camp rounder than Buddy Parker preferred.

This year the big bet in camp was triggered by a blasting, cracking report. Bingaman had bent over to tie his cleated football shoes. The bench splintered and collapsed from the enormous strain.

"Bingo's added a little weight," said Parker after an early practice. "Must weigh 400 pounds now."

"No," said Buster Ramsey. "He's not much over 330."

"He's closer to 400 than 300," Parker said. "I'll bet you a steak on that."

"It's a bet," said Buster.

There was a singular problem. Nobody could be sure of Bing's weight because there wasn't a scale in training camp that went over 300. Friday Macklem, the handy equipment man, was commissioned to find one to settle the wager. Macklem scoured Ypsilanti on his vital mission. Finally, a suitable scale was discovered. Macklem found one with a 400-pound maximum at the Ypsilanti Farm Bureau.

With some coaxing from Parker, Bingaman agreed to be party to the event. So the group drove over to the Farm Bureau. Bing stepped on the platform ordinarily used for weighing sacks of grain. The indicator sped around toward the maximum. It retreated some. It quivered and it finally stopped.

The needle pointed directly at 349-1/2 pounds. That figure became Bingaman's official program weight. The description — the 349-1/2-pound Les Bingaman — became famous.

By a mere eight ounces, Ramsey won the bet with Parker.

Bing's 349-1/2 pounds were compressed into a 6-3 frame. He was 4 feet 2 around the waist. The Lions played an exhibition game and were to fly to Birmingham, Ala. The pilot approached Nick Kerbawy and requested that Bingaman and Leon Hart, who weighed 260, be removed from the airplane.

"There's a short runway here at Little Rock," said the concerned pilot, "and I'm not sure we can take off with those two aboard." The danger was averted by putting Bingaman and Hart on another plane.

As usual, Parker did not believe in the status quo with a veteran championship team. Vince Banonis, John Prchlik, Pat Harder and Bill Swiacki retired. Yale Lary and Gene Gedman were in the service. The draft crop was leaner than it had been. Bill Bowman, a fullback, was the only rookie who could make the '54 Lions

as a starter. Bill Stits, Gerry Perry, Andy Miketa and Gil Mains were rookies on the roster.

Parker had done some rejuggling of his veterans, though. Torgeson now was the full-time center. Jim Martin had switched to defense and played linebacker beside Joe Schmidt. Doran remained on offense along with Box and Dibble, who would back up in the secondary, too. Sonny Gandee and Jim Cain, a 200-pounder, played at defensive end, with Fum McGraw and Bob Miller the defensive tackles and Bingaman anchoring the front five in the middle at guard.

Just before the season opened, there was a schedule hassle with the Browns. The Lions were to play their second game at Cleveland. But the Indians had won the American League pennant and would be home in the World Series on Sunday, October 3. The Browns had been evicted for that day. Edwin J. Anderson contacted Paul Brown and offered the Browns all the home team amenities — including the gate split — if he would agree to transfer the game to Briggs Stadium.

"I simply cannot agree to play before a hostile crowd," said Brown. So Cleveland switched its home game with the Lions from October to December 19 at Cleveland, one week after the close of the regular schedule for all the other NFL clubs. The date switch seemed nothing more than a routine annoyance when it was made. But it would become a change of strategic magnitude to the Lions in December.

Actually, the 1954 season was the least hectic in four years for the Lions. The season opened with a 48-23 victory over the Bears. Bill Bowman ran a kickoff back 100 yards for one touchdown. Walker ran a punt back 70 yards for another.

The next Sunday Parker spent like the average American pro football fan. He watched the

Rams and 49ers batter each other to a 24-24 stalemate on his living room television set in Dearborn. The Lions were off because of the Browns' postponement.

"I wish the Rams had won," Parker said, flicking off his television set after the game on the Coast. The Rams would be the Lions' next opponent — and Parker was superstitious enough to want the next week's team to come into a game with his team as a winner.

During the week, there were several serious coaching conferences. Bobby Layne's shoulder was nagging him again. On Wednesday, Parker and his staff made a decision. They kept it secret. Sunday noontime, Parker approached the stalls where the quarterbacks put on their uniforms. Layne was dressing.

"Tom, you're going to start," Parker said to young Tom Dublinski, the backup quarterback. "Try to concentrate on running the ball as much as you can. Bobby's shoulder is sore. You're going to have to do the job today. I know you can do it."

Dublinski, a third-year pro whose only prior starts for the Lions were in College All-Star games, gulped hard... and did the job expected of him. The Lions beat the Rams 21-3 behind Dublinski.

The added week's rest was the panacea for Layne's shoulder. In his next start, he passed the Colts silly. He threw three touchdown passes, two of them to Dorne Dibble. The Lions won 35-0 the second successive game in which the defense did not yield a touchdown.

The record was 3-0 — and harking back to the midpoint of the 1953 season, the Lions had won 10 games in a row. But San Francisco was off to its perennial quick start, at 3-0-1, while the Rams, with new rumblings of dissension, were lagging at 1-2-1. So the Lions took off again for their yearly two-game trip to the Coast. Again there would be another clash with

the 49ers with first place in the division at stake.

Just a year before, under similar conditions in a game as meaningful, Y.A. Tittle suffered a triple fracture of his jaw in Detroit. The 49ers' fans remembered. Perhaps somebody up front on the 49ers did, too. Early in the game Bobby Layne dropped back to pass for Detroit. He was buried by the red avalanche of the 49ers' defensive line. The loss was eight yards — and Bobby Layne. Layne didn't get up. Out cold, he was carried off the field. Without Layne, the Lions lost their first game of 1954. The 37-31 victory put the 49ers in first alone in the West with the Lions trailing at 3-1.

The Lions then went to Pasadena to practice for the game with the Rams. Layne recovered quickly, but Parker decided on a switch of quarterbacks again anyway.

"We'll probably start Dublinski against the Rams," said Parker at midweek. "But Layne will be in there."

Parker was not a hunch player, but Dublinski had beaten the Rams earlier, in his first professional start.

The key play in the game came when Norm Van Brocklin handed the ball to Skeet Quinlan, and then Quinlan had the ball taken from his arms by Leon Hart, who ran for a touchdown. That was the key score in a game the Lions won narrowly, 27-24.

The 49ers' seemingly annual fadeout had started. The Bears beat them 31-27. The Lions were back in a first-place tie at 4-1. The 49ers were 4-1-1.

On November 6, the midpoint of the schedule, the Lions beat the Colts 27-3 and became sole occupants of first place in the West. The Rams beat the 49ers 42-34.

When the 49ers played the return match in Detroit, the Lions squared the score. Layne and Dublinski combined to pass for 302 yards. The Lions left the 49ers for dead 48-7. Doak Walker

had a brilliant day prancing through the red-shirted defense. He ran for 194 yards on five carries, two pass catches and a punt return. He scored 18 points, and prompted Parker to say: "It was the greatest performance I've seen in coaching."

The Lions next beat Green Bay twice in less than a week, and their record was 8-1. Even a 13-13 tie with the Eagles didn't matter. With two games left, the Lions were the Western title winners for the third autumn in a row.

They relaxed against the Bears and lost 28-24. In the game Layne played only five plays because his nose was broken.

All the other teams were finished for the year except the Lions and Browns. They had the championship game coming up in Cleveland on December 26. But first there was the meaningless matter of playing the regular season game which had been postponed from October because of the World Series. In a raging blizzard in Cleveland, the Lions finished their season with a 14-10 victory.

The game that really counted was played in the same stadium the following week. Paul Brown did not have to be reminded that Buddy Parker now had a 7-0 edge over him in their personal coaching duel. And naturally the Lions did not have to be reminded that they only needed to appear on the field to make the Browns shake and fall apart. After all, it had happened as recently as the previous Sunday.

The Lions were favored to win their third straight championship. Bobby Layne was a national figure, a cover boy on national magazines.

But, on championship Sunday 1954, it all turned around.

Before the game, his eighth championship game in eight years, Otto Graham confirmed reports he would retire.

Graham had not thrown a touchdown pass

The same teams, the same turf . . . yet in the space of a week the fortunes of two teams – Detroit and Cleveland – would be reversed. Playing a regular season game postponed by the baseball World Series, the Lions and Browns met at Cleveland Stadium in the last week of the 1954 season. Jug Girard's catch of a Bobby Layne pass gave Detroit a 14-10 victory in the snow (left). Buddy Parker, tormentor of Cleveland's Paul Brown, now had seven consecutive victories over the Browns' coach. That would come to an end when the Lions returned to the same stadium one week later for the title game. Otto Graham passed (right) and ran for six touchdowns, giving Cleveland a crushing 56-10 victory.

against the Lions in the two previous championship games. Indeed, he never threw a touchdown pass against them in a regular season game, either.

The snow had melted in Cleveland. It was a pleasant Sunday afternoon. On the first play of the afternoon Bill Bowman, the rookie, cracked through the Browns' line for a 50-yard gain. "Cheese champions," the Lions had contemptuously called the Browns for their accomplishments in the East. Lew Carpenter fumbled the ball away but the Lions got it back immediately when Joe Schmidt intercepted a pass by Graham. The Lions then took a 3-0 lead on Doak Walker's 36-yard field goal.

Graham failed to move the ball and Horace Gillom punted back to the Lions. The same script from 1952 and 1953 with the same cast. But . . . a handkerchief fluttered to the grassless field. On the punt, Harley Sewell had roughed Gillom. The Browns kept the ball, moved 15 yards on the penalty against Sewell. Zip. Graham passed 31 yards to Ray Renfro for a touchdown. Cleveland 7, Detroit 3.

So . . . Bobby Layne started the Lions back. But Don Paul intercepted one of Layne's passes. Paul dodged a couple of Lions and returned the ball 40 yards. Graham passed 10 yards to Darrell Brewster for the second touchdown. Cleveland 14, Detroit 3.

The Browns quickly captured the ball again. Graham moved them inside the one, then scored the third touchdown himself. Cleveland 21, Detroit 3. And the game was seconds more than one quarter old.

Layne finally moved the Lions some in the second period, and Bowman scored from the 5. Cleveland 21, Detroit 10.

But then Mike McCormack, the Browns' middle guard, stole the ball from Layne as he faded to pass, and Graham scored from the 5. Cleveland 28, Detroit 10. Then Walt Michaels

intercepted Layne, and Graham passed 31 yards to Renfro for the fifth touchdown. Cleveland 35, Detroit 10 at halftime.

In the hopes of stirring something, Parker used Dublinski instead of Layne in the third quarter. The Browns destroyed Dublinski, too.

Layne returned and the miseries compounded. Graham scored his third touchdown, from the one, then Maurice Bassett scored on a 13-yard sweep. It was 49-10 after three quarters.

The fourth began with two more interceptions of Layne passes. The second set up another touchdown, mercifully the last. Cleveland 56, Detroit 10. Graham scored three touchdowns and passed for three others. Bobby Layne was intercepted six times, and the Lions fumbled the ball away three times.

In the locker room, Otto Graham again said his career was over. "That almost made me change my mind," he added.

"Why should a guy who can do what he did want to retire?" asked Paul Brown. "I don't want him to quit."

Otto Graham would be back for one more fling, persuaded to allow Brown to call all his plays for another year.

For the Lions, the fantasy of becoming the first team to win three championship games in succession was a ruptured reverie. Parker believed that winning three in a row was thoroughly impossible.

"There will never be a dominant team like the Yankees in this league," Parker said. "There are too many good teams."

On the day the Lions failed to win their third championship in a row, a young assistant coach had just concluded his first year in pro football on the staff of the Giants. Vince Lombardi was his name. In the 1960s, he would be head coach of the Packers – and in 1965, 1966 and 1967 they would win consecutive championships.

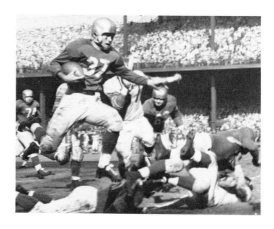

In two seasons, Parker had turned over more than half his ball club. He constantly brought in new players in hopes of perpetuating the Lions' championships into a dynasty. Only 16 of the players who won the 1952 championship game were still on the roster in 1956.

There were certain to be drastic changes for 1955. Les Bingaman was the first to retire, after seven years of bumping runners backwards from his territory at middle guard. In consort with Ramsey, Parker decided to change the Lions' defensive system. Instead of the five-man line with the two linebackers, the universal alignment of the era, Parker planned to try the new 4-3. There would be no successor to Bing. Rather, there would be a new position, middle linebacker. And Joe Schmidt, the brilliant young left linebacker, would be assigned to play it — and also to call defensive signals.

Cloyce Box, Fum McGraw and Bob Dove followed Bingaman into retirement. The Army took Bill Bowman and Gerry Perry. Tom Dublinski, feeling he was stymied playing behind Layne, jumped to Canada. So did Gil Mains, for a brief time. Parker traded LaVern Torgeson to the Redskins.

To replace Dublinski, Parker traded to get Harry Gilmer from the Redskins. In the draft, Parker acquired receiver Dave Middleton, two-way lineman Darris McCord and guard Jim Salsbury. And Parker juggled. Jim Doran and Jug Girard were at receiver, Leon Hart was at defensive end.

Something was missing when the Lions opened training camp in 1955. "Did you see Layne's waistline?" said Parker. The paunch protruding from the No. 22 jersey had been removed. Layne was down 12 pounds, to 195.

But Layne was having arm problems. He had strained his shoulder when he tried to restrain a bucking horse down in Texas by yanking at the reins. Early in training camp, the Lions sent

him to University of Michigan Hospital in Ann Arbor for treatment.

Layne opened the season, but he was never right. Later his knee was damaged. It was a lost season for Layne but it was worse than that for the Lions, who were beaten in their first six games.

In one game, Harry Gilmer passed 49 times and completed 24 — and the Lions lost to the Giants 24-19. They lost nine games, managing only victories over Baltimore, Pittsburgh and Green Bay. After three years of rule in the West, the Lions were dropped to last place.

At season's end there were rumors that the Lions would trade Bobby Layne to the Chicago Cardinals. "Not a chance," said Buddy Parker.

But Doak Walker announced his retirement after the terrible season. He had made his retirement decision before the season started. When he left, he had scored 534 points, more than any player ever to wear the Lions' uniform. In a six-year career, Walker — regarded as too small to play football when he joined the Lions as a rookie — was an awesome athlete who ran, passed, caught passes and kicked field goals and extra points.

Operating with his sixth one-year contract, Parker opened the 1956 camp at Ypsilanti with expectations of a renaissance by the Lions. Never had a team jumped from last place to first in one year. But the Lions of 1955 had taken the journey in reverse. So Parker wistfully believed the Lions could be qualified contenders in 1956.

Layne reported to the '56 camp with his shoulder and arm regenerated. "He's throwing with the old Layne sting," said Buster Ramsey.

The belief was that 1955 had been an accident caused by too many injuries and the loss of valuable young personnel. The Army returned Yale Lary, Gene Gedman, Oliver Spencer, Bill Bowman and Gerry Perry to

A series of unfortunate circumstances dogged the 1955 Detroit Lions, and when the season was over, they were in last place. Then Doak Walker announced his retirement. In an all-too-brief career of six years, he had been runner, receiver, option passer and place-kicker for the Lions. In the 1952 title game victory, he scored a 67-yard touchdown. In 1953, he kicked the deciding extra point. As a rookie in 1950, he led the league with 128 points scored, and his career total of 534 points is still the Lions' record. He was honored on "Doak Walker Day" at Briggs Stadium in 1955 (right).

Parker in time for 1956. And the draft was productive. The top choice was Howard (Hopalong) Cassady, the smallish redhead who had been an intercollegiate marvel at Ohio State. Don McIlhenny from Doak Walker's old school, Southern Methodist, was a second runner taken in the draft. Jerry Reichow was drafted as a future quarterback possibility with additional talent in running and receiving. Gene Cronin joined the defensive line.

This year Leon Hart was converted to fullback. Instead of just experimenting with the 4-3 defense, Parker and Ramsey decided to use it all the time. Ray Krouse was acquired in trade from the Giants to fit into the front four with McCord, Miller and Mains. Sonny Gandee was moved to linebacker to play with Schmidt and Bob Long, an acquisition from the Rams. The return of Lary helped solidify Chris' Crew — with David, Karilivacz and Christiansen himself.

Along with Walker, Hunchy Hoernschemeyer retired and Jug Girard followed him. So the Lions had a fleet of younger runners — Gedman, Bowman, rookies Cassady, McIlhenny and Tom Tracy — plus the converted Hart.

The season started with great expectations and faith . . . and considerable apprehension.

They reversed 1955 from the beginning. The 1955 club had lost the first six games and had been disgraced. The 1956 club won its first six games and was first in the West again. And, most important, Bobby Layne was the passer and winner of yore.

Two of the Lions' early victories were by four points, two others by three. It was the mark of excellence that a team could win so many games with so few points. There was speculation about the possibility of a perfect season, but then the Lions traveled to Washington to play the lowly Redskins.

Washington ambushed the Lions 18-17 and broke the winning streak. The Lions rebounded to beat the Colts 27-3, but on Thanksgiving Day the Packers and quarterback Tobin Rote came to Detroit. Green Bay was another also-ran, but Rote had a tremendous day while Layne floundered, and the Packers upset the Lions 24-20. The second loss enabled the Bears to slip into first place in the West.

The Bears and the Lions were matched in two of the last three games.

On December 3, the Lions ripped the Bears 42-10. Layne passed brilliantly. Gene Gedman ran magnificently. Dave Middleton caught seven passes for 176 yards, one a 48-yard touchdown pass from Layne. The Lions' defense was immense. It stopped Rick Casares, the NFL's leading rusher, with 42 yards. Chris' Crew restricted Harlon Hill, the league's most dangerous pass catcher, to one reception. With the victory, the Lions recaptured first place (8-2 to 7-2-1).

On the following Sunday, with Leon Hart bowling over tacklers at fullback, the Lions crushed the Steelers 45-7. The Bears, meanwhile, struggled past the Cardinals 10-3 and remained a half game behind. The winner on the next Sunday at Wrigley Field would qualify for the championship game against the Giants.

In the second quarter at Chicago, the Bears held a 3-0 lead on a field goal by George Blanda. The Lions were not concerned. Bobby Layne would get them going soon. On the first play of the second period, Layne handed off to Gene Gedman on a left end sweep. Layne dropped his hands to his sides and relaxed. He was watching Gedman when he was blindsided by Ed Meadows, the Bears' defensive end. Layne was out cold, cockeyed.

The Lions were enraged at the loss of their leader. First Lou Creekmur took a shot at Meadows. Then Bill Bowman did. Harry Gilmer battled valiantly to rally the Lions. He even got

George Wilson was a lonely man atop a stunned organization (left). He was the Lions' new head coach, succeeding Parker, who resigned abruptly at a banquet before the 1957 season. The new coach responded in spectacular fashion. He and a new quarterback, Tobin Rote, guided Detroit back to the NFL championship. There, they demolished the rival Browns 59-14. At right, Gene Gedman scores the second of eight Lions' touchdowns in the title game, following the block of Lou Creekmur (76) on Len Ford.

them into the lead for a bit. But the Bears crushed the Lions 38-21.

The 1956 season was an almost total recovery from 1955, but it ended in disappointment.

Parker once again announced he was going to quit football. But the Lions, through Anderson and Kerbawy, retaliated by appealing to Parker's judgment. They offered him what he had long desired — a contract longer than one year. But the two-year offer had been unauthorized. The Board of Directors, with long memories of the mistake with McMillin, vetoed the offer by Anderson and Kerbawy. Parker summarily rejected the new offer of one more year. It was reported that the Steelers wanted Parker if the Lions did not.

There appeared openly an anti-Parker faction on the board.

"A lot of us were disappointed over the way the Lions played last Sunday in Chicago," said an unnamed director in an interview in *The News*. "The unvarnished truth is the Lions were outcoached. Halas and his staff used their imaginations.

"And we have no assurance that the 1957 coaching will have as much luck as it had this season. Conceivably we could finish last, as we did in 1955."

But a pro-Parker director said, "Buddy's done a remarkable job this season and everybody knows it. Giving him a two-year contract doesn't mean a thing. When we gave McMillin a contract we were hiring an unknown quantity. We're not now."

Now the Colts, on the brink of contention themselves, showed interest in Parker, if he were to become unemployed.

On the day after Christmas, Anderson brought the Board of Directors together again. He advised that Parker be offered the two-year contract he wanted so much, at $30,000 a year. Faced with the departure of a winning coach,

the directors had less difficulty seeing his point.

Secure with a two-year contract, Buddy Parker began to restore the Lions for 1957. His first concern was at quarterback. Layne was 30 now. Buddy felt the injury to him at Chicago cost the Lions a championship. Now he wanted insurance, another veteran quarterback of No. 1 quality available for future emergencies. He was unconcerned about all the problems inherent in having two No. 1 quarterbacks on the same club — jealousy, factionalism, restiveness by the fans not the least of them.

The veteran Parker desired was Tobin Rote, the tall quarterback who had been so impressive in his duels with Layne for Green Bay. After a series of negotiations, Parker got his man just before the opening of the 1957 camp. The price was three veterans — McIlhenny, Spencer and Jim Salsbury plus rookie Norm Masters. Val Joe Walker came over from Green Bay with Rote.

Parker made one other major deal before camp opened in a new site in suburban Bloomfield Hills. He acquired fullback John Henry Johnson from the 49ers for Bill Bowman and Bill Stits. In the draft, Parker again was successful. He picked up Terry Barr to play defensive back, Steve Junker to catch passes, John Gordy to block and Ken Russell to provide depth for the offensive line.

On the evening of August 12, 1957, the Lions staged their annual Meet the Lions banquet at the Statler Hotel. Buddy Parker was invited to a private prebanquet party in a suite hired by D. Lyle Fife, a director of the club. Parker entered the suite and immediately began to seethe. Some of his players — including quarterbacks Layne and Rote — were socializing with the owners. It was a practice Parker detested. The cloying of the directors, their hero-worship of his athletes and their mass invasion of the locker room after Sunday games — had long annoyed him. He left the party angry and

headed for the grand ballroom for the banquet.

President Edwin J. Anderson told the fawning fans what they wanted to hear. "We are a definite contender for the championship," said Anderson.

Broadcaster Bob Reynolds was the toastmaster, and he introduced Buddy Parker. The coach leaned into the microphone and spoke:

"There comes a time in every coach's career when he faces a situation he can't handle. That time has come for me. Tonight I'm getting out of the Detroit Lions' organization. I've had enough. I'm through as coach of the Lions."

Parker turned abruptly and strode to his seat. There was the silence of shock.

Reynolds grabbed the mike. "I don't think Buddy means that," said the broadcaster. "I'm going to ask him to come back up here and talk to you."

From his seat, Parker replied: "I meant what I said. That's it."

Anderson took the microphone. "Buddy is upset by a few incidents that happened today," he said. "I think after I have a chance to talk with him, he'll reconsider and will continue as our coach."

Parker was surrounded by reporters.

"This is the worst squad I've ever had," he explained. "The team is dead. I don't intend to get caught in the middle of another' losing season, so I'm getting out."

A delegation of players — Layne, Schmidt, Christiansen and others — went to Dearborn to plead with their coach to return. He was unswayed.

After an emergency session, the directors named 44-year-old assistant coach George Wilson to succeed Parker. Not all of the directors were dismayed that Parker — who had coached the Lions to two championships and nearly a third — had quit on the two-year contract he had battled for so diligently.

As an assistant, George Wilson had worked with the Lions on a part-time basis only. He had been a rough hewn player for the Bears and was a vigorous man admired by the players.

"Following in the footsteps of Buddy Parker figures to be a big job," Wilson said. "I only hope that I can do half as good a job as Buddy . . . that would mean somewhere along the line I would win one championship, at least."

Wilson said he would solve the dilemma of two No. 1 quarterbacks by alternating Layne and Rote on a game basis. "Bobby will start one week, Tobin the next," said Wilson. But the plan was abandoned even before the end of training camp.

A few weeks after leaving Detroit, Parker returned to football. He became head coach of the Steelers, a downtrodden club.

Wilson busily engaged in adding veterans to the Lions to plug some weaknesses. He picked up Roger Zatkoff from the Packers to play right linebacker. He acquired Frank Gatski, who had played center for many years with the Browns.

On the morning of September 17, two weeks before the start of the 1957 season, two Detroit policemen stopped Bobby Layne for driving down Grand River Avenue, a main artery into downtown Detroit, with no headlights on. Later in the day, after missing practice while appearing in Traffic Court, Layne met with Wilson and Kerbawy.

"It's a rough deal for you right after taking over this club," Layne told Wilson. "I'll quit football if it will help."

"I want you to stay," said Wilson. "We need you."

Pleading innocent, Layne's trial was put off until December.

The Lions did not make an auspicious beginning in 1957. Wilson's plan was to go with the hot quarterback, Layne or Rote. With that arrangement the Lions played to a 3-3 record over their first six games.

One of the victories was a 31-27 victory over Baltimore that was to presage events in December. With 20 minutes to play, young John Unitas had outpassed both Layne and Rote. The Colts were in 27-3 command. Rote then threw a 14-yard touchdown pass to rookie Steve Junker, but the Colts still led by 17 points and there were only eight minutes to go. Bobby Layne was back in at quarterback now. He threw a 26-yard touchdown pass to Howard Cassady to slice the Colts' lead to 27-17.

With less than two minutes remaining, the Colts still had a 10-point advantage. Then Layne threw 30 yards to Cassady to the Colts' 1, and John Henry Johnson scored from there. With a minute and a half left, the Colts led 27-24. Unitas had the ball and intended to run out the clock. But Yale Lary forced Lenny Moore to fumble. Lary recovered with 50 seconds left at the Colts' 29. Layne passed once again to Cassady for a 29-yard touchdown. The Lions had overcome a 24-point deficit to win 31-27.

The stirring victory made the Lions 3-1 and it should have been a tonic. But on their annual trip to the West Coast, they lost both games to the Rams and 49ers. The Rams beat them 35-17. In San Francisco, the Lions provided a second miracle finish. Down 28-10 in the fourth quarter, the Lions were fired by Rote this time. He passed for three touchdowns — two to Jim Doran, one to young Junker. In a 9-1/2-minute burst, the Lions seized a 31-28 lead.

But they left too much time for Y.A. Tittle — 10 seconds too much. With that much time to spare, Tittle lofted one of his Alley-Oop floaters to kangaroo-legged R. C. Owens 41 yards away at the goal line. Owens vaulted over

David and Christiansen to catch the ball. The Lions were deprived of a victory 35-31. They returned home at 3-3, two games behind the 49ers in the standings.

Wilson boldly said the Lions were still in the race, that anything could happen to the 49ers. San Francisco lost its next three games. The Lions won two of their next three, including a 31-10 rout of the 49ers in the rematch.

On Thanksgiving, Wilson gave the Lions a halftime tongue-lashing, and they beat the Packers 18-6.

Layne was acquitted in court. Two afternoons later, he was playing against the Browns at Briggs Stadium. He was pass-rushed by the Browns' Paul Wiggin and Don Cole. Layne's cleats stuck and his ankle was shattered.

Rote got the Lions a 20-7 victory over the Browns. Even so, the Browns, after an absence of one year, won their division again that day. They won in reverse when Buddy Parker's Steelers eliminated the Giants.

Three teams remained alive in the West — the 49ers, the Colts and the Lions. Then the Colts were knocked out. Entering the final Sunday, the Lions were tied with the 49ers.

At Chicago, the Bears quickly went ahead of Detroit 10-0. Wilson blistered the Lions at halftime. In the second half, Rote rallied the Lions to three touchdowns. He won the confidence of his teammates, insecure with Layne on crutches. The 21-13 victory over the Bears sent the Lions into a Western Division playoff with the 49ers. Each had 8-4 records.

George Wilson took the Lions to California early to prepare for the playoff game at San Francisco. The game of Sunday December 22, 1957, was one of the most dramatic football games ever played. The 49ers streaked to a 24-7 lead in the first half. A field goal by Gordy Soltau made it 27-7. But two touchdowns by Tom Tracy and one by Gene Gedman brought

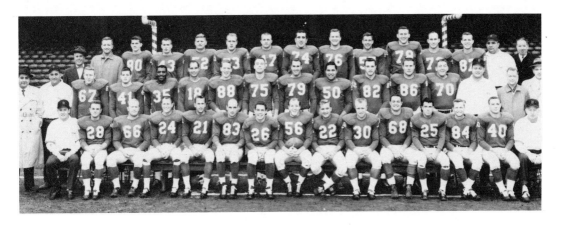

Detroit from behind. The Lions won it 31-27.

George Wilson was in the NFL championship game as a rookie head coach. His opponent was Paul Brown and his Cleveland Browns. For the fourth time in six years, the Lions and Browns would play for the championship.

The date was December 29, 1957, a cold, but sunny Sunday in Detroit. The Lions entered the game with memories of the 56-10 shellacking in the 1954 championship game.

Before the first period ended, the Lions were in 17-0 command. Martin kicked a 31-yard field goal on the first drive. Rote scored a one-yard touchdown on the second. Gedman scored a one yard touchdown on the third.

During the week, Wilson had diagrammed a special play, a fake field goal. Now, Wilson sent Jim Martin in to kick a field goal. He vigorously kicked his leg to make sure Martin kicked. Rote looked at the bench and decided to ignore the coach. He rolled to his right and lobbed the ball to Steve Junker for an easy touchdown.

Less than four minutes later, Terry Barr intercepted another O'Connell pass and ran it back 19 yards for a touchdown. Detroit was in front 31-7 at the half.

Lew Carpenter, the former Lions' runner, scored for the Browns midway through the third quarter. Detroit 31, Cleveland 14.

Wilson had cautioned about throwing deep on first down. But Doran — who had advised Layne he could get open for the winning touchdown pass in the '53 championship game — told Rote he could beat Ken Konz.

So on first down, against the coach's orders, Rote play-faked and passed to Doran running down the left sideline for a 78-yard touchdown. Detroit 38, Cleveland 14.

Before the third period ended, Rote passed to Junker again for a 23-yard touchdown. Detroit 45, Cleveland 14.

Seven seconds into the fourth quarter, Rote threw his fourth touchdown pass to Dave Middleton, a 32-yarder. Detroit 52, Cleveland 14. Rote left the game to a standing ovation from the 55,263 in Briggs Stadium. Jerry Reichow, the young No. 3 quarterback, replaced him, and passed 16 yards to Cassady for the final touchdown.

The final score was 59-14, and for the third time in six years the Lions were champions. Their winning share was a record $4,295.41.

Tobin Rote had proven himself a championship quarterback, just as Bobby Layne had. Rote completed 12 of his 19 passes for 280 yards and the four touchdowns. Joe Schmidt's defense intercepted five passes and recovered two fumbles.

"The players were thinking about the pasting we took three years ago in Cleveland, too," said Lou Creekmur.

There was a big party that night at the home of Bill Beckenhauer, the close friend of Bobby Layne, Joe Schmidt and Terry Barr. As usual, Layne was the life of the party. It was his last big party with his comrades.

Two games into the 1958 season, the era ended. There was a bold headline in *The News* on Monday, October 6: "Jittery Layne Fails Lions in Clutch." Layne was accused of being a bundle of nerves as the Lions squandered three scoring chances inside the 15 in the last quarter of a disappointing 13-13 tie with the Packers. That next day, a Monday, the Lions traded Layne away.

And on Monday night Bobby Layne left Detroit by airplane for the reunion with Buddy Parker in Pittsburgh.

The Great Games

December 27, 1953

More than any other sport, pro football is flavored by clashes of ideologies. Every team has its own character, its own philosophy, distinctive from that of its opponent.

From their inception in 1946, the Cleveland Browns reflected the mood of Paul Brown, their cerebral, autocratic coach who was one of the ingenious men operating in post-World War II football. They were a mechanical team, seemingly devoid of emotion.

And they were hugely successful. For four successive years from their inception in 1946, they were champions of the newly established All-America Conference. In 1950, the AAC became defunct and Paul Brown moved his champions into the prestigious NFL. The Browns immediately became the dominant team of the NFL. Scoffed at as upstarts from an inferior league, the Browns won the fifth successive championship in their five-year history their first season in the NFL. They beat the Rams, who had moved from Cleveland to Los Angeles, 30-28 in the 1950 NFL championship game.

At that time, the Lions were gradually starting a rebirth from their 1940s decade of disaster. In 1950, quarterback Bobby Layne joined the team and Buddy Parker rejoined the Lions as backfield coach under Bo McMillin. A year later Parker would become head coach. The Lions managed a 6-6 season in 1950 while the Browns were winning the league championship in their first NFL season. It was merely Detroit's third non-losing season in 10 years.

As they improved markedly in the early 1950s, the Lions offered a counterpoint to the Browns.

It was the Lions — members of the NFL since 1934 — who indeed became the upstarts. They were a happy-go-lucky team of rogues — impassioned and impulsive.

The respective quarterbacks of the Browns and Lions were the embodiments of their teams.

Dark-haired Otto Graham was an efficient quarterback and a meticulous passer. Off the field he presented a straight-arrow image. If he indulged in revelry, it was unknown. Blond-haired Bobby Layne was an undisciplined disciplinarian. Already his nocturnal escapades were legend in Detroit. His passes on the football field were not artistic. Certainly, they were not meticulous. Quite often, the passed football was scattered about.

About the only tendency Graham and Layne shared was a mutual ability to rally a team in the final minutes in the race against the clock.

Paul Brown insisted on calling the plays for Graham. He used a system in which he shuttled the guards from the bench to the huddle. They were messengers transporting Brown's play command to Graham by word of mouth. The shuttling guards were Chuck Noll and Lin Houston.

Graham accepted Brown's programmed play, spewed out the signal and enacted the operation with precision. It was an excellent method for the Browns because on December 27, 1953, they were involved in their eighth championship game in eight years.

"Otto Graham is perfectly capable of calling the plays," Paul Brown said a few days prior to the 1953 championship game with Detroit. "But I was a quarterback myself and not a very good one. I know how difficult it is for a quarterback to handle his own assignments and still give the proper concentration to play-calling."

The uninhibited Layne operated the Lions' huddle without such restrictions. Often there was a suggestion from Parker during a meeting at the bench. But Layne was not bound by it. In fact, Parker envisioned a day to come in pro football when all quarterbacks would call all plays audibly by code at the line of scrimmage.

The play-calling methods were reflective of the converse ideologies of the two teams from

Browns 0 3 7 6 16
Lions 7 3 0 7 17

cities on the opposite shores of huge Lake Erie.

The rivalry between the Lions and Browns, between Parker and Paul Brown, was just starting to flower. Brown was the most successful pro football coach of the time. But Parker was his archnemesis.

When the Browns arrived in Detroit the day after Christmas for the 1953 championship game, the personal coaching scoreboard between the two men read: Buddy Parker 5 victories, Paul Brown 0. The tally included preseason, regular season and Pro Bowl games, plus one prior championship game.

That previous championship game had been the year before in 1952. The Browns' streak of successive AAC and NFL championships had been broken in 1951, when the Rams beat them 24-17 in the championship game. Then in 1952, the Lions won their first divisional or conference title since 1935. Detroit had to defeat the reigning world champion Rams in a playoff to win that title and to qualify for the championship game against Cleveland. They did so with dispatch, 31-21, and then they won the 1952 championship as Layne out-dueled Graham 17-7.

The 1953 campaign highlighted the contrast between the Lions and Browns.

Detroit struggled throughout the season in the Western Conference, grappling with San Francisco and Los Angeles. Cleveland waltzed through the first 11 weeks unscathed. An unbeaten season beckoned, but with the title clinched, the Browns lost their regular season finale to the Eagles. They went into the championship game with an impressive record of 11 wins, 1 loss.

In training camp, the Lions had grievous doubts about repeating as world champions.

"We won't stand pat," Parker said when he assembled the Lions for training camp at the Michigan Normal College in Ypsilanti.

He had 23 rookies trying to qualify for his 33-man squad. Among them were Pete Retzlaff, Joe Schmidt, Charley Ane, Harley Sewell, Ollie Spencer, Gene Gedman and Lew Carpenter. Added to them were Jim Cain and Dorne Dibble, who had completed their tours of military service and returned to the team. All made the 1953 club — except Retzlaff, who would become a formidable performer for the Eagles after the Lions cut him.

The Lions' training camp was troubled from the start. Les Bingaman, the gigantic middle guard who anchored the Lions' defense, reported too gigantic. He was 350 pounds or more. Parker exiled Bing to the Fat Man's table in the dining room. There he existed on a solitary diet of cantaloupe.

Veteran Jim Hardy, Layne's backup quarterback, retired. Fortunately, a trade sending No. 3 quarterback Tom Dublinski to the reestablished Baltimore franchise was nullified.

"I don't know what it is," Parker complained two weeks into training camp as the Lions prepared for the College All-Star Game. "We've fallen into a slump. Layne is throwing wild and the blocking is lousy."

Vince Banonis, the veteran center, tried to dispel the gloom at Ypsilanti with a prediction.

"I'm saying we'll win another championship," he said.

Parker's dour look brightened on August 1 when the Lions managed a decent performance in a camp scrimmage. Schmidt, the rookie seventh-round linebacking candidate, helped his chances by intercepting two passes.

By the start of the 1953 schedule, he was a regular and five other rookies were on the roster. The Lions had not stood pat with a championship team — but the club was experiencing difficulty in synchronization. They managed three unimpressive victories, the third over the 49ers. But on October 18 the Rams

beat the Lions 31-19 in Detroit and the homefolks singed Layne with boos and a Goodbye Bobby serenade.

Two weeks later, after another close victory over the 49ers, the Lions were beaten for a second time by the Rams, 37-24 in Los Angeles in a game that featured play-after-play battling between the Lions' Jim David and the Rams' Bob Boyd. David was a villainous creature to the 93,751 fans in the Coliseum.

But they could revel in the Rams' victory and the plight of the Lions.

At mid-season, the Lions were 4-2. The Rams led the West at 5-1. Meanwhile, the 49ers were deadlocked in second with the Lions at 4-2.

A very unhappy Buddy Parker reflected over the second loss to the Rams and issued an atypical commentary:

"The Rams better not lose another game . . . That is if they want to win the championship."

Parker could have made the same observation about his own Lions. He didn't. He just silently thought it to himself.

The next six weeks were to become the perils of Buddy Parker.

"We're through with the Rams and 49ers, but they're not through with each other," Parker said with obvious relief.

In the first game of the final six, the Lions defeated the Colts 17-7. Meanwhile, the 49ers edged the Rams 31-27 for a three-way tie for first in the West. Each team was 5-2.

During the following week, Buddy Parker's father died in Texas. He went there for the funeral and missed the next game with the Packers. The Lions won it 14-7, principally because of their pass defense. The secondary, known as Chris' Crew because Jack Christiansen was its catalyst, intercepted four Packers' passes. Yale Lary, a second-year man, intercepted three of the four. On the same weekend, the Rams were held to a 24-24 tie by the

Chicago Cardinals, while the undefeated Browns aided the Lions by defeating the 49ers 23-21.

Parker's ominous proclamation of two weeks before was beginning to make him appear a clairvoyant. The Lions were now first in the West at 6-2, with the Rams a half-game behind and the 49ers a full game back in third.

But four games remained.

The Lions' next game was in Chicago, where they had beaten the Bears only four times in the previous 19 years of their existence.

It took a bravura performance by Layne, calling his own plays, for the Lions to win 20-16. He passed to nine different receivers in the game for 241 yards and ran for 71 yards more.

But it was once again the defense which rescued the Lions. Chris' Crew intercepted four passes for the second straight week. The last one, an acrobatic interception by Bob Smith, led to the Lions' victory. The Bears nursed a 16-13 lead into the fourth quarter but a nonjudicious play call cost them the advantage and the game.

Chicago's quarterback that day was an inexperienced 26-year-old named George Blanda. On third down Blanda gambled with a pass to retain possession. He stood in his own end zone and threw, but much too short and much too unwisely. At the 7, Tulsa Bob dove for the wayward pass and deflected the ball upward.

"The ball squirted into the air as I hit it but I rolled over so I could see it come down," said Smith. The Lions' deep back was lying on his back when it came down and clutched it before it hit the earth.

Three running plays netted the Lions only five yards to the 2. There Parker had a fourth-down decision. He shunned the field goal that would have safely produced a tie and

let Layne call a fourth-down play. Layne gave Doak Walker the ball and sent him around end. The gamble worked for a touchdown. The four-point victory maintained the status quo. The Lions remained slightly ahead as the Rams and 49ers also won.

Four days later it was Thanksgiving and the Lions were home against the Packers.

At halftime, Green Bay led 15-7. The Packers then took the second-half kickoff and marched toward another touchdown and a commanding advantage. But again the Lions' defense struck and turned the ball over. At the Lions' 3, Les Bingaman hit Al Carmichael and forced a fumble. Jim Cain fell on the loose ball for the Lions.

On the first play from scrimmage, Layne dropped back into his own end zone to pass. He missed Cloyce Box with it. So he called another pass play to the same receiver.

This time Bobby connected with Box, and Cloyce continued onward, 97 yards for the touchdown. After Jim Martin's conversion, the Lions trailed 15-14. But on the Packers' third offensive play, Bingaman, svelte for him at about 300 pounds, intercepted Babe Parilli's pass. Hunchy Hoernschemeyer quickly sprinted 41 yards to send the Lions into the lead. It became a 34-15 rout and Layne's pass from the end zone was the turning point.

"I knew we needed a lift," said Layne of his daring throw from the end zone.

Again Parker had made the correct decision. At halftime he had moved Box from end to left halfback.

The following Sunday the Bears helped the Lions with a 24-21 victory over the Rams, while the 49ers coasted over the Colts 38-21. The Lions now led the second-place 49ers by one game with the Rams in third, a game and a half behind. Again the clairvoyance of Parker's statement three weeks before was recalled.

A second death struck the Lions during the next week. Mary Lou Torgeson, the 24-year-old wife of Lavern Torgeson, died on December 4. The players were deeply saddened by her death. But preparation for the Sunday rematch with the Bears had to press onward. With Torgeson given a leave of absence to take his wife's body home to Washington, the Lions were without their defensive signal caller. The assignment was given to Joe Schmidt, the rookie left linebacker.

The defense had been responsible for the Lions' second-half good fortune and now there were fears it would break down without Torgeson, the veteran right linebacker. Jim Martin, the all-purpose journeyman, filled the vacancy.

In the locker room at Briggs Stadium, the Lions were solemn. Suddenly Doak Walker broke the slience. "A prayer for Mary Lou . . ." Still somber, the Lions went out and scored 13 points in the first half. Doak kicked field goals of 41 and 36 yards and Layne passed 38 yards to Dorne Dibble for a touchdown.

There was no breakdown on defense. With Schmidt calling the alignments with the skill of a veteran, the Lions held off the Bears in the second half. The early 13 points were sufficient. The Lions were winners for the fifth straight week, 13-7. Again Chris' Crew was immense. This time there were five interceptions with Christiansen claiming two to give him 11 in 11 games.

The Lions had some quiet hopes they could clinch their title on this Sunday. But the 49ers remained in the race with a 48-14 victory over the Packers. The Rams, though they routed Baltimore, were eliminated by the Lions' triumph. The Lions were 9-2, the 49ers 8-3.

"We never really expected help from the Packers," said Buddy Parker as he became a savant again. "Besides, it's nicer to win it yourself."

On their way to the title game, the Lions edged San Francisco in the Western Conference. Tragedy struck the team in the 11th week of the season; death claimed the wife of right linebacker LaVern Torgeson (far left). He was replaced by Jim Martin (left), and Torgeson's defensive signal calling duties were entrusted to the sensational rookie left linebacker, Joe Schmidt. Safetyman Jack Christiansen (right) made 12 interceptions in 1953.

At least a division tie was assured as the Lions prepared for their season finale at New York against the weak Giants. The Giants had had a terrible season and were a team in disarray. But they received an early shot of incentive on Tuesday. Steve Owen, their coach of many years, resigned under some pressure. The players would be ready to sacrifice themselves for their stout old coach as Buddy Parker cautioned the Lions. "The Giants will play their hearts out for Steve," said Parker.

Parker was equipping himself for any eventuality, with the Lions certain to play either a playoff with San Francisco or a championship game with Cleveland after the trip to New York. Russ Thomas, the regular scout, was assigned to provide espionage information on the Browns, who were 11-0 and were seeking to become the NFL's first unbeaten club since the 1942 Bears. On the West Coast the retired Jim Hardy was enlisted to provide details on the 49ers — should a Western playoff be necessary.

It was a chilly week in Detroit and Parker continued to stress defense, a defense which permitted only seven touchdowns in the five-game winning streak.

LaVern Torgeson returned from the personal tragedy of his wife's death and asked to play against the Giants.

On Sunday, the Lions had considerable difficulty — but perpetuated their winning streak and won their second title in two years. The Giants were their sixth consecutive victim after Parker had made his prophecy in the anguish of the loss to the Rams. He was reminded how wise he had been in his statement that the Rams had better not lose again or else. He had forgotten he'd ever uttered the statement.

"I must have been plenty mad when I said that," he said after the divisional title-clinching. "I had no crystal ball."

The Lions were 10-2, the best season in their history, preparing to meet the Browns for the second time in a championship game. Although the '53 record of 10-2 was superior to the 1952 champions' 9-3, the '52 Lions had gone through the season with fewer scares. Six of the 10 victories in 1953 were settled by a touchdown or less, the product of a stout defense which yielded just nine touchdowns during the six-game victory streak to the championship game.

The pattern of close, spectacular games did not change in the championship game at Briggs Stadium against Paul Brown's well-drilled Browns. Cleveland had failed on its final Sunday to go 12-0. Already assured of their Eastern title, the Browns were deprived of a perfect record by the Eagles, 42-27.

During the prelude to the championship game, Buddy Parker went into an analytical comparison of the '52 champions and his '53 club, and their circumstances.

"The seasons were entirely different," said Parker. "Last year we were coming up, just another contender. This year we were the champions. Everybody played us tough. Nobody played us easy all year.

"I have a feeling this team is better than last year's. It has better balance and is stronger defensively. I'm quite sure that next year's team will be even better than this one."

Buster Ramsey, the defensive assistant, spoke glowingly about the improvement of his unit. "I'm thinking of the improvement in the future of Joe Schmidt. Right now he's as good as any linebacker in the league . . . and he's just a rookie."

Across Lake Erie in Cleveland, Paul Brown drilled the Browns and slipped subtle reminders to them. They had lost the last two years in the championship game, first to the Rams and then to the Lions. The Lions had whipped the Browns five times in five meetings since the end of the All-America Football Conference.

While 54,577 watched in Briggs Stadium, the Lions went ahead 10-3 at halftime. That lead vanished in the second half because of two Lou Groza field goals and a touchdown by Chick Jagade for the Browns. At left, Walt Michaels of Cleveland brings down Bob Hoernschemeyer. The other Browns' players are Bill Willis (60) and Tom Catlin (50). At right, Yale Lary in pursuit of Browns' halfback Billy Reynolds. No. 88 is Darrell Brewster of the Browns.

The Browns were made 5 1/2-point favorites to dethrone the upstart Lions. In Cleveland, Otto Graham nodded silently as he operated the plays Brown instructed him to. In Detroit, Layne worked the plays himself, in accordance with the game plan provided by Parker, but Layne free-lanced and innovated and experimented. His arm had been bad over the second half of the schedule and quite often he skipped practice. But as Christmas approached, the arm strengthened and Layne threw his sometimes wobbly passes to his receivers every day.

One of his receivers was Jim Doran, a solid athlete from Iowa State. Doran had spent much of the year playing defensive end. Indeed, his teammates had voted him the team's most valuable player of the 1952 championship season for his performance at defensive end. But during the 1953 season, Parker had become dissatisfied with his pass receiving corps. So Doran was shifted back to offense, his original position when the Lions drafted him. He played infrequently the rest of the season and did not catch even a single touchdown pass.

"Box made 15 touchdowns last year," said Parker. "This season he scored two. We lost that quick touchdown, the kind that breaks a game wide open. That's part of the answer why it was more difficult this year."

Again Parker was treading toward the occult.

He frankly feared Otto Graham's arm. Otto, with a magnificent receiver in Dante Lavelli, had been the No. 1 passer in the NFL in '53. He completed 64.7 percent of his passes during the season. It was a phenomenal completion record. Together Graham and Lavelli were preparing for their eighth championship game in the last eight years.

This was Layne's second. And his arm was uncertain. Possibly because of the soreness, possibly because he seldom was accurate and precise until the clutch, Layne was deep in the

quarterbacking statistics as the NFL's fifth-ranked passer.

"Maybe he'll reach his season's peak in this game," said Parker as he watched Layne throw at practice on a day when a snowstrom forced the Lions to work out indoors at the University of Detroit's Memorial Building.

Another try at clairvoyance.

By Christmas Day, two days before the championship game, the odds favoring the Browns had been cut from 5 1/2 points to three. The Lions practiced outdoors. Afterwards each player received a present in a green and red Christmas envelope. It was a $300 gift from management.

On Saturday, December 26, commissioner Bert Bell arrived in Detroit. So did the Browns.

"Here possibly are the two best teams ever to meet for the championship," said Bell.

"The Lions and Browns are entirely different types of teams," said Brown. "Maybe we look better on paper. But they have a quarterback who runs and a field goal man in Walker who is just about as steady as Lou Groza."

On Sunday it was 34 degrees at Briggs Stadium. Eighteen years before, the Lions had won their first NFL championship in a partially empty stadium at the University of Detroit. The attendance was only 15,000 when Dutch Clark's Lions beat the Giants for the title. Now the streets downtown and leading in from suburbia were clogged. Throughout the two weeks of buildup for the game, there had been a brouhaha about the no-home-television rule. Commissioner Bell remained firm and the blackout remained. On this coolish Sunday, 54,577 customers packed Briggs Stadium and watched the Browns win the coin toss and choose to receive.

On the second play, Joe Schmidt blitzed in from left linebacker. He crashed viciously into Graham, the ball squirted loose, and Bingaman

plopped his 300-plus pounds atop the football at the Browns' 13.

Paul Brown was not the only cerebral head coach on the field this day. Buddy Parker, too, had thought of something special for this game. As the Lions went to offense at the Browns' 13, their line arrayed itself in an unbalanced formation — a rare ploy since the passing of the single wing era. With the added blocking strength on the strong side, the Lions pushed to the first touchdown on the ground. Walker scored it by running to the opposite side on the sixth play.

Striking quickly, the Lions then hoped their defense could contain the Browns. It did harass Graham with the pass rush and blitz. Otto was having a terrible day, but the Browns managed to move the ball some.

In the second quarter, Groza and Walker matched field goals. The Lions led 10-3 at halftime. As they walked across the field to their dugout runway, Leon Hart limped on a crippled knee. It was apparent he was finished for the game. Jim Doran was needed in the emergency.

Graham's passing malfunctions continued in the second half. But Paul Brown's quarterback was functioning well enough. Finally, the Browns tied it 10-10 on Harry (Chick) Jagade's touchdown in the third quarter.

Layne was passing better than Graham, but the Lions still failed to move the ball.

In the fourth period the Browns got close enough twice for Groza to kick 15- and 43-yard field goals. With fewer than five minutes left, the Browns were in front 16-10 and Groza kicked off into the end zone.

Layne assembled the Lions' offense near the goalposts.

The huge clock above the center-field bleachers told the Lions that 4:10 remained.

"Jest give me the time boys, and I'll get you downfield and back into that All-Star Game at Chicago," said Layne in his Texan's drawl. "Jest block."

Out of the huddle and up to the end of the line to the right trotted Jim Doran, the erstwhile defensive end. Aligned opposite Doran in the Browns' secondary was Warren Lahr, a veteran defender.

Layne took the snapback and fired out to the right to Doran, who had Lahr beaten. The first play of the drive gained 17 yards to the Lions' 37.

On the next play, Layne tried to pass to Dorne Dibble on the left. But the ball was dropped. So Layne tried his second-down pass to Doak Walker, his old high school crony. The pass was errant.

Now it was third-and-10 and the Lions gasping with less than four minutes to play at their 37. Layne called a pass to Doran again. At the sidelines, Parker's mind feverishly contemplated whether to punt if the third-down play failed to achieve the first down. He decided he would punt . . . if necessary.

Layne made the plans academic.

He dropped back again and looked right for Doran. Doran put a fake on Lahr, stopped abruptly and hooked. Layne's pass hit him in the chest, and Doran made it to the Browns' 45. An 18-yard gain. A first down.

"A buttonhook," Layne would say later. "We miss on that play and the game is over."

Now Layne dropped back again and passed to Cloyce Box at the 36. Nine yards. On second-and-one, Layne handed off to Hunchy Hoernschemeyer. There was no gain, and it was third-and-one. Layne again stepped into the huddle and called his own number, a quarterback sneak. He had to have one yard and he got three. Then he called time out and trotted to the bench to confer with Parker. Just over two minutes remained.

"Aldo Forte upstairs says Lennie Ford is

coming in fast from his end," said Parker. "A screen pass might work somewhere along the line."

While the timeout continued and the television commercials flashed across the screens of an expectant America, Jim Doran sidled up to Layne.

"I can beat my man," said Doran, "I can beat him on an up."

The whistle blew and Layne stepped into his huddle and called his play:

"Nine up . . . and block . . ."

Doran lined up wide right at the Browns' 33 and Layne took the snap. Doran streaked straight upfield, feinting at Lahr and slipping past him . . . by one step and then two.

Layne cocked, saw Doran open and fired a picturesque pass dead on target. Doran grabbed it behind Lahr and continued the remaining few yards into the end zone. With 2:08 to go, the Lions had tied it 16-all on Layne's 33-yard touchdown pass to Doran, the converted defensive end.

Doak Walker's placekick made it Lions 17, Browns 16.

Otto Graham had 2:08 left to pull out the victory for the Browns. He called the play Paul Brown had ordered and dropped back to pass.

In the Lions' secondary stood Carl Karilivacz, a 23rd-round draft choice who was playing in the championship game as a rookie. Karilivacz leaped as Graham's pass arched downward on the first play of the Browns' offensive series. His timing was excellent. He intercepted.

Layne, calling his own plays, ran out the remaining time.

The Lions were champions again. The Lions would fail miserably when they tried to make it three championships in succession against the Browns, but on this day their ideology had proved superior once again.

Bobby Layne had called the plays and Buddy

Parker's player moves had worked to perfection.

"Doran had been begging me to throw an up all day," said Layne. "Jim said he was sure he could get a step in front of Lahr. He called the shot."

And Otto Graham, the league's most proficient passer, completed only two of 15 passes all day. He had two intercepted.

"I just played a lousy game," said Graham. "I couldn't control the ball."

Dante Lavelli, Graham's favorite receiver, talked sourly nearby.

"Their pass defense wasn't especially difficult," he said. "I was loose a lot. We just didn't throw to the right men at the right time."

And Jim Doran, who had been the Lions' right man at the right time, next day went downtown to the club's offices to say goodbye and head home for Iowa.

As Doran walked to his car parked outside the club's building, he looked at the wheels and muttered angrily. It was just 24 hours after he had caught Layne's pass on a play they called together.

The car had a flat tire.

December 16, 1956

Whenever the Lions traveled to Chicago, they were accompanied by a natural fear of skulduggery. George Halas, the venerated Papa Bear, was a beloved icon in the mind of the Lions. It was just that they didn't trust him ... especially in his own lair, crammed Wrigley Field.

The Bears were a difficult enough opponent under even terms. At home Halas always managed to inveigle an edge for the team he had founded in 1920 when the NFL was born in a garage at Canton, Ohio. That was the popular belief among his opponents, at least. The Lions were not singular in this opinion. It was shared by all the other NFL clubs. It was feared that Halas would try to get away with some trick — and he often did.

So the Lions were typically wary and cautious as they prepared for their final game of the 1956 season. It would be at Chicago — and it would be more meaningful than the average football game between the archrivals.

The winner would advance to the championship game with the Giants. The Lions had reversed their miserable 1955 season with a magnificent 1956 campaign. Still shocked by the blitzkrieg 56-10 loss to the Browns in the 1954 championship game, the Lions started the 1955 season in an abyss. They lost their first six games, half the schedule, and staggered to a 3-9 finish, a plummet from first place to last in the Western Conference.

But in 1956, with Bobby Layne healthy again, the Lions won their first six games. At midseason, they were unbeaten and leading the West. It was a complete turnaround.

For the fifth time in six years, the Lions were a powerful club, perhaps the most powerful in the West. In contrast, the Bears had not won a divisional title in 10 years.

When the Lions briefly faltered on Thanksgiving — and Tobin Rote outdueled Layne for a 24-20 victory by Green Bay — the Bears slipped into first place. They had won seven games in a row followed by a tie. But they managed to maintain their spot at the top for only a week.

On December 3, the Bears made their annual visit to Detroit. Layne was brilliant and the Lions rolled to a 42-10 victory, regaining first place in the West.

Thus, all the drama and intrigue was staged for the season's final game two weeks later.

Both clubs won on December 10. The Lions waltzed to a 45-7 victory over the Steelers. Layne started, then Harry Gilmer, his backup, appeared so he could get himself prepared should there be an emergency the following Sunday. At Chicago, the Bears struggled to a 10-3 victory over their crosstown rivals, the Cardinals. It was a bitter game in Halas' Wrigley playpen and the Cardinals howled angry accusations when it was over. Two touchdown runs of 65 and 63 yards by the Cardinals' Ollie Matson were nullified by dubious penalties. Dubious in the minds of the Cardinals, anyway.

"Detroit better bring pistols when they come ... otherwise they'll get gypped," said a Cardinal whose name was unrecorded for posterity.

The Cardinals checked their films and announced they had discovered 23 flaws in the officiating, all in the favor of Halas' Bears.

Walter Wolfner, the Cardinals' owner, publicly accused Halas of heinous actions and malevolence.

"We hired six special policemen to patrol around our bench," said the outraged Wolfner. "It was useless. Halas had that band right there beating drums into our telephones."

Halas, smiling sardonically, piously denied any intent to sabotage the Cardinals' play-scouting system by jamming their communication lines with drumbeats.

But Buddy Parker was typically suspicious.

Lions	0	7	7	7	21
Bears	3	14	7	14	38

His Lions had a half-game lead with one to play. They were 9-2. Chicago was 8-2-1. The entire season was abstracted into this one game at Wrigley Field.

Parker was openly alarmed about possible sinister deeds by Halas on this critical Sunday.

"I wish I could do something about the bench at the Bears' park," said Parker warily. "But I guess that's George. Remember the time he cut the wires to the pressbox telephones on Green Bay?

"He's got a new one now. No kidding. Halas puts a 50-piece Navy band behind the visitors' bench. The drums keep thumping right into the telephones all the time. He's got the finest football field in the league. Halas really takes care of it. That field will be perfect Sunday and if it rains or snows, well, it will rain or snow on both of us.

"But the benches won't be the same. If he could, he'd have one of those fans of his sitting between our players. One time there I felt a tap on my shoulder. I looked around and it was some guy I'd never seen before. Just one of George's followers trying to get into the act. There are people in front of you and behind you and on the sides."

So it became a week of psychological pronouncements and clandestine practices.

Halas was on a sabbatical leave as the Bears' coach. He had handed the coaching job to Paddy Driscoll, an old-time associate. But Halas continued to control the Bears. He was, in effect, head coach emeritus and he watched over the preparations.

In Chicago, the Bears practiced indoors at an armory.

"We've got a couple of items for Sunday," Halas confessed to an early arriving Detroit visitor. "They're a surprise."

A little mental propaganda appearing in the Detroit press would aid the Bears' cause.

"Buddy has done a great job and if we can't win I'd like to see him do it," said Halas, continuing his psychological approach. "We're concerned about their defense primarily. That's what has held them together all season. Somebody's going to get to it sometime and I hope it's Sunday."

Halas went on to praise Dave Middleton, the young medical student who had devastated the Bears two weeks previous in the meeting at Detroit. He had become Layne's pet receiver. In that game, Middleton caught seven passes for 176 yards. In contrast, Chris' Crew had restricted Harlon Hill, the Bears' best receiver and probably the most dangerous in the NFL, to one catch. It was good for a token 13 yards.

"That was the best defensing I ever encountered," said Hill of the double-teaming scheme in which Christiansen, Jim David, Yale Lary and Carl Karilivacz shared the coverage.

Halas recalled how Layne had thrown two touchdown passes in the first game, a 48-yarder to Middleton providing the key touchdown in the second half. And Halas expressed concern over Layne's running ability. Layne had scored another touchdown on a 15-yard run off a fake pass play.

It was evident that Halas believed the Bears must neutralize Layne — render him ineffective — in order to beat the Lions and win the championship.

In Detroit, Parker, ordinarily a phlegmatic man, spoke candidly and confidently about the Lions' chances.

"It's an even-up thing," said Parker. "We beat them 42-10 before but we don't necessarily have to do it again. I realize that if Oklahoma played somebody 10 straight times they'd win 10 straight. But they're so much better they can win playing a bad game. There's not that much difference between us."

Parker did not delve as deeply into the realm

of occult pregame psychology as did coach Halas.

"This kind of game is no problem," Parker said. "The way the tempo runs on one like this you don't have to worry about the players' frame of mind. There's too much at stake. You can never tell just by looking at a player whether he's up or down before a game. You get fooled a lot. Then you get to a game like this. Our state of mind will be fine, don't worry.

"We are ready. For the first time this year I have every one of my players healthy."

Parker's major concern was what sort of problems the Lions would encounter when they reached Wrigley Field.

In the secrecy of the Chicago Armory, ancient Clark Shaughnessy, T-formation tutor of Sid Luckman, 41 years a coach, was in charge of the Bears' game plan.

He gathered the defensive personnel around him – Bill George, Ed Sprinkle, Ed Meadows, Joe Fortunato and their colleagues.

"Layne killed us when we played in Detroit," Shaughnessy told them. "This time we're going to have to rush him and hurry him. We're going to have to change our defense every play. We don't want Layne to know where our rushes are coming from. We have to rush Layne."

It was vividly clear to the Bears' defenders: Layne must be stopped or they wouldn't get to the championship game. They all nodded and agreed on this point as Shaughnessy talked and they listened intently. Among the most intense was Meadows, the roughhewn, black-haired defensive lineman who enjoyed trapping the quarterback.

Elsewhere in the armory, Ed Brown practiced his passing. He was the NFL's No. 1 passer . . . not a glamour quarterback, but effective. Hill faked and maneuvered and found himself alone on his precise patterns. Rick Casares, the NFL's No. 1 runner, practiced his bursts into the line.

Casares had been held to 42 yards by the Lions in their confrontation two week before. He had gained respect for the Lions' defensive line and the overall defense now under the command of Joe Schmidt, middle linebacker and a four-year veteran. Casares needed 64 yards in the finale to become the fifth 1,000-yard runner in the 37-season history of the NFL. But such a milestone was secondary in a game of such enormous importance. Halas, in an obvious ploy declared publicly that Casares would serve principally as a decoy against the Lions.

"We've been feeding him the ball," said Halas when Casares' quest for 1,000 yards was mentioned. "We're not going to do that Sunday. The Lions stop one man too easily. If Casares breaks that record, he'll have to get away on a long run. He has no chance of punching it out through the Lions' line."

Halas had some secret plans for the Lions, all right.

On Saturday, December 15, 1956, the Lions boarded the train for Chicago at Michigan Central Depot. The players dropped their belongings in their private coach, and headed for their special dining car. Their mood was carefree, almost joyous. Bobby Layne sat at a table and regaled his comrades with conversation in his deep Texas dialect.

The Lions were confident. For the fifth time in the six years of Parker's regime, they had gone into their final game with the Western title as the prize. They had proven themselves to be winners in these games. They were certain they could beat the Bears again . . . even in Chicago. The train trip was a joy ride.

At Chicago, Parker checked the Lions into the aristocratic Edgewater Beach Hotel on the far North Side. By coincidence, the Bears were having an alumni party at the hotel on Saturday night. Some of the Lions' party was invited

Some of the players in a 1956 drama to decide the champion of the Western Conference: (right) master strategist and George Halas confidant Clark Shaughnessy, with Bears' star receiver Harlon Hill; Dave Middleton, who caught seven Bobby Layne passes for 176 yards against the Bears in an earlier game that year, and Chicago's Rick Casares, the leading rusher in professional football that year.

inside. There was onimous talk that some accident would befall Layne the following afternoon during the game.

Sunday, December 16, 1956, was Buddy Parker's 43rd birthday. It would not be a festive occasion. The din created by the band angered him. But the Lions' apparent ennui at the start of the game did not concern him. Their trait was to start lethargically and allow Layne to rally them in time to win in the second half going away.

So there was no worry when Layne could not move the ball after the Lions received the opening kickoff. There was none, either, when George Blanda, kicked a 37-yard field goal to put the Bears ahead, 3-0, in the first quarter.

That was the score on the fifth play of the second quarter. Layne stepped into the huddle, analyzed the situation and called Gene Gedman's number on a sweep to the left.

Layne handed off to Gedman and turned to watch the ballcarrier on his circle route to the left. Layne's hands dangled nonchalantly at his sides, his participation in the play ended,

The last thing Layne saw was Gedman's rear end and churning thighs. Suddenly, all became blackness. Layne was face flat on the field, unconscious.

The Bears' plan was to place Layne under a pressurized rush. Ed Meadows had belted in on this play. His momentum continued after Layne completed the handoff to Gedman and watched the play unfurl. Layne was sent careening from a blow from the blindside. He did not see Meadows charge into him.

The darkness did not lift for Layne until the second half.

The Lions were furious at what they regarded as a cheap shot. Lou Creekmur shifted sides to engage Meadows on the next play and it was a cruel collision. There were penalties and grabbing and punching. Meadows was ejected before

the end of the second quarter when he kicked at Creekmur and engaged in a fistfight with the Lions' Bill Bowman. Later the Lions' Gil Mains was ejected when he landed a fist on the chin on one of the Bears, Bill Bishop.

It was a violent, brutal football game. From antiquity, the Lions have claimed they were a beaten team that day because they lost Bobby Layne when he was kayoed by Ed Meadows. But this was not totally true.

Indeed, the Lions, under the aegis of little Harry Gilmer, went ahead soon after the Layne-Meadows incident.

Gilmer had been a magnificent college passer at Alabama. But he was merely a journeyman pro quarterback and later he would coach the Lions of the mid-1960s through two terrible seasons. He was a thorough student of the game and a keen passer.

Soon after Layne became *hors de combat*, Gilmer rallied the Lions to a go-ahead touchdown. He hit Jim Doran with a 14-yard pass, then Bowman with an 18-yarder for the touchdown.

But then, as Halas had foreshadowed, the Lions' defense suddenly became vulnerable for the first time in 1956. Casares managed the long run Halas had mentioned for a 68-yard touchdown and a 10-7 lead. Then J. C. Caroline, whom Halas had switched from defense to offense, scooted nine yards for a touchdown. The Bears had the situation in control by halftime 17-7.

In the third period, Lary intercepted Brown and Gilmer delivered the Lions another touchdown. He passed 12 yards to Middleton, before Leon Hart bulled into the end zone. The Lions had a chance — and it was just the type of situation that Layne had thrived upon for years. But he was just starting to regain consciousness in the locker room.

The Lions' defense was asleep. Halas

After handing off to Gene Gedman, Bobby Layne watched the halfback run. In that moment, the lights went out on Layne. He had been blindsided by the Bears' Ed Meadows. A thoroughly shaken Layne was helped off the field. Acts of recrimination followed, and Meadows was ejected after an altercation with Lou Creekmur. Harry Gilmer replaced Layne and threw a touchdown pass to Jim Doran, putting Detroit ahead 10-7. Then, a Lion's defense that had managed to stop Casares (below, being tackled by Carl Karilivacz as Joe Schmidt comes up) fell apart. Casares ran 68 yards for a touchdown to put his team ahead to stay.

exploited Harlon Hill's abilities with brilliance. At times Hill lined up in the backfield and ran with the football. Once he threw a pass. Other times he was at his normal end position. The Lions had neutralized his receiving in the first game. But now he roamed with freedom. Hill was totally in the clear behind Chris' Crew when Brown spied him in the third period. It was a 44-yard touchdown pass — and it broke the Lions' backs.

The game turned into a rout. Bobby Watkins scored on a seven-yard run, Joe Fortunato on a 27-yard pass interception. The Lions managed one more touchdown on Gilmer's nine-yard pass to Dorne Dibble.

But by then the critical game of the year had degenerated into a riot. Lions fought with Bears. Halas' fans poured onto the field and got into the battle with the Lions.

The final was Bears 38, Lions 21. Casares finished with 190 yards on 17 carries, a bonafide member of the elite 1,000-Yard Club with a season total of 1,127. Gilmer had played gallantly in vain. Scampering around, away from the Bears' menacing rush, he kept the Lions in the game offensively. But the defense broke down.

The final indignity was the serenade to Buddy Parker from Halas' 49,086 customers — Happy Birthday to you, Happy Birthday to you . . . Happy Birthday, Dear Buddy . . . ''

Parker displayed white anger because of the one play on which his quarterback was set upon by an aggressive — probably an overaggressive — football player.

"Meadows should have brought a blackjack," said Parker in the locker room on his unhappy birthday.

"We're a one-man ballclub offensively. I don't mind the Bears winning. They were up. But they said they'd get Layne and they did and I wonder if this is football."

Edwin J. Anderson, the Lions' president, was a man with bushy eyebrows. He always wore a Tyrolean hat with a feather in the band. He was incensed.

"I offer no alibis," said Andy, an affable person on most occasions, "We've had a better season that we expected. The Bears were up higher than we were.

"But Ed Meadows should be barred from football."

Layne returned home to Detroit with his teammates. He entered Detroit Osteopathic Hospital with a concussion.

"I didn't see Meadows before or after he hit me," said the subdued leader of the Lions. "I never saw anything. I never heard anything. The lights just went out, that's all."

Meadows, the villain of the piece, told Sid Luckman, an assistant coach for the Bears, he was surprised Layne had a concussion. He had not been penalized for the Layne affair. But he was in an ensuing sequence when he kicked the revenge-minded Creekmur, who was on the ground. Then Meadows was attacked by Bowman.

Meadows maintained complete innocence over Layne's injury. Meadows spoke after returning from a hospital where he had a broken tooth fixed.

"I shot in after him, running at full speed," he said. "He had his back to the line every time with the ball and I didn't know whether he still had the ball or not.

"Believe me, there was nothing deliberate about it. Sure, I was trying to tackle him and I always try to tackle hard. But as for me being out to get him, there's nothing to that at all."

Commissioner Bert Bell, before he was in receipt of a three-page letter of protest from Anderson, said: "I don't believe any player would maliciously try to hurt anyone. I don't know what the play was. There was no penalty

Leon Hart's touchdown, aided by the block of Lou Creekmur (below) brought the Lions to within three points, 17-14, in the third quarter. A bomb to Harlon Hill then broke the backs of the Lions, and Chicago rolled to a 38-21 victory. Protests from the Lions followed along with denials by Meadows that he had meant to disable Layne. For the angry Lions, there was some consolation when Chicago played the New York Giants for the NFL championship a week later. New York won 47-7.

called. I talked to referee Ron Gibbs and the officials said they didn't see anything in the situation."

In Detroit, the incident had become a *cause célèbre*. Newspapers headlined the story on the front page and villified Meadows. Parker, as was his wont, announced again that he would quit the game of pro football.

"That rioting by the fans should stop," said Parker. "It's taken a long time to build up pro football and when you have to put up with those fans ruining everything, it's going to ruin the game. It's the second week in a row that the fans have taken over that same field. It makes you wonder whether it's worth it or not."

In his seasons after replacing Bo McMillin in 1951, Parker had been rewarded only with six successive one-year contracts. He had boiled for years, since the Lions had an incipient dynasty, that he couldn't get a long-term contract as head coach. Now the Lions would offer Parker a two-year contract in hopes of keeping him.

The furor continued. Anderson's missive to Bell charged Meadows with deliberately slugging Layne. "That's a lie," spouted Halas. The Lions further suggested that Meadows be barred from football. Bell bristled back at the Lions after viewing films which showed Meadows roughing Layne, but not slugging him.

"The Lions ought to look at motion pictures of the game and get any other evidence they think they have before accusing that boy of deliberately injuring another player," said Bell from his commissioner's office in Philadelphia.

The Lions charged the act as being premeditated . . . and viewers of the movies were inclined to agree to this point.

"I wasn't surprised to find out it was Meadows who got me," said Layne.

Six days after the riotous game in Chicago the Lions abjectly apologized for their charges against Meadows. Parker telephoned Halas at his office in Chicago.

"I regret telling the press that you encouraged dirty playing," said Parker to the Papa Bear.

"I probably wanted to win that game more than any other in my coaching career . . . not for personal satisfaction but for the players who did such a tremendous job in almost succeeding in making the unprecedented jump from last place to first within a year.

"I still think Meadows made an illegal play, but I never said he slugged our quarterback. There are bound to be a few illegal plays in a game that means so much to everybody."

"I wasn't surprised that he called me," said Halas. "It proves again the kind of sportsman he is."

On Christmas Eve, Parker announced, "I won't quit football. I can't leave something I've done all my life."

Two days later Parker achieved his breakthrough. The Lions gave him a two-year contract for 1957 and 1958 at a $30,000 annual salary. He smiled at last.

And two days after that the Giants obliterated the Bears 47-7 for the NFL championship the Lions believed could have been theirs.

Buddy Parker watched it on TV, content in his new two-year security. But in the course of future events, it turned out the game the Lions played and lost in Chicago at the end of 1956 — the game in which Bobby Layne was clobbered, precipitating controversy and malicious charges — was the last Parker would ever coach for the Detroit Lions.

The following August, with 1957 training camp barely started, Parker ripped up his two-year contract and quit his job again. This time he meant it and it was final. The 1957 team he claimed he couldn't control would win the championship with an historic comeback — despite another injury to Bobby Layne.

December 22, 1957

Halftime at San Francisco . . .

As the football teams moved toward the end zone runway at Kezar Stadium, where the fans ofttimes dropped garbage on the athletes below, there was a public announcement of importance to all.

"Tickets are now on sale for next week's championship game with the Browns," boomed the public address man. The seagulls continued their graceful sorties over the decaying adobe stadium. And the 60,000 title-deprived fans in Kezar in the city by the Bay unloosed a maddening cheer.

Their beloved 49ers, never before so much as a divisional title winner since their establishment in 1946, were at the very brink. Y.A. Tittle, Hugh McElhenny, Billy Wilson and their other heroes of the moment had the Lions down 24-7 in this playoff for the Western Conference title of the NFL.

So, as though homed in by the announcement that next week's tickets were on sale now at intermission, thousands left their seats. They formed queues at the ticket kiosks and bantered with unconcerned gaiety. This, indeed, was the 49ers' day at long last.

"Tittle, three touchdown passes already," said a ruddy-faced fan, prepared to buy four tickets to the NFL championship game. "Betcha he throws three more in the second half. Can't believe the Lions are so lousy."

The Lions, beaten and disgusted and without Bobby Layne, fled to the safety of their locker room. A helmet was thrown, there was a soft curse. Then there was utter and gloomy silence.

The only noise came from through the wall, from the next locker room, where the 49ers were unable to restrain their celebration.

"We could hear them laughing," a quarterback named Tobin Rote would mention years later. "The walls were paper thin and as we sat there we could hear them laughing and yelling about how they were going to spend their championship game money. We couldn't do much but sit there and listen to them."

The somber mood of the Lions turned to seething anger.

"Listen to those SOBs," growled Joe Schmidt.

In a corner, Bobby Layne, his broken ankle mending in a cast, drawled something about the game not being over yet.

Tobin Rote's head drooped. Nearby a cherubic, seldom-used reserve running back named Tom Tracy sat impassively. There was a glint in the eyes of first-year coach George Wilson and his insides burned with fury.

Still, the circus — the mocking merry-making — next door in the 49ers' locker room continued.

"The wife's got my dough all spent," shrieked an ebullient voice. "Wants a new car."

The noise would stop only when it was time for the 49ers to return to the brownish Kezar turf and finish the rout. Thirty more minutes, and after years of frustration, they would be in the championship game. Outside, the ticket sales were brisk.

And so a season started in turbulence and filled with considerable glory was ending in despair for the Lions. And in humiliation on national television in a playoff game which had turned into a lopsided waltz.

"OK," said George Wilson, "you haven't quit before. Don't now."

His words had a hollow tone.

The Lions — Tobin Rote, Joe Schmidt, Tom Tracy — put on their grayish silver helmets, fastened their chin straps and went outside. The mocking laughter of the 49ers subsided so the game could progress.

After the destruction of Bobby Layne in the loss at Chicago in December, 1956, Buddy Parker decided it was mandatory the Lions

Lions 7 0 14 10 31
49ers 14 10 3 0 27

acquire a second top-caliber quarterback. Parker was positive the loss of Layne in that game had cost the Lions the 1956 championship. So he screened the league, determined which veteran quarterbacks were available and opened trade negotiations. Parker liked Tobin Rote, who had conquered the Lions for Green Bay the previous Thanksgiving.

On July 26, 1957, shortly before the opening of the training camps, Parker concluded his lengthy talks with Lisle Blackbourn, the coach of the Packers. Rote was acquired from Green Bay for four veteran Lions — halfback Don McIlhenny and linemen Ollie Spencer, Jim Salsbury and Norm Masters. The Packers threw in a defensive halfback, Val Joe Walker, lest the deal seem too lopsided against the Lions.

"If we had had Rote on the bench last year in the game at Chicago, the result would have been different," said Parker in defending the trade, which on the surface was a slap at Bobby Layne.

"Rote always has been great under pressure.

"It took us three months to get him and then it looked like the deal had fallen through. I didn't think they were serious about trading Rote. But then they called us and said we could have him."

Layne had been an icon in Detroit since 1950 — and now, suddenly, he was threatened by another quarterback. A touchy situation had been created. But Parker believed he could handle the situation all right.

Layne felt no resentment. And immediately Rote meshed with the camaraderie for which the playful Lions were famous.

Two weeks later Layne and Rote were among the players Parker discovered, with drinks in their passing hands, at the pre-banquet party in the Statler Hotel. Before the night ended, Parker had quit as the Lions' head coach, in his famous "I can't handle this team any more"

speech at the Meet the Lions affair in Detroit.

George Wilson inherited the playboy ballclub and its hazardous two-quarterback situation.

"It's working out much better than the combination of Sid Luckman and Johnny Lujack when I was with the Bears," Wilson said before training camp was ended. "When Rote is on the bench, he's trying in some way to help Layne on the field. It's no different when Rote is playing and Layne is on the sideline."

Wilson announced plans to start the season by alternating quarterbacks, Layne in the opener vs. the Colts, Rote in the second game vs. his old Green Bay teammates.

The season started with the Lions losing to Baltimore and a young quarterback, John Unitas, 34-14. Then they won their next three games. The third was the rematch with Baltimore — a young team just growing into contention in the West with the Lions and 49ers.

With sheer brilliance, young Unitas outdueled both veterans, Layne and Rote, for 40 minutes on a gray October Sunday in Detroit. Johnny U. threw four touchdown passes. With five minutes to play in the third quarter the Colts were in control, 27-3.

Rote replaced Layne and threw a 14-yard touchdown pass to Steve Junker. It did not seem very important at the moment, late in the third period.

Re-enter Layne in the fourth quarter. With eight minutes to go, the Colts led 27-10.

For two years, Howard (Hopalong) Cassady had been an outcast among the tight, unified Lions. His teammates resented the crushing publicity of his collegiate exploits at Ohio State. They resented as much his failure to match those exploits in the pros. He was considered another collegian with an over-inflated reputation.

Now, with eight minutes left against Baltimore, Layne glared at Cassady in the huddle.

He ordered him out on a deep pattern. Layne threw, and Cassady caught a 26-yard touchdown pass. It sliced the Colts' lead to 27-17.

No longer was Baltimore's lead insurmountable. But then Layne was intercepted by Andy Nelson on the Lions' next series. A moment later the defense forced Alan Ameche to fumble and Jim David recovered.

A moment after that, Colts' coach Weeb Ewbank and Wilson were given the standard two-minute notification. On the field during the lull, Layne went over strategy. He sent Cassady deep again. Layne threw and Cassady had to vault to reach the ball. He caught it and tumbled at the Colts' 1 – a 30-yard advance. On the next play, John Henry Johnson scored and the Colts' lead quickly had been slashed to 27-24.

But Unitas merely had to run out the remaining 90 seconds with some ball control. Two runs lost yardage and on the third Yale Lary grabbed Lenny Moore by the elbows. Lary compressed the elbows into Moore's ribs. Presto, the ball squirted out and Lary let go and dropped on it. With 50 seconds to play, the Lions had the ball again on the Colts' 29-yard line.

Back in the huddle, Layne once again commanded Cassady to go deep, along the left sideline. Then Layne, the blond, game-rescuing specialist, arched the ball to Cassady at the goal line. Another touchdown – a 24-point deficit obliterated in less than 20 minutes – and the Lions won 31-27.

The victory was vital. It kept the Lions and 49ers in the race, tying them with the Colts atop the West.

"This team has proved to itself it can beat anybody it wants to beat," said Wilson.

"The 1953 championship game was wonderful," said Layne, who had proven he retained his game-stealing flair, the quality which enabled him to overshadow Rote. "But this one is bigger now for George and for all of us."

The Lions now embarked on their two-game West Coast junket. They lost to the Rams in the first game, then went up north to play the 49ers. Another defeat could be disastrous.

Now it was Rote's turn to prove he could rally a team in the fourth quarter. The Lions trailed the 49ers 28-10 when Rote was given the rescue mission. Rote passed 31 yards to Jim Doran for a touchdown. Then he passed 13 yards to Junker for another. Then, with 80 seconds remaining, he passed eight yards to Doran for another touchdown. Three touchdown passes by Rote in 9-1/2 minutes and the Lions again had managed to overcome a massive deficit. The Lions were in front 31-28.

But with 10 seconds left, Y.A. Tittle lofted a balloon into the end zone from 41 yards out. R. C. Owens climbed up some invisible ladder, over Jack Christiansen and Jim David, and caught the ball. It was the 49ers' Alley-Oop play. They beat the Lions 35-31. The arched pass to Owens was the 28th thrown by Tittle that day and the 21st completion.

The Lions made the seven-hour flight home in deep despair. Their trick was stealing victories in the last minute. Now they were victims of such a happening.

"It's like having your heart cut out," said Bobby Layne.

It was worse. The '57 schedule was half over and the 49ers were dominant in the West with a two-game bulge over their pursuers. They were 5-1; the Lions and Colts were 3-3.

"We're not out of it," said George Wilson. "With quarterbacking like that I can see how the 49ers keep winning. But this is a different kind of year. Anything can happen."

It did. The 49ers lost their next three games. The Colts won their next three. The Lions won two and lost one of their next three. With three

games remaining the Colts led the division at 6-3, with the Lions and 49ers tied at 5-4.

On Thanksgiving Day, the Lions were having their annual problem with the Packers. Green Bay led 6-3 at the half. George Wilson spoke at halftime in the locker room.

"You guys are a disgrace. You ought to be ashamed. I'm sick of watching you. You're supposed to be a football team and you're nothing."

Wilson berated his athletes for perhaps 10 minutes, then sent them back onto the field.

Stung by the oratory, John Henry Johnson rumbled 62 yards for a touchdown early in the third period. Harley Sewell's block opened the hole. The game turned, the Lions won, 18-6.

"He was so mad," Lou Creekmur, the offensive left tackle said of Wilson, "I wanted to leave. I was afraid he'd hit somebody and they'd hold me as a witness."

"It was Thanksgiving," said Gene Gedman, the runner, "but it was no place for Puritans."

"It's the maddest I've been all year," said Wilson. "They were fumbling the championship away and it really burned me."

The following Sunday the Colts and 49ers won again. The standings remained static.

December 8, 1957, was a raw, gloomy day in Detroit. The Lions were rooted in a blue lethargy again — their regular first-half malaise — in their game with the Browns. In the second quarter, Layne retreated to pass. He implanted his foot in the earth at Briggs Stadium. His protection broke and he was bowled over by Paul Wiggin and Don Colo. Layne's ankle snapped.

The words of Buddy Parker, on the day of his final deal for the Lions, echoed: "If we had Rote on the bench last year . . . the result would have been different."

Layne was carted off and taken to Detroit Osteopathic Hospital. The Lions were down to a single quarterback again — Rote. At halftime, the Lions, shocked at the loss again of their spirit leader, held a precarious 3-0 lead. Wilson again tried halftime oratory, plagiarizing from an old movie he once saw in which Pat O'Brien was cast as Knute Rockne.

"Win one for Layne," Wilson implored. "He's won plenty for you."

The comment broke the Lions' despair and their lethargy. Led by Rote, they beat the Browns 20-7 to remain in contention.

Three hours later Layne was propped up on an operating table waiting for surgery to repair his broken ankle. A television set was turned on, bringing in a black-and-white picture from San Francisco. The Colts were playing the 49ers and Tittle, like Layne, was an injury victim of the enemy pass rush. John Brodie, a rookie, was trying valiantly to rally the 49ers. Brodie scrambled, dashed away from Gino Marchetti and Art Donovan, and desperately looked for a receiver.

"Throw it, throw it," rooted Layne, propped up in the hospital, across the country in Detroit. Brodie finally threw it . . . Hugh McElhenny caught it. And the 49ers beat the Colts 17-13.

With just one game left for all three, the day's games had resulted in a three-way tie for first in the West. The Lions, 49ers and Colts were tied at 7-4.

On the final Sunday, the Lions revisited Chicago and Wrigley Field for the first time since the infamous incident in which Layne was knocked incoherent by Ed Meadows.

There was motivation more powerful than avenging a year-old grudge, however. For the sixth time in seven years, the Lions entered their final game with the Western title involved. And confused by the spread formation thrown at them by the uncanny George Halas, the Lions dropped quickly behind. At halftime

the sluggish Lions were losing to the Bears 10-0.

It was time for another piece of harsh rhetoric by George Wilson. He lambasted the Lions, indicated they were quitters, called them names.

Tobin Rote produced three touchdowns in the second half. The key was a nine-yard pass to Dave Middleton to send the Lions into the lead. The Lions won, 21-13 ... and then had to sit back and wait.

Out on the West Coast, the 49ers beat the Packers 27-20. It meant the Lions and 49ers would be tied at 8-4. But down in Los Angeles, the Rams upset the Colts 37-21. A three-way tie and a complicated playoff was avoided. On the next Sunday, the Lions would merely play off with the 49ers in San Francisco. The winner would be the host team to the Browns, who had qualified for their 11th league championship game in their 12th season of existence.

On Tuesday, December 17, the Lions flew West from Willow Run Airport near Detroit. Amid riotous circumstances in San Francisco, every ticket to the playoff at Kezar Stadium had been sold. The Lions had won their last three games with rallies in the second-half. This had been Bobby Layne's trick ... But Tobin Rote had learned it. Quickly. And George Wilson, as the hurry-up successor to Buddy Parker, had become a halftime orator of some renown. He spoke on the Westward-bound airplane:

"Our conditioning is paying off. We have been running more in practice than ever before.

"No, most halftime talks aren't fiery. We ate the boys out a little bit at halftime against Green Bay. We had Bobby Layne's injury to talk about against Cleveland. All I said in Chicago last Sunday was we had only 30 minutes to do the job or the season was over."

Out in San Francisco, the papers quoted 49ers' coach Frankie Albert. "We'll beat the De-troit Lions next Sunday," he predicted simply.

The Lions felt some contempt for the 49ers. They had lost at Kezar on Tittle's last-play Alley-Oop to Owens. But they reversed that result two weeks later in the rematch at Detroit. The Lions devoured the 49ers 31-10.

"They were the easiest team we've played," some of the Lions said after the rematch. But that was in Detroit. In visits to Kezar the Lions had won only twice in eight years. Additionally, the 49ers had Tittle, their quarterback-leader, back. The Lions brought Layne along solely for morale-boosting purposes.

The Lions bivouacked in Palo Alto, down the peninsula from San Francisco, at rustic Rickey's Hotel. Through the years, Rickey's has been the locale for some of the Lions' wildest escapades and zaniest incidents. But on this week, there was only preparation for football. The Lions practiced at Stanford.

Three days before the game, Wilson attempted to assemble a backfield. Rote was at quarterback, in Layne's place. Of the runners, John Henry Johnson and Cassady were lame. Wilson stationed the roly-poly Tracy in with the first unit — lest he be needed on Sunday. Tracy was totally healthy for the simple reason that he had seldom played all season.

"He's our secret weapon," said Wilson. "He says he's been ready for 12 games."

The next day after practice, Wilson said: "If we win, we'll get the job done with our defense plus Rote and the receivers."

It had taken time for the veterans — those who had been with the Lions from the 1952-53 championship seasons — to accept Rote. Layne had been their champion, their winner. They felt safe with him at quarterback. They felt a bit insecure with Rote.

Before the last game, a number of veterans confessed their apprehension to Doc Greene, the eminent sports columnist of the *Detroit*

Y.A. Tittle was the boss of a San Francisco team on the way to the 49ers' best season since entering the NFL in 1950. At left, Tittle sneaks over for a touchdown in San Francisco's 35-31 regular season victory over the Lions at Kezar. Detroit defenders are Yale Lary (24) and Joe Schmidt (56). There was no clear-cut choice for quarterback on the Lions in '57. New coach George Wilson alternated Rote and Bobby Layne, and the ability to bring the team from behind was by no means the sole province of Rote. In the fourth week of the season, the Lions trailed Baltimore 27-3, but rallied behind the passing of Layne to rookie Howard (Hopalong) Cassady (right). Detroit won 31-27.

News. For eight years, the Lions had not won a big game without Layne as the galvanizing factor. But now Rote had won such a game at Chicago.

"The Rote deal panned out pretty well for us," W. Nick Kerbawy, the general manager, stated one night at Rickey's.

"We should do better the next game," said Wilson, reaffirming his personal faith in Rote. "Now we've won with him. It's natural."

The phenomenon of Bobby Layne in Detroit had entered its last phase — although this fact was unrecognized at the time, as the Lions prepared for their 1957 playoff in San Francisco.

In the grandstands at Kezar Stadium, satisfied customers placed red and yellow tickets for the next week's NFL championship game into their pockets. Occasionally, they put their hands inside their coats. They traced the borders of the tickets with their fingertips. It was most reassuring.

It had not been much of an artistic spectacle on the barren field below. But it was so exciting because the beloved 49ers had so thoroughly dominated the visitors from Detroit.

R.C. Owens had not scored a touchdown since his Alley-Oop game winner against the Lions seven weeks before. But midway through the first quarter, Tittle and Owens collaborated again. He outjumped Jim David in the corner to catch Tittle's 34-yard lob pass. The 49ers had struck for a 7-0 advantage. Three minutes later they struck again to make it 14-0. McElhenny, streaking out of the backfield, dashed between David and Yale Lary. There, Tittle connected with him on a play that consumed 47 yards.

The Lions' secondary had become a sieve. The offense was sputtering. Rote managed a drive of 61 yards culminated by a three-yard pass to Steve Junker, the rookie tight end. It was 14-7. But Tittle marched the 49ers 88

yards on the return foray. He pitched his third touchdown pass to Billy Wilson, a 12-yarder. Then before the intermission — and the announcement that tickets were on sale — Gordy Soltau kicked a 25-yard field goal. The Lions had inflicted terrible self-damage with two fumbles and an interception off of Rote.

The 49ers had assumed their 24-7 halftime advantage with consummate simplicity. It had become a laughing matter for the 49ers. And laugh they did as the Lions eavesdropped and fumed.

The Lions, it was true, had gotten to the playoff as a team talented in second-half heroics. But this second-half syndrome was cracked immediately at the start of the third period . . . while the 49ers' partisans were still bragging to each other about their good fortune during the halftime ticket sale.

The second half opened with the Lions kicking off. On the first scrimmage play, McElhenny streaked outside and twisted into the open through the Lions' defense. Hugh went 71 yards before he was trapped and brought down at the Lions' 9. Any great expectations the Lions had after their halftime humiliations had to be tempered by fact. The Lions were in jeopardy of surrendering a fourth touchdown to the 49ers.

Tittle took the 49ers into their huddle while across the line Schmidt sought to flag the sagging defense. Schmidt's defense held. It held firmly at the Lions' three. Albert ordered another field goal and Soltau kicked the simple 10-yarder. Now the 49ers were in 27-7 command.

Once again the Lions' offense faltered. Rote could get nothing going and the Lions had to punt. Tittle envisioned another scoring march for the 49ers. But he fumbled at the 49ers' 27.

Bob Long fell atop it for the Lions. Six minutes remained in the third quarter and with

Some of the heroes of a great comeback which propelled the Lions into the NFL championship: Tom Tracy (left), who scored two touchdowns in the space of 89 seconds; Gene Gedman (right), whose touchdown tied the 49ers 27-27; Jim Martin, whose field goal made it 31-27 (after Joe Schmidt's interception and runback), and Darris McCord (far right), who cut down quarterback Y.A. Tittle for an 11-yard loss, ending San Francisco's counter-comeback.

21 minutes left in the game, the Lions still trailed by 20 points. Only absolute collapse would keep the 49ers from the destiny of their first divisional title and the championship game.

So there was no alarm when the Lions started battering into the 49ers' defensive line after Long's recovery. By now, Wilson had removed the ailing John Henry Johnson, whose power was lost.

"Tracy," Wilson said — and the stumpy, seldom-used substitute went into the backfield.

Eight plays transported the Lions to the 1. On the ninth play, Tracy carried for the touchdown. The score was San Francisco 27, Detroit 14. Less than 19 minutes remained.

Schmidt's defense gathered around Wilson and Buster Ramsey, the defensive aide, as Jim Martin kicked off to the 49ers.

"Christ, we can get 'em now," said Wilson. "But you guys have to get to Tittle, you have to control McElhenny, you have to play. You have to do it for us."

"Hell yes, let's go," said Joe Schmidt.

And Schmidt's unit stopped Tittle on three plays. The 49ers punted the ball back to the Lions. At his own 42, Yale Lary raised his right arm and signaled for a fair catch.

Rote huddled the offense and called a fullback plunge. Tracy crouched in the backfield, then darted forward as Rote accepted the snapback from Frank Gatski. Rote faked a pitch wide to Gedman and whirled. The handoff was completed and Tracy, low to the ground, bolted into the hole opened by Sewell's block. He was through the line, legs churning. He was open, cutting and turning through the 49ers' secondary. Fifty-eight yards Tracy ran, 58 yards to the end zone. Twice in 89 seconds the sulking benchwarmer had scored touchdowns. Unbelievably, the Lions were behind by only 27-21. And it was still the third quarter.

Wilson repeated his impassioned speech to the defense and Schmidt repeated his mutterings.

Martin kicked off, then smeared Joe Arenas at the nine. Again Tittle was stifled by the Lions' defense. Again the 49ers punted. Again Lary signaled for a fair catch, this time at the Lions' 46. It was still the third quarter.

Again Rote huddled the Lions while the 49ers' defense prepared to key on Tracy. Rote took the snap, dropped back and passed. Downfield, redheaded Steve Junker caught the football, finally dragged down after a gain of 36 yards. Now Rote pitched out to Tracy for 10 more yards.

The fourth quarter started and the drive continued, slowly, inexorably. On the fifth play, with the 49ers waiting for Tracy, Rote handed to Gene Gedman. He shoved into the end zone from two yards out. It was 44 seconds into the fourth quarter. With three touchdowns in the space of 4 minutes, 29 seconds the Lions tied the score at 27-27.

Jim Martin's extra point gave the Lions a 28-27 lead.

Once more the defense — Schmidt, Gil Mains, Darris McCord, Roger Zatkoff, David, Lary, Christiansen, Karilivacz — gathered around Wilson and Ramsey. They were delirious.

"It's not over, it's not over," said Wilson, pleading. "Don't forget what Tittle did to you guys in the first half. Don't give him any more easy stuff. Get to him, get to him."

And again Martin kicked off. Now the Lions' defense went onto the field to hold the tiny lead. Fourteen minutes remained.

Four more times Tittle would have the football with the chance to score and win and allow the now subdued Kezar fans to use the tickets they had lined up to purchase at halftime.

Four times, dramatically, Schmidt and his defenders took the ball from the 49ers.

Joe Perry fumbled and Gil Mains recovered. But the Lions could not capitalize.

Next, Karilivacz intercepted a pass by Tittle. Rote pushed the Lions to the 49ers' 3. But Tracy, seeking his third touchdown, fumbled and Bill Stits recovered for the 49ers.

Tittle had to throw and he did. Joe Schmidt intercepted a pass and, running like a linebacker, he headed toward the 49ers' goal. He was halted at the 2. Three thrusts for another touchdown failed. Wilson sent Martin in to kick a 14-yard field goal. The score was 31-27 . . . and now a field goal by Soltau would be of no use to the 49ers. Tittle had to get them a touchdown. Two minutes remained.

Magnificently, Tittle moved the 49ers, three times on screen passes to McElhenny. Using his three timeouts in the manner of Bobby Layne, Tittle took the 49ers to the Lions' 49 with 1 minute, 17 seconds left.

Schmidt asked the Lions' defense for one more stand. On the next play, Darris McCord broke through and tumbled Tittle for an 11-yard loss. Tittle's timeouts were gone and the clock continued. He hurried the ball into play. This time Mains put on the rush, chasing Tittle back. The pass was launched, but it fluttered and floated. Roger Zatkoff, the right linebacker in the Lions' 4-3 defense, caught the pass. It was the defense's third interception of Tittle in 10 minutes.

Only 50 seconds remained and the Lions now had the ball and the 49ers had no more timeouts. Rote ran out the clock with quarterback sneaks into the line.

The Lions were in the championship game for the fourth time in six years.

They returned to the locker room, where at halftime they had listened to laughter and mocking from next door. They were 31-27 victors, and George Wilson was a championship game coach in his first season. The team Buddy

Parker said he couldn't handle and quit on before the season had not quit on itself.

"It's the greatest comeback team I've ever seen," said George Wilson. "I've never seen any team battle back in the second half like this one. We thought the Lions had a great comeback team in 1953. This one is better."

Tom Tracy gained 86 yards on 11 carries. Tobin Rote passed masterfully in the second half and inspired his offense. Junker caught eight passes for 92 yards. Ken Russell, a rookie tackle, did an outstanding job of pass blocking with Charley Ane injured.

"Our bench made the difference," said Aldo Forte, the offensive line coach. "Look at Tracy and Russell and Rote."

"How about that?" said Bobby Layne, tossing away his crutches. "Tobin pulled another one out." Layne grabbed Rote. "Boy," said Layne, "you sure played a helluva second half."

"Tracy's long run was a beauty," said Rote. "I gave him the ball off tackle after faking a toss to Gedman. It was the same play Bobby worked with John Henry Johnson when we got that big touchdown against Green Bay on Thanksgiving."

"The blocking was perfect," said the ebullient Tracy. "It was a trap play. Harley Sewell belted the end (Ed Henke). I veered to the right and cut back to the left. Gedman screened me on their halfback (Dickie Moegle) the rest of the way."

The Lions' charter landed at Willow Run early Monday morning. The airline put out a red carpet for the players to walk on. They tried to get Tom Tracy to leave the plane first, to a hero's welcome. But Tracy hid in the back and was among the last to walk down the ramp.

On Sunday in Detroit, the Lions won their third championship in six years with a 59-14 massacre of the Browns. Tobin Rote threw four touchdown passes and scored one himself.

November 22, 1962

Alex Karras took aim, wound up and fired. The silver gray missile streaked across the room and whizzed past the head of its target. It clattered against some metal, fell and spun like a top, finally becoming motionless.

This much is known because Karras admitted throwing his helmet at Milt Plum in the agonizing moments immediately after a 9-7 loss at Green Bay. Indeed, Karras boasted of his action. Years later he still rued his faulty aim.

"Sure, I threw my helmet at Miltie," Karras said over lunch one afternoon four years later. "I missed him by that much."

Karras held his fingers two inches apart.

"I could have torn his head off, that bleep, bleep. He's nothing but a milk-drinking quarterback. I wish I got him that day.

"And Joe Schmidt was across the room after him, too."

Schmidt has denied that he ever tried to assault Plum in the locker room at Green Bay on October 7, 1962. But the legend persists.

What actually happened late that afternoon remains secret, unrecorded in the archives of the Lions. Karras has admitted his deed. Schmidt has denied the act credited to him. George Wilson, the coach, tried to make himself the scapegoat — and never really convinced anyone he should be blamed.

But on that day Milt Plum — a quiet, pipe-smoking man — proved he was not properly fashioned in the lineage established by Bobby Layne.

Ever since Bobby Layne was unceremoniously traded away — nearly in disgrace — to Pittsburgh after the second game of the 1958 season, the Lions had been searching for a quarterback. The 1958-59 seasons were dreary and Tobin Rote, the hero of the 1957 championship, had become unpopular with his teammates. After playing out his option in 1959, Rote jumped to Toronto in the Canadian League. He resurfaced later in the American Football League. The Lions tried to make do with Earl Morrall and Jim Ninowski. But Wilson discovered flaws in both of them. He figured the Lions could have beaten Green Bay for the 1961 championship if they had had a better quarterback.

So on March 29, 1962, Wilson concluded a major trade with Paul Brown in Cleveland. In a six-player deal, Plum, disdainful of Brown's messenger play-calling methods, went to Detroit. Ninowski returned to the Browns, who had traded him to Detroit in 1960.

Plum led the NFL in passing in 1960 and 1961, and Wilson figured he was the passer the Lions needed to cope with the Packer menace. With Karras, Roger Brown and Wayne Walker added to the club and Schmidt still the best middle linebacker in football, the Lions were a defense-fortified club again.

Plum's debut in Detroit made Wilson glow. Plum pitched the Lions to an opening 45-7 victory over the Steelers, quarterbacked by the aging Bobby Layne. Plum outdueled Layne — and adding to the irony, Wilson was the coaching victor over Buddy Parker.

The following Sunday Plum again produced 45 points in a rout of the 49ers. The defense, which griped perennially about the offensive impotency, was ecstatic. In the third game, Plum scored the winning touchdown at Baltimore on a masterfully executed 45-yard quarterback draw. After the 29-20 victory, the Lions' defensive quarterback critics believed Plum was Bobby Layne incarnate.

The fourth game of 1962 was on October 7 at Green Bay. With Plum as their quarterback, the Lions regarded themselves as the Packers' superior.

And for 59 minutes the Lions were a better team than Vince Lombardi's Packers. The game was a bitter and brilliant display of defen-

Packers 0 0 0 14 14
Lions   7 16 3 0 26

sive football, as most Lions-Packers bouts are.

Schmidt, Karras and their comrades thwarted Jim Taylor and Paul Hornung on the ground. They neutralized Bart Starr's passing. On the Packers' first series, the Lions stopped the drive at their 7. Hornung kicked a 15-yard field goal for a 3-0 Green Bay lead.

In the second quarter, Schmidt caught Starr on a blitz and shook the ball loose. Karras recovered the fumble at the Packers' 34. Plum drove the Lions to the 6. Then Danny Lewis circled end for the go-ahead touchdown. Walker's extra point sent the Lions into the second half with a 7-3 lead. Hornung kicked a second 15-yard field goal in the third period to trim the Lions' lead to 7-6.

That was the score when the Lions regained possession near midfield in the final two minutes.

"Keep control of the ball and get a first down if you can," Wilson said as Plum led the offense onto the field.

Two runs contributed little to the ball-control concept, although they did use some time. On third down Plum stepped into the huddle — and a pass play was called. The man who actually called it never has been satisfactorily identified. But several Lions frowned in surprise at the play selection. Terry Barr, the all-pro flanker, was to slant inward on a post pattern, taking cornerback Herb Adderley with him. Then Barr was supposed to cut outside toward the corner.

In calling a pass, the Lions shunned the safety factor. Another run would consume time. Then a punt by Yale Lary, best in the NFL at the time, would pin the Packers deep in their own territory. Perhaps near their goal line. With less than a minute left.

This forward pass was to become one of the most devastating plays in the Lions' history. It inspired internal anarchy on the team for seasons to come.

Plum took the snap and Barr maneuvered against Adderley and slanted in. In the pocket, Plum anticipated Barr's cut to the corner. He threw the ball toward the appointed spot. But his receiver never got there. Barr slipped on his cut and tumbled into the mud. Adderley, without opposition, retreated and intercepted the wayward pass at the Packers' 42. With no Lion nearby he ran the ball back 40 yards to the 18 before he was tackled.

It was the final minute of the game. The Packers cautiously advanced the ball to the 14. Then Hornung kicked his third field goal of the afternoon from the 21 — with 27 seconds left. The Lions had lost their most important game since 1957 in the most heartbreaking fashion. The defeat polarized the team.

Karras used his helmet for a cannonball aimed at Plum's head. There would be everlasting enmity between the two. Schmidt's enraged behavior was not documented. But he never forgave Plum. Five years later Schmidt became head coach and in desperation he had to use Plum much of the year as his starting quarterback. Even then the relationship was not cordial and Plum confessed one day, "Joe never forgets, does he? He carries a grudge."

According to most reports pieced together in the days of despair after the 9-7 loss, only the quick intervention of George Wilson saved Plum from bodily harm. Wilson supposedly chased the angry defenders away from Plum's locker. Then, when the press finally was admitted inside, Wilson publicly accepted responsibility for the risky pass call. He tried to take all the blame — but it was a hollow gesture that the Lions themselves never believed. The general feeling was that Wilson, after years without a satisfactory quarterback, now at long last had one, and wanted to shield Plum.

"I called the play," said Wilson. "There's no sense trying to second guess now. Just so long

as Milt doesn't get blamed for it. It was my play."

But in the moment of anguish and personal danger, Plum himself admitted some guilt because he failed to obey his intuition.

"George called for a pass," said Plum quietly. "But I called the pattern. Maybe I shouldn't have listened to him. Something inside told me we should have been running."

The pattern selected was certainly not wise. Barr, one of the superior receivers in football, was asked to make two cuts.

"I had to slant in, then slant out," he said. "My feet went out from under me when I started to make my cut. If I hadn't fallen, I'm sure everything would have been okay."

"Sure, I saw Adderley over there," said Plum. "But Terry was behind him. Then the pattern called for him to cut back out. I threw where he would have been if he hadn't slipped."

If he hadn't slipped . . .

"I saw Barr cutting in," explained Adderley. "I knew what he was going to do, so I just waited. I was surprised when he fell. Then the pass was right in my hands and I just took off."

The sting of the defeat could not be lessened. But there would be a rematch with the Packers on Thanksgiving Day in Detroit.

But before the Green Bay rematch, there were six other games to be played. The next week, Plum — placekicking for the first time as a pro when Wayne Walker had two field goals blocked — won the game against the Rams. He succeeded on field goals of 42 and 31 yards in a 13-10 victory.

The Lions were clinging to their three-point lead with slightly more than two minutes left, possessing the ball at their 38. It was third down and again the Lions needed ball control.

In the huddle, a pass again was called as Lions shuddered at the memory of the contretemps of the week before at Green Bay. Calmly, Plum dropped back and passed. The play worked.

Gail Cogdill caught a 12-yarder. Acquiring the first down, the Lions ran out the clock.

But the following week they were beaten by the Giants in New York, 17-14. Joe Schmidt was hurt and Detroit dropped two games behind the unbeaten Packers. Now they needed help from an outside source to catch Green Bay — even if they should win the Thanksgiving Day rematch.

"Somebody's going to beat Green Bay for us," Wilson promised.

But nobody did. Vince Lombardi's legions continued to win every Sunday. They were 10-0 when they arrived in Detroit for Thanksgiving and the game the Lions had vowed they would win.

"It's this simple," said Wayne Walker. "We're a better team than they are."

After the loss to the Giants, the Lions beat the Bears and talked about the rematch with the Packers. They went to the West Coast and beat the Rams and 49ers again — and talked about the rematch with the Packers.

"We're just getting ready for them," said Joe Schmidt.

"If we can beat them somebody else will beat them, too," said George Wilson at one of his Monday press luncheon briefings. "We have the best receivers in the league and the best defense. We can catch them."

And the Lions beat the Vikings — and talked about the rematch with the Packers. Beating the Packers on Thanksgiving had become an obsession . . . and finally the week of the rematch arrived. It was a short week of preparation — as always, just Monday, Tuesday and Wednesday to practice.

"The people can help us," suggested Walker. "When we come out on the field, they can let loose, make noise, let us know they're for us."

Wilson labored on his defense.

"Our plan is basic," he told the defense.

"You have to get to Bart Starr, you have to keep getting to him, you have to rush him, keep him from throwing, don't give him any time. It's up to you guys. Get Starr and we can win . . . and then we'll be back in it. Somebody else will beat them for us. But first we have to show they can be beaten."

At dusk on Wednesday night, a line started to form outside the bleacher entrance on the corner of Trumbull Avenue. People straggled up in twos and threes, with camp chairs and Thermos jugs filled with hot coffee and assorted spirits to ward off the chill of a nightlong vigil. The 3,000 remaining bleacher tickets were to go on sale in the morning. By 11 o'clock Wednesday night, the line stretched down the street. The crowd soon became unruly, as Lions' fans often are. Police were summoned and they quelled a minor disturbance outside the ticket windows. Finally late Thursday morning the gates opened and the mob entered the aged ballpark.

At last!

Thanksgiving was a gray, sullen day, and a light snow was falling.

The Packers were unbeaten in 10 games. They were believed to be invincible, except in Detroit. Green Bay had the highest scoring offense in the NFL with 304 points in 10 games. The Packers had the least scored-upon defense with 74 points. Only once had they been in danger — the 9-7 game against the Lions, who damaged themselves with a pass interception at the most inopportune moment.

Across the United States, viewers flicked on their television sets, some past noon and others, in the West, about as soon as they arose.

The atmosphere was electric. Could the Packers continue through their schedule unscathed? Or would the Lions' promise of grandeur, made in the despair of the 9-7 loss at Green Bay, come true?

"This is it," said George Wilson plainly to his athletes in the locker room. "You are a better all-around team than the teams that won championships here 10 years ago. Go at them, put the pressure on Starr!"

Adrenalin flowing, the blue-clad Lions streaked through the tunnel and out the dugout and onto Tiger Stadium. They were greeted by the thunderous roar of 57,598 faithful.

Early in the first quarter, Bart Starr counted off his cadence. Across the line, 11 wild-eyed men stared at him, ravenously hungry to attack him. The ball was snapped and Starr dropped back to pass. Immediately, he was set upon by seven predatory beasts. He was swarmed under for a 15-yard loss on his first pass play. The tone of the game had been established. The Lions intended to blitz heavily with their linebackers — Schmidt, Walker, and Carl Brettschneider.

It had been written that the offensive line Lombardi created in Green Bay was pro football's best in 20 years. But on this day Fuzzy Thruston could not contain the savage rush of 300-pound Roger Brown. Jerry Kramer could not halt the enraged Alex Karras in a dogfight between two ancient antagonists. The Packers' tackles could not neutralize the overwhelming rush from the Lions' defensive ends, Sam Williams and Darris McCord. Ken Iman, the Packers' fill-in center, could not help being overwhelmed by the blitzing Schmidt.

Midway in the first quarter, the Lions' punt rush forced Boyd Dowler to shank a kick only 15 yards. The Lions were set up at the Packers' 39. On third down, from his split position out to the left, Gail Cogdill streaked downfield on a fly pattern. He beat Jesse Whittenton on one side and Willie Wood on the other. Plum's pass was perfect, Cogdill caught it behind the coverage and continued to a 33-yard touchdown.

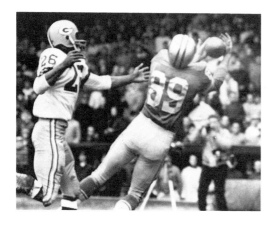

The Lions were ahead 7-0 after 8 1/2 minutes and their believers created bedlam.

With 2 1/2 minutes remaining in the first quarter, Tom Moore, in the Packers' backfield because of the injury absence of Hornung, was set upon by the Lions' predators. He coughed up the ball and Brettschneider pounced on it at the Lions' 47. Plum drove the Lions gradually to the Packers' 27. In the first minute of the second quarter, he split Cogdill to the right. Cogdill was matched up against Adderley, the villain of the 9-7 defeat. Plum threw and Cogdill, gaining a step, dove for the ball in the end zone. He clutched it in both arms as he was airborne and landed, keeping the ball within his grasp.

The 27-yard touchdown pass put the Lions into a 14-0 lead after only 16 minutes of play.

Again the wild-eyed Lions lined up opposite Starr. On the first play, Roger Brown crashed through and Starr fumbled the ball. Sam Williams scooped it up and pranced into the end zone for the Lions' third touchdown. Detroit had the Packers behind, 21-0, after 16 1/2 minutes.

Less than two minutes later, Starr was in his own end zone, trying to pass. Brown dropped him for a safety. It was 23-0 Detroit.

The Lions had scored two touchdowns and a safety against the team considered invincible in a span of 2 1/2 minutes.

And, then it was the Lions' defense — the front four rushing and the linebackers blitzing — that prevented the Packers from making more than a token effort.

Plum kicked a 47-yard field goal on the Lions' first series of the third period. It was 26-0.

The Packers' two touchdowns in the fourth quarter were anticlimactic. Willie Davis scored on a fumble recovery. Jim Taylor scored the second on a four-yard run.

The Lions succeeded, 26-14. The Packers were no longer invincible. Plum had redeemed himself and Roger Brown became All-Pro in one game on national television.

The defense, with its blitzing and looping and twisting, dumped Starr 11 times for 110 yards in losses on attempts to pass. Jim Taylor had entered the game with 1,121 yards in the first 10 games, the NFL's leading ground gainer. The Lions neutralized him by holding him to 47 yards for the day.

"I've never seen anything like it," said Joe Schmidt, who had swarmed over Starr so many times on blitzes. "We killed them."

"We got sick and tired of hearing and reading in the papers and magazines about the Packers being a wonder team," said a gratified George Wilson.

"They were past us before we could find them," said Forrest Gregg, one of the great blocking tackles in pro history in his years at Green Bay. "I never saw anyone get off so fast with the snap of the ball. They came out stunting. They blitzed almost every play and we couldn't seem to recover."

"We were due to lose one," said Ray Nitschke, the Packers' middle linebacker. "But one is all we'll lose."

He was correct. The Packers finished the year 13-1 and beat the Giants for their second successive championship of the Lombardi years. The Lions, 9-2 after the victory over Green Bay, finished 11-3. They lost their final game 3-0 to the Bears. Their three losses were galling — one by two points, two by three. The 11-3 record was the best in club history.

Karras, Schmidt, and Wilson were eternally convinced the best team in pro football in 1962 was the Detroit Lions. They proved it to themselves in hand-to-hand combat with the Packers. But nonetheless, the Lions finished second again.

November 26, 1970

The autumn of 1970 was historic for pro football. The American Football League had evaporated to become part of a 26-franchise conglomerate under the single NFL banner. Old AFL clubs, which had fought a battle for identity and acceptance for 10 years, operated with the NFL as members of the newly arranged American Football Conference. Three old-line NFL clubs, the Colts, Steelers and Browns, joined them to create 13-club balance in the two new conferences.

The war between the leagues and the four truce years of realigning were ended. For the first time in 1970, former AFL clubs — now known as AFC — played old NFL teams in regular season crossover games.

And 1970 was also historic because a place-kicker with half a foot — a birth defect — boomed a last-play field goal 63 yards. Naturally, Tom Dempsey's longest field goal in history beat the Lions, 19-17, for the expansion Saints, on the last play of the game.

But 1970 was historic most of all because of George Blanda and his miracles. Blanda was an ancient foe of the Lions. As a member of the Bears, Blanda had been a quarterbacking enemy of Bobby Layne two decades before, during the Lions' boom seasons.

Now in 1970, Blanda was 43 years old — and because of his heroic deeds on a succession of five Sundays he was pro football's player of the year. Players 20 years his junior were outdueled, outplayed by the gaffer with the graying hair who stole games for the Oakland Raiders with last-ditch dramatics.

At a moment in history when long hair on males and the wild-living of youth became the vogue, George Blanda, in his 20th pro season, became a folk hero. He not only became the idol of the abused over-30s . . . but of those in the sedentary over-40 cult, too. Indeed George Blanda was nine years older than his head coach, huge, ruddy, 34-year-old John Madden.

Blanda's theatrics, staged for Sunday afternoon television audiences, became a fixture of athletic Americana. His exploits were utterly astonishing.

They started innocently enough on October 25. The Raiders were playing the Steelers. Subbing for the injured Daryle Lamonica, Blanda rescued the Raiders with three touchdown passes and a field goal.

Next Sunday the Raiders traveled to play their AFL archenemies the Kansas City Chiefs. Hostilities were commonplace in this series. With the Chiefs ahead, 17-14, in the waning minutes, a free-for-all erupted but Blanda had witnessed such events before and remained static on the bench. He remained there until Madden commanded him onto the field after Lamonica had driven the Raiders against the clock to the Chiefs' 41. Then Blanda, with the self-assurance of 20 seasons in the business, kicked a 48-yard field goal with three seconds to play. His field goal produced a 17-17 stalemate. The tie positioned the Raiders in first place in the AFC West.

On November 8, the third Sunday of this miraculous five weeks, Lamonica was hurt again against the Browns, whom Blanda despised from the years he played for George Halas in Chicago. The Browns had mercilessly crushed the Bears, and Blanda, several times. They led the Raiders 20-13 as Blanda, the surrogate quarterback, marched his offense downfield. Pressured, he threw a 48-yard pass to Warren Wells, then kicked the extra point to tie the game at 20-20 with 1:39 left. With three seconds left he kicked a 52-yard field goal to make the Raiders 23-20 winners.

On the fourth Sunday, the Raiders journeyed to Denver. Madden instinctively put Blanda into the game to replace Lamonica with 4:01 remaining and the Raiders trailing the Broncos,

Raiders 14 0 0 0 14
Lions   0 14 0 14 28

19-17. The Radiers began from their 20. Blanda threw six passes and completed four of them. The fourth was a 27-yard pass to Fred Biletnikoff for the winning touchdown. Raiders 24, Broncos 19.

One week later, the Raiders and San Diego Chargers were tied 17-17. Lamonica drove his team into field goal range. Then Blanda kicked a 16-yard field goal for the 20-17 victory This time four seconds remained in the game.

Thus, in eclectic fashion, George Blanda singularly determined the outcome of five pro football games in five weeks, to the benefit of the Oakland Raiders.

In the sixth week the Raiders traveled again, to play the Lions in the traditional Thanksgiving day match at Tiger Stadium.

While Blanda was providing his weekly machinations, the Lions were sagging. They had begun the 1970 season with great expectations.

After so many seasons of languor, they finally developed an offense. Bill Munson was their catalyst at quarterback. The Lions started their season with a 40-0 victory at Green Bay. After six games, they were 5-1 and eagerly awaited their first confrontation with the Vikings. Minnesota had won the Central Division the previous two seasons, beating the Lions in all four games.

Now first place in the NFC Central awaited the victor. The Lions, with an incipient phobia about Minnesota, crumbled against the Vikings, 30-17. It was the same day Blanda's field goal tied the Chiefs and dispatched the Raiders into first place in their division.

On the following Sunday, the Lions went to New Orleans. Munson was intercepted three times. Nick Eddy twice fumbled the ball away on kicks. In the fourth quarter, Joe Schmidt gave Greg Landry a battlefield promotion to No. 1 quarterback. The Saints led 16-14 with time rapidly vanishing.

Landry smartly guided the Lions against the clock 86 yards to the Saints' 9. He also did it too quickly. In youthful exuberance, Landry called the necessary time out with 14 seconds still on the clock. Errol Mann kicked an 18-yard field goal to put the Lions ahead, 17-16, with 11 seconds left. Too much time remained. The Saints fielded the kickoff and managed to get off one pass, a 17-yarder from Bill Kilmer to Al Dodd who went out of bounds at the Saints' 45. With two seconds to go, Dempsey stepped back to his 37 and kicked a monumental 63-yard field goal. The Lions were losers again while Blanda beat the Browns with a touchdown pass and a 52-yard field goal in the final 99 seconds of the game.

Reeling now, the Lions went to Minnesota for the rematch. There remained a flickering chance they could still win the division.

With three quarters played, the Lions had the Vikings beaten, 20-10. But they were beaten, 24-20 — beaten for the sixth straight time by the Vikings.

On the same day, Blanda beat Denver with an 80-yard drive and a 27-yard touchdown pass in the final two minutes.

Their third straight loss — making their record 5-4 — absolutely devastated the Lions. Tears flowed again in the visitors' locker room at Minnesota.

"We're done now, we're finished," moaned Paul Naumoff, the exceptional young outside linebacker, grasping Jim David, the defensive coach during Schmidt's years.

"Those last seconds are turning into nightmares for us," said Lem Barney, the cornerback.

"Two weeks in a row, it makes you wonder," said center Ed Flanagan. "I've never seen a year like this."

"I can't explain to you how much it hurts," said Wayne Walker, red rims around his moist

Thanksgiving Day, Detroit, 1970 . . . the year of union between NFL and AFL. Into Tiger Stadium swaggered the unreconstructed Oakland Raiders. They came to heap more troubles on the heads of the Lions, who in recent weeks had lost for the fifth and sixth times in a row to Minnesota, and been the victim of Tom Dempsey's epic 63-yard field goal (right), giving the New Orleans Saints a 19-17 victory. The Lions were beginning to wonder if their destiny was theirs to command, especially now that they had to contend with George Blanda (below). The 40-year-old miracle worker had produced five consecutive weeks of last-minute heroics.

eyes. "They don't want it any more, they don't hustle any more . . ."

In this year of amalgamation, the second-place team with the best record in each conference would qualify for the playoffs. But even that possibility died in Minnesota. Only Mike Lucci, Schmidt's successor at middle linebacker, was so pretentious as to say the Lions retained a playoff chance.

"It's like everything else," said Lucci, his mood angry. "If we can get the momentum turned around we could win five in a row, be 10-4 and make the playoffs. I still believe we have a good football team.

"It would be easy to quit. We won't quit. I promise you that." The final five games were against the 49ers and Raiders (four days apart in the same week), the Cardinals, Rams and Packers. It was hopeless, another season of pathos for this once-ambitious team.

It remained hopeless even after Landry threw three touchdown passes and the Lions beat the 49ers, first in the NFC West, 28-7, the next Sunday. On that day, Blanda saved the Raiders for the fifth straight week with his 16-yard field goal that beat the Chargers.

And so it was that the Raiders, first in the AFC West, swaggered into Detroit, bellicose and cocky, for the Thanksgiving Day matinee. The Lions knew the Raiders by reputation only. But then the Raiders had little knowledge of the Lions, either.

The Lions had not won in their annual Thanksgiving Day game since the revenge 26-14 victory over the Packers in 1962. Now they were on the edge of elimination from the playoffs. One more loss and they were mathematical goners.

As usual, Thanksgiving Day was raw with the threat of snow. On the field, the Raiders swaggered through their calisthenics and pregame ritual. George Blanda, the oldtime adver-

sary, was given a hero's welcome as he tried his practice placekicks. He had popularized being over 40.

Al Davis, his white trenchcoat flapping in the wind, approached Russ Thomas, the Lions' general manager. Davis pointed to a plexiglass isolation booth stationed between the two benches. The manufacturer, envisioning boom sales to NFL clubs, had asked the Lions to test it for him. It was a heated cage in which numbed players could warm themselves when they weren't on the field.

Davis complained that the Lions would have an unfair advantage if they tested the device on a day they were playing the Raiders. He was correct, of course . . . and Thomas consented to have the Lions stay outside in the cold, too.

Again the nation watched Thanksgiving Day football from Detroit.

The Raiders kicked off and Bobby Williams was blasted by two Raiders. The ball squirted from his grasp and fell to the dirt at the Lions' 24-yard line, where Marv Hubbard recovered it for the Raiders.

One of the differences during the years of enmity between the NFL and AFL was the defensive pass coverage. In the early AFL years the NFL scoffed at the porous secondaries. AFL games were played with scores of 41-38 and the old guard NFL regarded this as pure comedy. The NFL had the stronger pass coverages, it was felt — the superior defensive philosophy. In the NFL, Lem Barney had become the best cornerback in his rookie year. Sage NFL quarterbacks seldom dared concentrate their pass offense at the strongest segment of the Lions' defense.

But the Raiders' game plan was to attack at Barney. Daryle Lamonica was the Raiders' Mad Bomber, an apropos nickname for his affinity of throwing the bomb at any time, frequently in the direction of Fred Biletnikoff. Biletnikoff

had been a Lions' draft choice during the years of league warfare. He was one of many never-to-be-Lions who signed with the new league rather than the NFL.

Impassively, Biletnikoff emerged from the huddle and flanked himself to the right. He was one-on-one against Barney. Biletnikoff broke toward the goalpost and took Barney in with him. Then he cut and veered toward the corner. Barney was beaten by several strides. At the corner, near the goal line, Biletnikoff caught Lamonica's 24-yard touchdown pass. One play, one touchdown pass. With 29 seconds played, the Raiders were ahead 7-0.

The Lions punted on their first series and Lamonica started from the Raiders' 25. After nine plays the ball rested at the Lions' 21. Again Lamonica called a pass play.

Biletnikoff was matched up, one-on-one, against Barney. Again he cut for the post, pulling Barney in with him. Then he changed direction to the corner. Lamonica connected a second time. The Raiders were in 14-0 command — and only 6:56 had been played.

In Tiger Stadium, the home and visiting benches are located on the same side of the field. In between there is a no-man's land in which players sometimes stray and on this day where the unused plexiglass heating booth was situated. Wayne Walker looked down toward the Raiders' bench. He nudged Mike Lucci and pointed. Lucci looked. They saw several Raiders smirking, some laughing, others holding conversations and then giggling.

"Those bastards are laughing at us," said Lucci.

"And listen to those fans booing us," said Walker.

Lucci and Walker reported the information from the Raiders' bench to their teammates. But the Lions' offense sputtered again. Lucci and Walker returned to the field with

The Raiders added insult to injury when, after Fred Biletnikoff twice beat the Lions' Lem Barney on touchdown passes from Daryle Lamonica, the Raiders' bench appeared to be mocking the Lions. On his next drive, however, Lamonica threw to the side of the field away from Barney, and Detroit's Dick LeBeau intercepted (left). The Lions' defense then set upon Lamonica and got the ball for Greg Landry (right), who had just replaced Bill Munson as starter at quarterback two weeks earlier. Detroit's first touchdown came on a pass from Landry to Altie Taylor. Landry tied the score with a pass to his airborne tight end, Charlie Sanders (next page).

the rest of the defense, determined to hold.

Lamonica started marching the Raiders downfield. They advanced inexorably into the Lions' territory, toward their third score — either a touchdown or a field goal by the venerable Blanda.

Deep in Lion territory, Lamonica threw — this time to his left, away from Barney. At the 6, Dick LeBeau, in a season of personal renaissance, intercepted the pass.

"Get it going, Greg," Joe Schmidt told Landry. "Just be careful and don't run with the damn ball so much yourself."

Landry obeyed part of the command. He got the Lions' malfunctioning offense started. But he ignored — as he always had — Schmidt's pleas for him not to run. When the Raiders' linebackers dropped deep into pass coverage and his receivers weren't open, Landry ran — and ran — and ran. He ran into the open field as though he were a running back, addling the Raiders' deep coverages in the process.

And when he could, he threw the ball.

From their 8, Landry marched the Lions downfield, running and throwing. Then from the Raiders' 12, he sent Altie Taylor out of the backfield as a receiver. Taylor, falling backwards over the goal line, caught the pass for the Lions' first touchdown.

Detroit's sport fans long have been a fickle group — quick to boo and hate their local team, and just as quick to change in midgame to cheers and love. There is no ambivalence — only boo-hate, cheer-love. And now 56,597 infidels who had spent the first quarter booing began cheering.

The Lions' defense, angered by the mocking laughter from the Raiders' bench, now bedeviled Lamonica. It halted the Raiders and forced a punt. Craig Cotton, Ed Mooney and Charlie Brown of the special teams barged through to rush Raider punter Mike Eischeid.

Marv Hubbard, the back blocker, retreated, trying to pick up Cotton, the first man in. Eischeid's punt hit Hubbard and the Lions had possession at the Raiders' 38.

"Plenty of time, Greg," yelled Schmidt as the Lions' offense dashed onto the field. "You got two minutes. Get the ball in there. We need the touchdown."

Landry called a reverse to Mel Farr. Farr, a brilliant runner with an injury-filled, ill-starred career, dashed 18 yards to the 20.

Charlie Sanders sauntered back to the huddle slowly, painfully, as always. He had become the most gifted tight end in pro football. But he always felt hurt . . . until he went for a pass that was a little too long or short.

"You know," said Greg Landry, "when I'm in trouble I'm always going to look for Charlie."

So Landry called a pass and looked for Charlie. He threw the ball toward the goal post. Near the goal line, Sanders became airborne. The ball was just slightly long. Sanders reached out and seized the ball in one hand. As he slid ahead in the end zone, he covered it with his other hand. It was the most picturesque catch of the year. Errol Mann kicked the extra point and the score was tied 14-14.

"I saw the ball and said 'I don't have a chance,'" said Sanders. "Then I said, 'What the hell, I'll dive for it like I was taught in high school.' It hit and stuck."

It was 14-14 at halftime and the score remained unaltered through the third quarter. Twice the Lions fumbled the ball away. But on third-and-18, Landry isolated Farr against a linebacker on a flare pass. Farr outran his man, caught the pass, broke Dan Conners' tackle and traveled 58 yards to the 8.

"Greg did a good job of finding me because the pattern was supposed to go deep," said Farr, whose body became racked and bloodied every time he played football. "But I had to cut

in short when the linebacker bumped me over."

Landry now assembled his offense at the Raiders' 6-yard line. It was early in the fourth quarter, the score still 14-14 . . . and over at the Raiders' bench George Blanda removed his cape and started to unloosen his 43-year-old right arm. This was becoming his kind of game. The Lions' defense hadn't allowed Lamonica past midfield since the first quarter.

"Be ready, Charlie," said Landry in the huddle, pointing to Sanders.

Landry dropped back and the Raiders' linebackers watched him cautiously. He could run again and maybe helmet-butt his way to the end zone. Instead, Landry threw.

In the end zone, Sanders flopped backwards and caught the ball. The six-yard touchdown pass — Landry's third of the day — put the Lions in front, 21-14, with 11 1/2 minutes to play.

Eleven minutes were left, ample time for the George Blanda Weekly Magic Show. Blanda entered the game and completed his first three passes, producing two first downs as the Raiders marched to the Lions' 40. Then Blanda completed a fourth pass, to his tight end, Ray Chester. Chester got behind safety Mike Weger and rumbled 37 yards to the Lions' 3. A first down. Few noticed a yellow handkerchief at the line of scrimmage. Chester had been caught stepping ahead too quickly. The long gain was nullified. The third-down play failed. An almost certain score down the drain, the Raiders punted.

As the Raiders' offensive unit and the Lions' defense criss-crossed to their respective benches on the same side, Wayne Walker sidled past George Blanda.

"Not today, oldtimer . . ." said Walker quietly with a straight face. Walker, 33 by the playing records and 34 by his birth certificate, continued his journey to the bench as Eischeid

punted on fourth down to the Lions' six.

Landry immediately made Walker's message emphatic by running and passing the Lions 94 yards to their fourth touchdown.

Upstairs, Bill McPeak, the Lions' offensive coach, spoke into his telephone mouthpiece. He had sent in the play on third-and-18, when Farr beat the linebacker for a 58-yard pass gain. Now he suggested a deep pass straight upfield — provided the Raiders played bump-and-run. Schmidt beckoned a reserve receiver, a short, wiry athlete named Chuck Hughes. Hughes trotted onto the field and spoke to Landry.

Then Hughes lined up right and streaked downfield. It was a gamble because the Lions were trying to control the ball with their one-touchdown lead and four minutes left. They had the ball at their 34, third-and-nine.

Landry's pass was thrown at a spot, and Hughes was a trifle late reaching it. He dove and as he landed he caught the ball in his outstretched hands for a 42-yard gain at the Raiders' 24.

"If they went bump-and-run I was supposed to go," said Chuck Hughes, who would die of a heart attack on this same field less than a year later during a football game. "Kent McCloughan bumped. So I took off. I didn't think I made a good move."

But it was the fourth airborne catch of the game by the Lions. Three plays later, Farr cut off right tackle from the 11 and pranced into the end zone, spiking the football into the ground as he did so.

The Lions led 28-14 with less than two minutes to play. The game was even out of the range of George Blanda.

On this day Wayne Walker played his 169th game with the Lions — setting the club's longevity record. It was his most satisfying game.

"They were over there laughing when they

got those two touchdowns," said Walker, still angered afterwards. "I've been here 13 years and we haven't always had good teams, but nobody laughed at us before on the field. It was like laughing at my mother. This team is the only loyalty I have and they were smirking and smiling and laughing at us."

At the game's end, Mike Lucci dashed toward John Madden, the Raiders' coach.

"You ought to wait till you've won the ball game before your guys start laughing," said Lucci.

"That's what I said to Madden," Lucci related later. "Except I spiced it up more."

"I wonder how much they're laughing right now," said Joe Schmidt, "It didn't look too bright for the homefolks, though, when they went 14-zip."

"I feel good because the fans got to me," said Sanders. "The booing — that was the main thing that fired us up. The people put us down. We figured then we'd try to see if we could win it for ourselves. It proved what Joe Schmidt had been telling us — we've got a helluva team."

"We showed a little class, a little class," said Lucci, whose defense became so stingy after the double stinging. "They thought it was going to be a cakewalk in the first quarter."

"They thought they were delirious, 14-0 in front two minutes into the game," said Alex Karras.

"I felt if we lost another game we were out of it," said Landry, who had bested John Brodie and George Blanda four days apart.

The Lions had returned from oblivion with their two victories over San Francisco and Oakland. Landry had become their young leader.

Against the Raiders, he completed 10 of 15 passes. Seven times he broke away from the Raiders' intense pass rush and ran for gains totaling 77 yards. He engineered touchdown drives of 92 and 94 yards. Most important, he made first downs 10 times in 13 situations.

"Landry did the best passing since I've had the team." said Schmidt, "the best in my four years. It was the best passing and catching combined. We made some fantastic catches.

"Greg gets trapped back there in crucial situations and I don't like to see him run. But he will . . . and once he got by the line he was okay."

"We even had an option in for me," said Landry. "It was a designed play, just like a college play. We worked on it for this game.

"And Charlie . . . after his two catches today, I'd be a fool if I didn't look for Sanders. But if I threw a little better he wouldn't have to make such great catches."

And the postmortems turned again to the Raiders and their first-quarter mockery.

"You don't have to see it. You can feel it," said Sanders. "It's like saying they don't respect you for your job. It's like an executive laughing at you for being a ditchdigger. You never know how the tables are going to turn."

It was a joyous holiday — and the Lions continued onward. They beat St. Louis, first in the NFC East, 16-3. Then they defeated the Rams, who were temporarily first in the NFC West, 28-23. Green Bay was the fifth straight victim 20-0. The Lions finished 10-4 — as Lucci surmised they might be — and made it to the playoffs as the runnerup team. It was the Lions' first playoff appearance since 1957. Though Dallas beat Detroit 5-0 in the playoff opener, the Lions viewed the setback as temporary.

The 28-14 victory over the Raiders and George Blanda on Thanksgiving Day — a miracle game itself — was the stimulus which accounted for the Lions making the playoffs.

"It's the first time in a long time we don't have to eat chicken for Thanksgiving," said Mike Lucci. "We can eat turkey."

Their come-from-behind victory over the Raiders was the beginning of a surge by the Lions which got them into the 1970 playoffs. There, they fell to the Dallas Cowboys 5-0. It was Detroit's first appearance in post-season play since the 1957 NFL championship. Dallas' Walt Garrison maneuvers behind Ralph Neely's block on Lions' linebacker Mike Lucci.

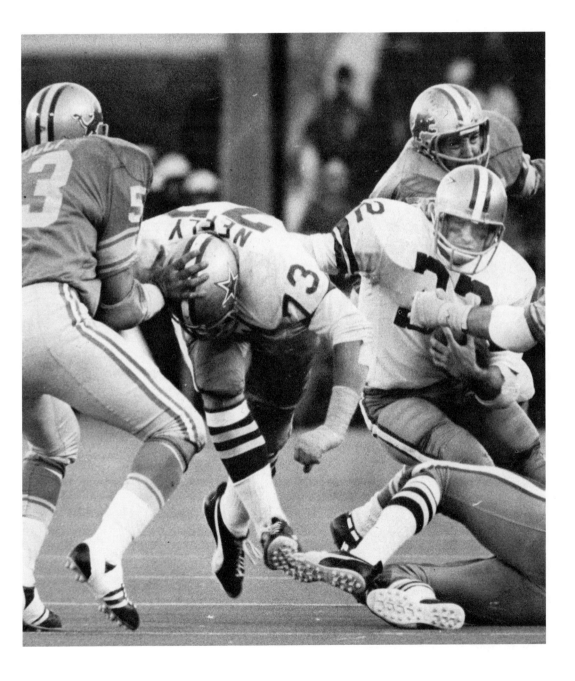

The Memories

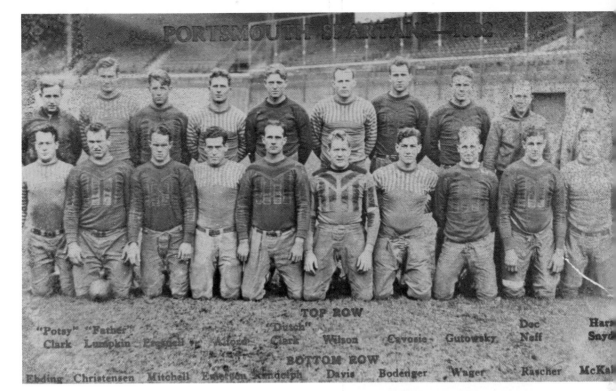

TOP ROW

"Potsy" "Father"   "Dutch"   Doc   Harry
Clark Lumpkin Presnell Alford Clark Wilson Cavosie Gutowsky Neff Snyd

BOTTOM ROW

Ebding Christensen Mitchell Emerson Randolph Davis Bodenger Wager Rascher McKal

The Lions originally were Portsmouth team, which played indoor game in Chicago in '32.

Classic profile (left) and classic stylist: Earl (Dutch) Clark led five Lions teams.

Ace Gutowsky's runs (right) weren't enough; Bears beat Lions to win in West in '34.

BEARS · 19
LIONS · 16
Detroit '34

10¢

NATIONAL LEAGUE FOOTBALL

Philadelphia Eagles vs Detroit Lions

A game program with Whizzer White, a Lion in 1940-41, featured on cover.

1935 Lions and Dutch Clark (7) were champs in second season in their new home.

Buddy Parker (4) leads Dutch Clark (7) in Lions' tie with '36 College Stars.

Byron (Whizzer) White, left, led NFL in rushing in 1940 with 514 yards.

Les Bingaman was a standout 349½-pound middle guard who played from 1948-54.

Quarterback Bobby Layne paid little heed to his waistline or his statistics; all he did was lead Lions to three titles.

Lions' program from '40s; in those days the team's snarl was worse than its bite.

The Lions Fanfare magazine was a gallaxy in '50.

Buddy Parker coached Detroit to 47-23-2 record in 6 seasons.

The Lions' dynamic duo of the early '50s — Leon Hart, Doak Walker

Jack Christiansen led Lions' secondary.

Steve Owens (next page) won '69 Heisman, became Lions first 1,000-yard runner.

Jim Doran made winning TD catch in '53 title game.

Hip, shoulder and leg injuries have slowed
Mel Farr; when healthy he's one of the best.

Greg Landry (right), virutally unknown when drafted
in '68, has become top-rated quarterback.

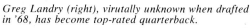

Nick Pietrosante
holds Lions' rush
records with 3,933
in seven seasons.

Paper Lion (left),
by George Plimpton,
was a Walter Mitty
look at game and
'66 best-seller.

Lem Barney and
Dick LeBeau
are two in long
line of strong
Lions cornerbacks.

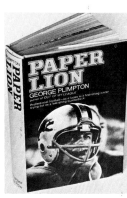

Lou Creekmur (76) and Leon Hart (82) were among stars on Lions' line in 1950s.

Charlie Sanders, a peerless tight end, averaged 36 receptions a season in first five years with Detroit.

Lem Barney, returning an interception, became an instant sensation at cornerback.

Jack Christiansen, defensive back, 1951-58. Inducted in 1970.

Dutch Clark, quarterback, 1934-38. Inducted in 1963.

Bill Dudley, running back, 1947-49. Inducted in 1966.

Bobby Layne, quarterback, 1950-58. Inducted in 1967.

Alex Wojciechowicz, center, 1938-46. Inducted in 1968.

The Players

Earl [Dutch] Clark

Position: Tailback
Years: 1934-38
Height: 6-0
Weight: 180
College: Colorado College

The bubble gum cards provided a profound image for young boys acquiring their first intimacy with pro football in Detroit.

The city was baseball-oriented, and the heroes of the time were Charlie Gehringer, Hank Greenberg, Tommy Bridges, Goose Goslin and Mickey Cochrane. They were the Tigers. And they won the city's first world championship in sports in October of 1935. In various poses of batting and throwing, their pictures appeared in washed out colors on the bubble gum cards of the era.

But then there appeared for the first time, one autumn in the middle 1930s, bubble gum cards featuring the lesser-renowned pro football players. They were newcomers, upstarts. A boy's introduction to pro football and its athletes was on these cards. For a penny, one could be purchased in a package also containing three slices of too-sweet bubble gum.

There is a vivid memory of a solid-looking football player in a pale blue jersey with the silver numeral 7 across the chest. The subject's hair was parted almost down center, and it was curly, with a crescent lock dangling off his forehead. There was the caption: "Dutch Clark, Detroit Lions."

Dutch Clark is an impressive name, a name that conjures notions of leather pads smacking and footballs being passed and kicked. Many of the sports fans of Detroit acquired their first knowledge of professional football from the reverse side of Dutch Clark's bubble gum card.

His given name was Earl Clark and he played quarterback for the newest of Detroit's championship teams.

In a six-month period from late 1935 to early 1936, Detroit was known across the nation as the City of Champions. In an unprecedented sweep, Detroit's Tigers won the World Series in October, the Lions won the NFL championship in December and the Detroit Red Wings won

hockey's Stanley Cup in April.

The Lions were merely two years in residence when they won their first NFL championship with a 26-7 victory over the New York Giants in 1935. Dutch Clark scored a touchdown on a 40-yard run and he was the catalyst in the Lions' victory.

They had come to Detroit as a prefabricated team the year before, and they induced a ready-made superstar to rejoin them in their new location. Dutch Clark had played for them in Portsmouth, Ohio, where they were nicknamed the Spartans. The Spartans never won a championship — but they usually were a contender.

George A. (Dick) Richards, a Detroit radio station proprietor, purchased the Portsmouth franchise and its assets (players) for $15,000. Among them were Ace Gutowsky, Glenn Presnell, Ernie Caddel, George Christensen, Ox Emerson and Frank Christensen. Also included in the purchase price were the playing rights to Earl (Dutch) Clark — should he decide to return to pro football.

Richards was a flamboyant man and he knew the sport from a business angle. If pro football were to succeed in its fourth try in Detroit, the Lions needed a player of star magnitude. So Richards lured Clark, the former all-pro tailback in Portsmouth, from retirement. Clark had not played the 1933 season, the final year in Portsmouth, purely for financial reasons. He could not afford to play professional football.

"Until Clark came along pro football in Detroit was looked upon as a novelty," wrote one sports historian of the 1930s. "Its chances of survival were slim because it was too close to collegiate gridiron centers, but Dutch changed all that."

Clark, who was unrelated to head coach Potsy Clark, had been something of a Horatio Alger type in college. He played small-time football for Colorado College in the late 1920s. Yet his exploits as a runner, passer and kicker became so well-known he was selected on the Associated Press' All-America team in 1928. He was the personal choice of Alan Gould, then the sports editor of the AP. Because AP's team was one of the more prestigious All-Americas selected annually, Gould caught considerable flak for selecting Clark and ignoring more famous quarterbacks who played for major teams.

But when he became a professional, Clark vindicated Gould's unpopular iconoclastic choice. He became an all-pro quarterback at Portsmouth in 1931 and 1932, when it was still a primitive sport. Then when he returned to pro football with the Lions in Detroit, Clark again was selected all-pro in 1934, 1935, 1936 and 1937. He was the last of pro football's dropkick stylists. He was NFL scoring champion in 1932 with 55 points, in 1935 with 55 again and in 1936 with 73.

"He looks like the easiest man on the field to tackle," said Bronko Nagurski, a contemporary all-pro with the Chicago Bears. "The first time I tried to tackle him I thought I'd break him in two. But when I closed my arms all I was holding was air."

"Dutch was the hardest man in football to tackle," said Red Grange. "His change of pace fooled the best tacklers."

Dutch succeeded Potsy Clark as head coach in 1937. For two seasons, he was player-coach. But there were numerous rifts with owner Richards. Anticipating he would be sacked, Clark quit the Lions and became head coach of the Cleveland Rams.

In 1963, Clark was elected a charter member of the Pro Football Hall of Fame in Canton. He was selected in the first group, which included Grange, Nagurski, Sammy Baugh, Mel Hein, Don Hutson, George Halas, Curly Lambeau, Ernie Nevers, Cal Hubbard, Johnny Blood (McNally), Jim Thorpe and Fats Henry.

What about the furor created when you were picked as an All-America while playing at Colorado College, which hardly qualified as one of the nation's powers?

"Alan Gould picked me on Associated Press in 1928 over Howard Harpster of Carnegie Tech, the big shot on most of the All-America teams. Of course, Gould got abused quite a bit about it. It was a great break for me because I later went into professional ball and everything I did gave Mr. Gould the opportunity to blow it up a little bit."

How did you get to Portsmouth?

"I was out of school a year. I graduated in June of '30 and I coached basketball and football at the school for a year. And Potsy Clark took over the Portsmouth franchise as a coach and his brother, Stu, was coach at Denver University. I had played against him four years at Colorado College and he thought quite a bit of me. I had never thought about playing professional football. He told Potsy I would probably make a good professional player. So Portsmouth wrote me and it was right during the Depression when nobody had a dime. So I decided to go back and try. I kept telling myself it was financial, but I kind of wanted to try to vindicate myself — or vindicate Gould — to see if I could play."

You played in Portsmouth in '31 and '32 and then sat out '33. What did you do that season?

"I coached at Colorado School of Mines in Golden, Colorado. At the time, as I say, it was during the Depression, and you had a hard time getting your money, you had to fight for it. If they owed you a little bit, you'd be lucky to get it. I thought it would be best, so I quit. Then in '34 the franchise was moved to Detroit and Potsy persuaded me to play. I had laid out a year and I don't think I was quite as good a

There were two Clarks important to the early days of the Detroit Lions. One was Earl (Dutch) Clark, the great broken field runner and dropkicker; the other was George (Potsy) Clark (right) who was head coach from 1930 to 1936, first of the Portsmouth, Ohio, Spartans and then the Lions after the team was moved to Detroit. Dutch and Potsy were not related.

ballplayer in Detroit as I was when I was at Portsmouth. I still got lots of publicity out of it."

What are some of your recollections of playing in Portsmouth, which had to be a quaint type of place for a pro team?

"Everybody made their own schedules in those days. In other words, we might schedule the Bears three or four times in a season. And maybe not play some of the others at all. We had very few ballplayers. I don't know how many you were allowed, but at one time we got down to where we were playing with 14 players because they didn't have the money to pay us. Potsy would go around and say, 'Shall we hire another one?' And everybody would say, 'No.' You just went in and played and if you got hurt you kept playing. I was there just two years, but every year it seemed there were different teams in the league. They would take a flyer at it and lose money and drop out. It wasn't a balanced league at that time with the exception of the Giants and the Bears and the Packers, who always seemed to be there."

What about fan support?

"We got more out for practice than we did for the games. The steel mills were out then and in Portsmouth itself there was a big shoe plant and they weren't working. Hell, we'd get 4,000 or 5,000 people out there to watch us practice and at game time we'd be lucky if we had 2,000."

In '32, Portsmouth was involved in that indoor playoff game in Chicago, which became the forerunner of the modern championship games. What was that like?

"They played against the Bears in the Coliseum in Chicago. I didn't play in that particular game. When I went back to Portsmouth I retained my job as basketball coach at Colorado College. I played football in the fall and then came home to coach basketball. The snow was bad. I didn't know whether they were going to play it or not. It was an all-mixed-up affair until right at the end when they finally moved it indoors."

After the franchise was moved and you rejoined it in 1934, it was an immediate success in Detroit.

"We won our first 10 games and we had seven shutouts in a row at the start. Then the last three games we lost by three points apiece. We lost 3-0 to Green Bay and then twice to the Bears — 19-16 and 10-7. The Bears were a real good ballclub in those days."

And then in '35, the Lions seemed destined for a dismal season. You were only 4-3-1 before a late-season rally in which you beat the Packers and tied and beat the Bears and then beat the Brooklyn Dodgers to get into the championship game. What about '35, the Lions' first championship year?

"We started out very poorly. In fact, I don't think we had as good a ballclub as we had a couple of other years. But other years we didn't win it. We started off badly in '35. Boston was in the league then and we beat them a couple of times early in the season. Then we got a few breaks toward the end and we won it. After a couple of very bad ballgames early in the season, I thought we played considerably better. Then we had that game with the Giants for the championship."

In those early years, what was the day-to-day routine of a pro football player? For instance, what was the practice routine?

"We practiced on that old field Wayne University had. It was over around Second or Third Avenue. At that time we dressed at Webster Hall Hotel. They had a swimming pool, locker rooms downstairs and that's where we dressed. Then we'd go over and practice and then walk back along the streets in uniform. The majority of players just wore their cleats over there, four

or five blocks. For a while when we first came here we used to go out to Chandler Park in a bus to practice. I remember during the time of the championship game with New York, we were having trouble practicing. We even took a bus to the State Fairgrounds and practiced inside that coliseum out there. And then we played our games in the University of Detroit's stadium. It wasn't until 1938 we moved downtown to Briggs Stadium for our games."

Today, of course, they have the extravagant prelude to the Super Bowls. The coaches often complain about it. What was the atmosphere before the 1935 world championship game with the Giants?

"Potsy kept you ready. But he always had a few jokes. He was a little bit like Duffy Daugherty, who used to coach at Michigan State. He'd get you in the huddle and tell you jokes. But he'd work you hard. He got you ready for the ballgame. We had a pretty good ballclub, of course. In those days it was so damn different than it is now. We had to play it both ways. We had kids who were terrific offensive ballplayers and poor defensive ballplayers. Today they couldn't play it that way. They couldn't play defense today. And vice versa. Some were a little better on defense than they were on offense."

Teams today spend the night before all games, even when they're playing at home, together at hotels. In '35, what did the Lions do the night before their championship game?

"We never changed anything at all. We stayed right where we were living. Potsy had the idea that this was just another ballgame for you. He didn't take you off someplace and get you all excited. He said, 'This is a game just like any other and we're going to take it like any other and we're going to win it like any other.' Everybody just led a normal life; that was one thing he was very insistent about before any

kind of game that might have been extra special."

What other recollections do you have about that first championship game?

"It was cold and snowy, but Potsy was a type like Bud Grant in Minnesota. You couldn't holler about it. He'd run you around the track if you hollered. Nobody said anything. The game was played in a snowstorm. I remember scoring a touchdown and Gutowsky and Caddel scored touchdowns and Buddy Parker scored the fourth touchdown. I think we got $288 for winning."

The NFL Record Manual says $313.35 was the winning share. You were called a quarterback, yet in strict single wing nomenclature of the time you were the tailback. Correct?

"I was the tailback. Or quarterback because I called all the plays. Frank Christensen was the blocking back — that was the quarterback in the single wing on most teams. Potsy didn't do it that way. He had the tailback call the signals. If I happened to be out and Presnell was at tailback, he was calling signals. Press filled in at tailback and he also filled in at wingback. I played at wingback sometimes at Portsmouth and I yelled like hell. I used to play against Turk Edwards, the big tackle who played for Boston and I had to block him and he damn near killed me. He had a bad leg and he wasn't letting anybody get near that leg. Geez, I thought he'd tear my head off. So I screamed to Potsy. I said, 'I don't belong out there, I'm a tailback.' So from then on we finagled around to get Presnell out there."

You were the last of the dropkickers in pro football. It has become a lost art. Why?

"I presume I was the last. I don't think there were any after me. The last year I played I placekicked. The ball was getting smaller and it was harder to dropkick. Dropkicking wasn't hard for me. I'd been doing it all my life since high school. The ball was different then, it was rounder. When they slimmed the ball to help the passers it became more difficult to dropkick."

How far could you kick a field goal with a dropkick?

"I couldn't dropkick far — not nearly as far as I could placekick. Forty yards would be a long one for me dropkicking although some people dropkicked longer than I did. But they did it a little differently. They dropped the ball at a little bit of a slant so they could get under it. I dropped my ball almost straight down."

At the same time you were dropkicking, Glenn Presnell was placekicking for the Lions because he had a 54-yard field goal in 1934 which was the NFL record for 19 years.

"Glenn placekicked and I dropkicked. If it was out too far Glenn would try it. His 54-yard field goal was against Green Bay at Green Bay. We beat 'em 3-0 and they came back a few weeks later and they beat us 3-0 in Detroit."

Who were the greatest players you played against in those days?

"Of course I always start out with Nagurski because I think he was one of the best. Cal Hubbard I thought was a great ballplayer. Of course Don Hutson, the greatest pass receiver. When he first came into the league he had to play defensive end, you know. He was hard to run against. We used to run our off tackles — he weighed about 170 — and we figured we'd have no trouble against him. He'd get his little old body in against that tackle and he'd keep it there. So you couldn't get to him to block him and when you tried to run around him he was so damn fast he'd run right with you outside. Then after a couple of years they got a quarterback at Green Bay. They played the Notre Dame style and the quarterback played blocking back and then on defense went to defensive end and they moved Hutson to

safety. Mel Hein was great with the Giants. I thought Mel was the finest man in back of the line that I ever played against or ever saw play. Ken Strong of the Giants was a great ballplayer in those days."

The game wasn't as specialized as it was to become. You had to go both ways. What was your position on defense?

"I played safety. We played a 6-2-2-1, that's all we ever played. That was a six-man line, two linebackers, two halfbacks and a safety. I was the middle man and we played more or less of a zone. Most teams at that time played seven-man lines. We played a six, which I thought helped us. It was a little different and they hadn't practiced against it too much. And then in the middle '30s, about '36 or '37, that damn Steve Owen in New York started a five-man line with three linebackers with Hein playing in the middle. And they gave people fits with that five-man line. Nobody was used to playing against it."

What sort of game plans were prepared in those days?

"Well, we didn't have game plans. We just had a few plays. We put in a few little extra innovations to the same plays that we had but actually we were going off nine running plays and nine passes. And then there were little innovations that we would add to ourselves, we'd maybe add an X to a play, you see. That would mean the play would be run the same except something different on the end of it would come up.

"As for game plans as such, we had no such thing. We were going off tackle or we were spinning. The thing that was going the best for us was the thing that we stayed with. We were never ones to keep jumping around and try everything because we had it. If it was going good we kept using it. I had times when I used to run Gutowsky five or six times in a row on a

spin play, because I knew when I came back in the huddle they're figuring, 'Well, he's run it three times in a row, he's going to go to something else this time' So I came right back with it again. And if it didn't work, we'd go to something else."

And of course there was no such thing as a playbook then?

"Well, no. We had notebooks. Almost everybody had notebooks and wrote the thing down that they were thinking."

How was it you became coach in 1937?

"Potsy and Richards. Richards was a funny guy, you know. He and Potsy were always having trouble. Potsy quit a half a dozen times and Richards fired him a half a dozen times. And Richards would offer me the job. He'd say, 'Take over, Potsy's quitting, I'm gonna fire him.' So forth and so on. I'd say, 'Ah, you'll get along all right.' It went like that for several years and they'd always get back together. Until one time Potsy actually got so mad that he quit. And Richards said to me, 'You want the job?' I happened to be in California at the time and I talked to Potsy and I said, 'Look, I don't want the job, your job. You're gonna get back together again. Why I won't even go talk to him.' He said, 'Nope, you go ahead and get it because this time we're through.' So I went over to Richards and he gave me the job."

You had a problem or two with Richards yourself.

"I always had problems with Richards."

He'd second-guess?

"Well, yeah, he didn't know anything about it. But he didn't like the way we played. We were a running ballclub, we had ends like John Schneller and Ed Klewicki – big, tough kids who blocked well, and he wanted you to get out there and run a thing like Green Bay did with Hutson. Have an end down there catching those balls. Well, we didn't have that type of

ballclub. So he'd have his chauffeur bring messages up and leave them in my mailbox. When I got home at night there'd be a few of them there. Then he got sick and they sent him to California. People who were running the team – they were also running his radio station for him – said, 'Don't worry now, he's a sick man and he's got to get out of it.' So they sent him to California.

"But he still had the telephone, you know. He was always on the phone. And he had a fellow who worked there – well the only person I think I ever disliked in my life. I don't dislike anybody. I think everybody's a pretty good guy. But this guy used to call Richards and tell him all about it. He was a broadcaster up there at the station, Harry Wismer. And Harry was Richards' boy, you know.

"One time we were in Chicago playing the Bears and I took the kids in after our warmup and was talking to them. We were just goin' over things. Goddam if a loudspeaker doesn't come on and there's Richards on the thing giving them a pep talk. Wismer had been standing there and he just flipped it on. As it happened we won the ball game and it helped a lot because after he got through they all laughed. When you were playing the Bears in those days you didn't need any pep talk. You were out there for your life anyway. His pep talk kind of loosened them up, made it a little better ballclub that day."

So you split with Richards after the 1938 season and Potsy came back to Detroit from the Brooklyn Dodgers. What caused you to split?

"I went to New York. I was at a draft session at that time. He had called me from the West Coast and given me the names of some ballplayers to draft. So that's who I drafted. Then afterwards he called me on the phone and said, 'How could you pick a guy like that?' I said,

'You told me to draft him.' But he wasn't happy with it. So Bill Alfs — he was vice-president of the radio station and also vice-president of the ballclub — was talking to me back there at the meeting. He said, 'Dutch, I think he's liable to fire you at any minute.' There was a man there from Cleveland. They had had a coach over there whom they were very unhappy with and they let him go, a man named Hugo Bezdek. So they offered me the job and, after talking with Alfs, I thought, I'm going to get fired here, anyway, so I took that job at Cleveland. I was over there with the Cleveland Rams for four years."

You didn't play with Cleveland, though?

"No, I was gonna play, I was thinking of playing. But Richards, he said, 'You can't play because we still have the contract here in Detroit.' And if I wanted to play I had to turn around and give them a fullback named Johnny Drake, who was a great ballplayer. So I just forgot all about it and I never played again."

Was it true that Richards hired Steve Hannegan, the publicity agent famed for his gimmicks in the '30s, to provide you with what today is known as an image?

"I guess he did. I didn't know anything about it. But he said he was going to hire somebody to publicize me and I said, 'What the hell you talkin' about, you're crazy.' I said, 'If I deserve publicity I'll get it.' I didn't know anybody. But he evidently did. I didn't know Steve Hannegan. I don't know if I ever met him or not. But I did talk a lot to a person named Bob Harron — he was with Columbia University, with Lou Little for a long time. Bob Harron was a wonderful person and I know he wrote some stories about me that were in the papers in the East. He worked for Hannegan, too, so I presume it was true."

Buddy Parker was a teammate of yours on the '35 champions when he was a rookie and then he went to the Chicago Cardinals and ultimately returned to Detroit to become coach of the Lions in the club's greatest years. What about Buddy?

"Buddy was a good ballplayer. I traded him, you know. Of course, he was one of my best friends. Richards kind of made me trade him. I traded him for Bob Reynolds, the big guy from Stanford who now owns part of the California Angels baseball team and some radio stations. I traded Buddy to the Cardinals and it almost broke Buddy's heart.

"But it was the best thing that ever happened to him because he did well and then went into coaching. He never would have gone into coaching in Detroit. He wasn't the type of person here that he became when he got down to Chicago. He'd hang around with Gutowsky and those guys here and they liked to play the horses and things like that. And he wasn't thinking of football as much as he did when he got to Chicago. I think he played more football down there and he got a chance to break in as an assistant with Jimmy Conzelman. It was the best break he ever got. Bo McMillin brought him back as an assistant coach in 1950 and when Bo left the next year, Buddy ended up running the team."

Lou Creekmur

Position: Tackle
Years: 1950-59
Height: 6-4
Weight: 250
College: William and Mary

Even a quarterback with the consummate passing and leadership skills of Bobby Layne would have been ineffectual without his bodyguards from pro football's Silent Service. Layne's pass protection generally was excellent. He was afforded ample time to drop back, search for a receiver and release the football.

With Layne in the lead, the Lions became pro football's dominant team of the early 1950s. With the offensive line pass-blocking for him, Layne became the dominant player. Lou Creekmur, a tall, well-spoken left tackle and sometimes guard was the dominant blocking lineman in Layne's cordon of protectors.

Creekmur, from William and Mary, typified the athletes who battled in the pit — the violent zone where the offensive line collided on charge with the defensive line. Pro football is a trendy sport, of perpetual innovation and change. Formations change. Concepts change. Terminology changes. The action — the collisions and the grunting and the groaning — in the pit remains static, angry and brutal. Elbows fly — and Lou Creekmur admits flinging some. Offensive hands grasp defensive jerseys to impede the pass rush. Creekmur admits to have used his hands in an illegal manner on occasion.

Basically, the offensive linemen are unrecognized by the viewing public. But they are noticed and they are appreciated by the quarterbacks, who stand in the pocket, and the runners who try to dart through miniscule holes in the pit.

Creekmur's talents as a protector of Layne and a blocker for Bob Hoernschemeyer, Gene Gedman, Pat Harder and Doak Walker were certified in the Lions' list of all-pros. Creekmur was voted to all-pro teams as either a guard or tackle every season from 1951 through 1957, with the exception of 1955. He was absent that year simply because in an emergency he was transferred to the defensive line in midseason.

Even so, 1955 was one of eight years Creekmur was invited to play in the Pro Bowl.

Creekmur played in all four of the Lions' championship games with the Browns in a seven-year span in the '50s. Three were victories and the exultation of championship winning remained indelible and clear.

"I always enjoyed beating the Browns," Creekmur said. "The guys on this team, they were terrific. Three players come to mind first — Bobby Layne, Doak Walker and Jim Doran. Doak was the finest fellow I ever met. Bobby was the sparkplug. He is the greatest competitor I ever saw. He made a lot of money for all of us."

But without Lou Creekmur and his colleagues on the offensive line, Layne could not have done it.

Creekmur played 10 seasons with the Lions, starting in 1950 and concluding his career in 1959. But years later he returned to football as a color analyst on the radio network of the Miami Dolphins. A champion as a player during the Lions' Great Years, he was in the booth when the Dolphins became the first pro football team to go 17-0 in their Super Bowl VII season of 1972-73.

You joined the Lions in a circuitous manner. You weren't a draft choice out of college. How did you get to Detroit?

"Originally, I was a draft choice of the Philadelphia Eagles and the Los Angeles Dons when they still had the All-America Conference. My class graduated in 1948, so I was eligible for the draft then. But I stayed over one more year at William & Mary and worked on my master's degree. I then was thrown into that All-America Conference pot with Bob Hoernschemeyer, Y. A. Tittle and all those other guys in 1949. The reason that I probably ended up with Detroit was I played in the first Senior Bowl Game at Jacksonville, Florida, in

January 1949. I was on Steve Owen's South team and Bo McMillin was coaching the North. I was playing behind some boy from Oklahoma whom Owen had preference for and finally he let me get into the game playing defensive right tackle. I had a pretty good day playing defense. Then I blocked a punt going right over Doak Walker. McMillin was the Lions' coach and I guess he liked what he saw so at the end of the game he asked me if I would be interested in playing for Detroit if I were drafted by Detroit. They picked me up in that draft out of the hat."

Bobby Layne, of course, was the Lions' greatest quarterback — and one of the greatest ever. Yet without you guys on the offensive line to protect him there would have been no Bobby Layne story.

"That's true. But Bobby probably made the offensive line as good as we were. Bobby had an affinity for chewing your rear end out. If you ever missed a block, not only did you know about it, but all the other guys on the offensive team and everybody on the bench knew about it. On top of that, the 50,000 fans up in the stadium all knew about it, too, because he told you right then, out there in front of the whole crowd. And it was so embarrassing that we all made a pact that we would never miss a block that would ever disturb Bobby Layne. There were some great football players in that line — fellows like Charley Ane, Harley Sewell, Dick Stanfel. It was a good, sound, basic line."

How did Bobby chew you out?

"He never failed to take note of the man who would make the tackle or rough him up on a pass or something like that. He'd look at that number and know exactly who was supposed to block that man. Then he'd immediately pull you out of a crowd and start chewin' right there, lookin' up at you with that finger in your face, just rantin' and ravin'. And it would really

make you feel like two feet tall. And if you knew you missed a block, you couldn't say anything. One time he started chewin' Charley Ane out so bad they almost had to pull Charley off Bobby. He was ready to go at it."

Offensive linemen are supposed to be virtually anonymous. Fans seldom recognize them and give them credit. But in Detroit it seems Layne made you guys noticed.

"He sure did. I'll tell you, the treatment off the field he gave us couldn't have been better. He would take us out for a steak and really realize that without the guys blocking for him he didn't have much. He treated us with such respect and . . . well, it sounds funny to say this, but the whole team showed such a love and respect for each other we would break our backs for each other. We had such camaraderie that we were one big happy family. Some of the closest friends I have still are some of those Lions."

Did you feel offensive linemen in your time did not get the publicity, notoriety and praise that they should have?

"I don't think that we ever dwelled upon it. We knew that we got it from Aldo Forte, our offensive line coach, and from Buddy Parker and from Bobby Layne and our backfield. We were just as proud as could be when a guy like Hoernschemeyer or Doak Walker scored, knowing that we helped him get over that goal line. Here again it goes back to what I just said, we were such a close team. There was no big star and no guilt feelings that it was Walker getting the publicity or Hoernschemeyer or Layne or Cloyce Box getting publicity. We were all a part."

In '55 the Lions were 0-6, when you were moved to defense in midseason. Why did you go on the defensive line?

"I moved to defense because we didn't have anybody to replace Les Bingaman. This was the

Two associates of Lou Creekmur on the forward line of the Lions in the glory years of the '50s: center Charley Ane (far left) and guard Harley Sewell. The retirement of Les Bingaman (right) in 1955 left a 349½-pound hole in the middle of the Lions' defensive line. An experiment which moved Creekmur there as the replacement failed, and he returned to his old tackle position. By 1955, the man in the middle was a linebacker, not a lineman, and his name was Joe Schmidt.

year Buddy Parker started experimenting with the man over the middle dropping back and covering in a zone against the pass. I just couldn't do it. I wasn't fast enough moving backwards and laterally. And that's when they started with the 4-3, and the man over the middle became Joe Schmidt."

What was the influence of Schmidt on the club?

"Oh, it was just great — after he was accepted. The first year that Joe broke in everybody was upset that Joe Schmidt was being kept and they had traded Dick Flanagan to Pittsburgh. We wondered why we were keeping this young kid. He only weighed about 215, 220 and we just couldn't understand Buddy keeping him. After Joe started playing with such reckless abandon that he would continually be able to smell the ball, and go to it, everybody accepted him 100 per cent. He became the leader. There were so many great defensive players on that club at one time — Schmidt, Fum McGraw, John Prchlik, Jack Christiansen, Yale Lary and Jim David. We had superb personnel and Joe just kept them in control. He was a great leader."

What was your reaction the night Buddy Parker got up at the "Meet the Lions" banquet and said he couldn't handle you guys and quit?

"Utter shock. I think that everyone was completely knocked off their feet. Buddy cornered the executive committee, at that time we had a players' executive committee, and he got all of us together the following day and apologized. He pretty much told us that he just lost his head. I think he was a little upset with our participating in get-togethers with the owners. Buddy liked to feel that this was his team. He didn't like the interference that we used to get from owners. He liked to keep us in a compact group to ourselves. I think it was just a spontaneous reaction on his part. I believe he had no idea he was going to do it.

You retired after the '58 season, then you returned in the middle of the next season. Why did you return?

"I came back after four games of the '59 season and played eight. How that came about was really comical. I retired at the end of '58 because of business. I was with a trucking line in Detroit, and worked as a district manager through the entire 1958 season. While I was still playing I was running a terminal. So the boss says, 'You gotta quit.' So I hung 'em up.

"Then in 1959 they planned to have a picture session down at a hotel and wanted us to bring our bosses by. So I brought my boss by to this luncheon. And George Wilson, the coach then, walked up to the front table and said, 'Hey, Lou, we could use you out there.' And I, very jokingly, said, 'Any time, George, just let me know.' Well I got back to the office and there was a call from George. He says, 'Lou, can you and the boss come down?' The boss and I go down to the Lions' office and George lays it on the line to me. 'I'd like you to come back,' he said. I said, 'The boss is right here, it's his decision, not mine, George.' My boss says, 'Hell yes, go on and play.'

"I signed a contract on Wednesday but couldn't practice. Thursday was my first practice in full pads and we had a scrimmage. On Friday we practiced a little, then caught a plane and went out to Los Angeles. Saturday we loosened up a little bit in L.A. On Sunday, I started the game and George said all I was gonna do was play a quarter to get the feel of it. Well, we were ahead in the first quarter, so I stayed in the second quarter and finished the half.

"We got back to the locker room and George says, 'I don't want to break up a winning combination. This is the chance to win the first game of the season. Lou you stay in there.' So I

stayed in and played the third quarter and looked over at that bench at the end of every single play, thinking, 'Boy, he's got to take me out soon.' To make a long story short, I finished the game.

"Lou Michaels, the defensive end who I'd really had a great time with the year before, just beat me to a pulp because I wasn't in good condition. I crawled off that field. The next day we went up to Palo Alto and on Tuesday I couldn't get out of bed. But it was probably the most important season of my 10 years 'cause if I had not played in 1959 I wouldn't be covered by the pension."

You mentioned your matchup with Lou Michaels. What were some of the other memorable matchups in your career?

"Don Colo was a fierce competitor, a great defensive tackle with Cleveland. Lenny Ford with Cleveland. He and I used to have a lot of fun together. At times he was one of the best football players on the field and at other times when he was lazy you could really have yourself an easy day with him. But he was a great competitor.

"There were so many stories. We played Cleveland so many times. But one game we played them in a snowstorm in '52 or '53. I broke Lenny's thumb during the regular season. Then we played them in the championship game, all of a sudden we found them in a 6-1 defense. Lenny was playing out there, way out there. I had nobody in front of me, nobody to block and I kept hollering to him the whole game, 'C'mon in here Lenny, c'mon in here, c'mon rush the passer.' And he wouldn't come near me.

"I never did find out why until we went out to the Pro Bowl together. We rode the same plane out and killed a couple of bottles of champagne together and that's when I found I had broken his thumb in the game before. He

said, 'I wouldn't come near you. You find out I had a broken thumb you'd pull it right off me.'

"Ed Sprinkle and I had some good tie-ins. He was a great defensive end for a little guy. He never weighed more than 220 when he played for the Bears, but he was all elbows and knees. I still have half a tooth in my mouth because of Ed Sprinkle. And Leo Nomellini with the 49ers, he was a good one, too."

There were people who watched you and said something about your elbows.

"Ha, ha, ha, ha . . . well, I used to throw a few. In fact, one of the reasons I think I made it to the Pro Bowl was the coaching I received from Marvin Bass when he was my line coach at William and Mary. He was a firm believer in throwing that elbow.

"Hardy Brown had the reputation of coming around and tearing peoples' heads off with his ability to drop that shoulder and hit 'em right across the face . . . I coldcocked Hardy Brown one year. I've never thrown a better elbow. Knocked him out cold. And we must have run that film back, oh at least 20 times, watching Hardy Brown get knocked out cold."

"I caught Clayton Tonnemaker once and I don't think Clayton or I will ever forget it. Doak Walker had come around the end and had just slipped down. Clayton was going to make sure he didn't get up and was just startin' to come down with both knees in the middle of Doak's back. And the timing was just perfect for me. I was on the other side of Doak and I caught it just in time and I let one ride. And at that time they had those big, thick plastic masks — big, thick bar — well, I came right through that bar on Clayton. It must have ended up in the upper deck, knocked Clayton cold, gave him a bloody nose, two black eyes and must have knocked out a couple of teeth. And, boy, did my elbow hurt.

"I guess another one I busted was that boy

Ed Meadows. Meadows was the one who hurt Bobby. He was playin' on the end opposite the man I would be blocking on the Bears. He came around and caught Bobby and put Bobby out of the game. I grabbed the other tackle on the right side and I switched over to the right side on the very next play. I told the tackle, 'Take my position, let me play that one.' And Meadows — man I've never thrown a sweeter one. I broke his nose and his jaw, gave him two black eyes, the whole works. The very next play he swung and hit me right on the side of the helmet and immediately the official called it, fined him 50 bucks and kicked him out of the game."

Parker said the injury to Layne that day cost the Lions the '56 title.

"The play was just as dirty as could be. Bobby handed off the ball on a sweep and just stood there watchin' it and Meadows really unloaded on him. It really upset us. That's what I mean about the closeness — how we'd protect each other and care so much for each other. Hell, you couldn't help wanting to go over there and make restitution for what he had done to Bobby. We couldn't get Bobby back in the ballgame, but I'll be damned if I was going to let that son of a gun get away with it."

Did you ever get caught for holding?

"Many times. I'll tell you, when I quit in '58 Doc Greene wrote a column in the *Detroit News* on my holding and I said, 'Heck, Doc, I probably held on every other play.' And he put it in the paper. And then I came out of retirement in 1959 and those officials really were lookin' for me.

"You get to the point as an offensive lineman, it's so frustrating that a defensive lineman can pound on you and pound on you, hit you with fists, elbows, everything and anything and you can't do a thing about it except according to the regulations. You're supposed to keep your hand into your jersey. Well, you had to do something. So you'd gamble and grab and hold. But I never really held much with my hands. I developed a knack of holding with my elbows, knees, feet, head — any place where I could make a junction with my body and the other guy's."

In that same column, Doc Greene wrote about an incident you had with Charley Powell of the 49ers.

"Charley was provoked because just as he was ready to get by and get to Layne, I leg whipped him. I really used to be able to get those heels around. I'd hit the guy right in the shins. They thought they were gettin' by and all of a sudden they'd end up with their faces in the mud. And, oh man, you talk about gettin' people upset! So by the end of the game they'd really be so mad they'd be ready to fight.

"Well, if I timed it right and I did somethin' on one play, by the next play I knew the guy couldn't stand it any longer and he's gonna really try to take my head off. I'd just nonchalantly walk up to the official and say, 'Mr. Ref, watch Charley Powell, he's been sluggin' me all afternoon.' I'd go back up on the line and say somethin' to him just before the play. And it never failed — whoever it was would throw a big roundhouse. And here would come the flag and here would be 15 yards. And we did it one year when we were behind by one point with San Francisco . . . Charley threw one at me, we got the 15 yards, put us right in the area for a field goal. Jim Martin comes in and kicks one and we beat 'em by two points. He cried like a baby."

Bobby Layne

Position: Quarterback
Years: 1950-57
Height: 6-1
Weight: 190
College: Texas

Long before the advent of Joe Namath, Bobby Layne was a bon vivant quarterback in Detroit. He was blond, slightly pudgy and he talked in a raspy Texas dialect. Layne was pro football's wassailer nonpareil and his nocturnal escapades became part of the Lions' championship legend. His fans were legion. So were his detractors on many Sundays — at least for most of four quarters. It was then that Bobby Layne was the finest quarterback of his era. Swiftly, precisely, confidently, he pulled out multitudes of ball games with cunning use of his arm and the final moments of the clock.

Bobby Layne played football and lived life in a grand, gregarious, flamboyant style. Years before it became fashionable for an athlete — before such words were even used to describe them — Layne exuded machismo, Gemutlichkeit, sangfroid, chutzpah. With theatrical flourish and some verbal assurances to his fretting teammates he could turn almost certain defeat into sweet, sweet victory.

With his flair, Layne established quarterback standards which still apply in Detroit. Through years of trial and error, all succeeding quarterbacks — and there was a procession of them — were judged against Bobby Layne. Only one could ever match up to any degree — and Layne personally scouted him and recommended him to the Lions. He is Greg Landry, the Detroit quarterback of the '70s. Landry arrived a decade after Layne left, exiled to the Steelers on a Monday morning after a poor performance the afternoon before.

In eight seasons in Detroit, Layne played for three world champions and another conference champion. During a career which started in 1948 and lasted through 1962, Layne overlapped the quarterbacking eras of Sid Luckman, Sammy Baugh, Frankie Albert, Bob Waterfield, Norm Van Brocklin, Otto Graham, Charlie Conerly, John Unitas and Bart Starr. As a passing artisan, he probably could not match his contemporaries. Layne seldom was a high percentage passer. Sometimes his throws fluttered and wobbled. But Layne had no peer as a man who could inspire a team to victory.

It was 1950 when Layne, then 24, arrived in Detroit after one year with the Bears and another with the New York Bulldogs of Kate Smith and Ted Collins. He had been drafted by the Pittsburgh Steelers out of the University of Texas, where he had been coached by the famed Dana X. Bible. The Steelers made him their first-round choice. But they were the last holdout in pro football's metamorphosis from the archaic single wing to the T-formation. Layne did not want to be a single wing tailback, so he asked to be traded. Art Rooney, the benevolent owner of the Pittsburgh franchise, obliged him. He traded him to George Halas' Bears. In his rookie year of 1948, Layne languished behind Luckman and Johnny Lujack. Next year the Bears sent him to the New York Bulldogs, an All-America Conference team which had moved from Boston to New York. Layne learned pro quarterbacking under fire as the Bulldogs' No. 1 quarterback in 1949. It was a most frustrating year for the young, blond Texan. The Bulldogs played to a 1-10-1 record. At the end of the season, Layne asked again to be traded — and again he was obliged.

He was traded to the Lions, where an ailing and irascible Bo McMillin was the head coach. McMillin was just assembling the manpower that would soon become a championship team under Buddy Parker.

In 1946, the Lions were 1-10. Then came seasons of 3-9, 2-10 and 4-8. In 1950, Layne's first year and McMillin's last, the Lions were 6-6. In 1951, the first year under Parker, they were 7-4-1. In 1952, they went all the way. They beat the Rams in a playoff after both finished 9-3 in the West, and then won their first championship in 17 years by beating the Browns.

In six years, the Lions won three championships and lost another championship game — and then one day in 1958, Layne was gone, banished. He rejoined Parker in Pittsburgh and played five more years. He was still a legend, a reveler, an inspiration — but he was never a champion again. Today Bobby Layne is identified singularly with the Lions and Detroit.

There have been a lot of stories about Bobby Layne, on and off the field. Are all the stories true?

"Once those things get started, they're hell to stop. If I had one regret about when I played it would be that one thing. I had kids growing up at that time and it didn't help any. I would say that lots of ballplayers were probably doing the same thing I was doing. I just happened to be there at the time it started and, like I say, it's hard to stop the stories. When you get a reputation like that, hell, you can go some place and drink two beers and you know what happens. But it was my fault because I exposed myself to it.

"But you and I know, you can't play professional football 15 years without being able to perform. In Pittsburgh my last five years, I lived with Ernie Stautner and we had a standing rule that we would raise hell on Monday and Tuesday. On Tuesday night at 12 o'clock we'd quit everything. From then until the game was over we didn't do anything — just stayed home and watched TV. We'd go out and eat, but there were no parties."

There are stories you'd go out Saturday night before a game.

"That's not true. Oh, we did when I was real young and we'd do it in the exhibition season. But we never took advantage of Buddy. He didn't check us and all that stuff. He said just plain don't embarrass me, don't be seen out.

Oh, Hunchy (Hoernschemeyer), Dib (Dorne Dibble), Jug (Girard), Bing (Les Bingaman), and me, we'd play an exhibition game somewhere and then we'd have a good time after. But mostly it was a real serious group. Damn few of that group took advantage of Buddy."

Joe Schmidt talked about the camaraderie you had then.

"Every Monday, anybody who was hurt had to show up at the stadium and get treatment. So every Monday we'd all go to the Stadium Bar, which was across the street from the stadium. Doak Walker never drank but he'd always be there. He just wanted to be a part of it. We had fun together. The worst thing that can happen to a bunch of players is to have two go one place and talk about two other guys and blame somebody for a loss. We would get together every Monday and if we'd had a loss, hell, by Tuesday, we'd be ready to go back to work and think about the next game and not be blamin' somebody. Actually, we still have a closeness. We're all still friends."

You were probably the most proficient quarterback ever at driving a team down the field against the clock, pulling out the game. What special quality is needed to do this?

"Well, Buddy Parker was responsible for that. He was the first coach who worked on this in practice. He was the originator of the two-minute drill. He would come on the field with a watch and he'd say 'Okay, you've got a minute and 30 seconds, you've got one time out left, see what you can do.' So we would actually practice this up and down the field. So when it came up in a game you didn't panic. In our playbook, the first page was about gambling. The second page was about the two-minute offense. It said the most important part of a ballgame was two minutes before the half and two minutes before the game was over. You've seen these teams that don't do anything

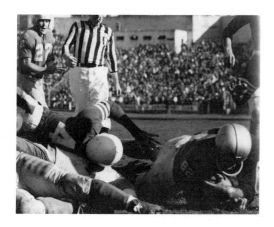

for the first part of the game, then look great in the last minute or so. We were like that a lot."

It seems as if Parker was ahead of his time as a coach.

"He stayed ahead of it. That's one reason the Lions were winning then. Buddy was great here in Detroit. In Pittsburgh, he didn't have the players and he overworked himself. He got kinda tough because he was not winnin' and was tryin' so damn hard and it was a losin' battle.

"When I reported over there he called me into the office and he said, 'Look, I've got this many players' and he went over the whole team and he explained to me how many can win. 'Frank Varrichione,' he said, 'we've got a helluva tackle in Varrichione. There's Stautner and Jimmy Orr.' We went down the list and it was pretty thin. But he inherited that kind of deal. He had more quarterback meetings, more meetings trying to accomplish this thing. By this time he was gettin' up at an age where his nerves weren't as good as they were over here. Things bugged him. He was tryin' to make a championship team when he didn't have championship material.

"My God, over here after we got rollin'... look at our draft choices. We got guys like Yale Lary, Joe Schmidt, Harley Sewell all in one year. You get a nucleus and you start draftin' five or six of these guys in a year, till you start gettin' old, you're gonna win."

But you never were big on rookies, were you?

"You should never get real close to a rookie. Cause if they get cut they'll come cryin' on your back. So, we just kinda waited until they made the club, then they were part of us. All of them can't make it."

Bo McMillin was one of football's most famous personalities. Yet his three years of coaching in the pros in Detroit were disastrous.

Why did Bo do that badly, and what was he like?

"I can't say anything about Bo because he was a sick man when he was here. We didn't know it. But his coaching techniques compared to Buddy's were like night and day. There's a lot of coaches like this — the old school and they're not gonna change. They've been in the coachin' profession for years. I had this in college with Mr. Bible. A good man. But when they get old they get set in their ways. I told you about Buddy at Pittsburgh. He wasn't the same guy."

According to stories written in 1950, you gave an ultimatum that you wouldn't play for Bo in 1951. Is that true?

"The truth is one of our owners — and I won't recall his name — called us together. We had a luncheon. There were the team captains — myself, Cloyce, Johnny Greene, Doak — what they would consider the leaders. We had a luncheon near the end of the season. And this person asked us what we thought it would take — they were dyin' for a winner here. They were just graspin' and tryin' to get a winner for Detroit. He took our opinions, what we thought it would take to be a winner. But I never said that about Bo."

What did you players tell this owner?

"We did tell him we decided we thought we could win with Buddy Parker. We knew we could."

Parker, who had been an assistant, came in and you had a better season in 1951.

"We had a real great chance until the last game. We beat the Rams 24-22. All we had to do was beat 'Frisco in the last game to win the whole thing. I will say this, we got a lot of people hurt in the Los Angeles game and we went to 'Frisco and got beat four points. We came that close in '51, missed tying the Rams in the division by a half-game.

What are some of your more vivid recollec-

Layne's quarterbacking cohorts on the Lions, Harry Gilmer (left) and Tobin Rote (right, in the 1957 NFL championship game against Cleveland at Briggs Stadium). Each became a starter after Layne was injured, Gilmer in 1955 and Rote in 1957.

tions of the first championship season, 1952?

"In '52 we started out losing two of the first three and they were Coast teams. After the third game, Buddy called us all together right there in Briggs Stadium and he said – just before practice, everybody was down, low – and he said, 'Hell, we can win this thing.' Then he said, 'Tell you what, you win the next' – I can't recall the number of games – 'if you win the next so many games' – like three or five – 'and I guarantee you we'll be in first place.' And we did, and we were. We finally had to have a playoff game with the Rams, but everything he said was right. He could see it." (The Lions actually won their next five and eight of their remaining nine to tie the Rams and then won the playoff to play the Browns for the championship.)

And '53?

"That was an even better team. But '54 was probably the best team we ever had. It was the most amazing thing in the world. We had two games left and we already had it won. We got too goddamn complacent. I mean, we didn't have to play. Those last two weeks we had a game with Cleveland, one with the Chicago Bears. We already had the division won. Hell, those last two or three weeks was like a big holiday. You could imagine having two tough games like that and already having the division won. We beat Cleveland 14-10."

You beat Cleveland in the snow in the regular season finale in 1954.

"Yeah, then we went back over there and they beat the livin' hell out of us for the championship. Nothin' ever happened . . . I musta had six interceptions. The first time we had the ball I hit Dibble. He was going for a touchdown and dropped it. First play of the game, Bowman runs a takeoff and runs I don't know how far. Second play I roll out and hit Dibble . . . he drops it. You could just kind of see from those plays what was going to happen."

The Browns won it 56-10. Then in '55 you went zero and six in the first half of the season.

"Everything happened to us. Our first game we get Stanfel and Sewell and Jack Christiansen injured real bad. It was just terrible, awful. But we came back in '56."

In '56, you should have won it.

"That was the year Green Bay beat us here with Tobin Rote at quarterback. Also we had a game with Washington and we got beat 18-17. Those two games cost us, cause they were dog teams."

That season ended in Chicago with the Meadows incident and you lost the game and finished a half-game behind the Bears.

"We beat the Bears over here, by some horrible score, then played Pittsburgh and then went back to Chicago to play the Bears for the whole thing."

What was your reaction when Buddy traded to get Tobin Rote from the Packers the day after camp started the next summer?

"Really not anything. Tobin and I became good friends just as Harry Gilmer and I had been good friends the previous two years. I've always said it's nice to have two so-called equal quarterbacks, but I don't think you can have two No. 1 quarterbacks. Damn few successful teams have ever had two of equal caliber. But if one gets hurt – and I broke my leg and ankle that year and Tobin stepped in and took 'em to the championship – that's the good side of it. I always said you don't have two presidents of General Motors and you don't have two Presidents of the United States. You've got to have one man that runs it. All those years the Rams had Van Brocklin and Waterfield they didn't win. They really had the horses, but they didn't win except one time in '51."

Before the start of the '57 season Buddy got up to speak at a banquet and said, "I can't

handle this team. I quit." And that's what he did.

"We were stunned. In fact, we got together that night — Joe Schmidt and myself — and went out and got Buddy. He was packin'. We didn't think he was serious. Joe and I were captains of sorts. We went to Buddy's office and we begged him to stay with us. 'No.' he said, 'after what happened tonight I have nothing to do but what I'm doing.' He said, 'I've been here long enough,' and he said it was time to go and there were too many people meddling with it.

"I'll tell you what it really started over. It started with training camp. Leon Hart wouldn't show, wouldn't come to training camp that year. And Buddy said, 'The hell with him if he doesn't want to sign.' And the club directors came to Leon and they said, 'You'll make us look bad' — because he'd been a No. 1 draft choice. It wouldn't have made us look good if we cut him or traded him. That started the rumblin', I'll tell you.

"And then another thing, Buddy wanted to draft a fullback when Hunchy quit. He went to the draft meeting ready to draft Joe Childress from Auburn. We needed a fullback. And certain people told him to draft Hopalong Cassady. That was the story of it right there — when they started runnin' it. And Buddy told us that. He said, 'I can't run it anymore, so it's time to leave. It has nothin' to do with tonight.' Buddy was this type of person. Things would build up inside of him and he couldn't stand to get beat. Things kept buildin' up and he finally couldn't take it anymore."

You and Doak Walker had a longtime relationship, high school teammates, college opponents when Texas played Southern Methodist, then pro teammates again on some championship teams.

"We were real close. We grew up together, played together all through high school, High-

land Park in Dallas. We were about to get drafted, the war was about over and we didn't know what to do. We joined the Merchant Marine together. We stayed in the Merchant Marine for about 10 months. And we were in New Orleans and we went to radio school. We were officers, warrant officers. We were gonna ship out and the war ended.

"We had always decided we'd go to the University of Texas together, play together in college. It just so happened that weekend SMU was playin' Tulane in New Orleans and Rusty Russell, who was our high school coach, was now at SMU. We were goin' back to school, we were goin' to Texas. So Rusty told Doak, 'If you're goin' back to Dallas just get on the train with us and we'll give you a free ride.' Well, somewhere between New Orleans and Dallas he talked Doak into goin' to SMU. So on Tuesday I go to Austin and enroll at Texas. We won the conference that year."

You were drafted by Pittsburgh.

"They were playin' the single wing and I was not a good enough runner to play over there. So they traded me to Chicago — that was when they had the bonus pick and I was the bonus pick — and they traded me to the Bears for Ray Evans, a boy from Kansas. I played with the Bears that first year — Lujack, Luckman and myself. A Jewish boy, a Catholic boy and me. Halas was real fair to me. He was an honest guy, I really liked him. He called me and said, 'Bobby, I cannot afford to keep three quarterbacks at your salary. I thought Sid was gonna retire but he wants to play some more and he's been good to me.' He thought Sid was gonna quit and he'd have Johnny and myself as quarterbacks.

"Football wasn't a real moneymaker then. So he traded me to the New York Bulldogs. It was not exactly one of my greatest experiences. We won one game outta 18 and I would've quit.

I had already made up my mind, I wasn't gonna go back to New York. I was gonna quit football. I went up there weighin' about 195, 200. I came home, I weighed 167. I went to Dallas to see Doak, drivin' back from New York. He didn't even know me. It was a miserable, horrible year. And I was young and lost in New York. My son, Rob, was a little baby. I just marked the days off the calendar until it was over. Then luckily I got traded over here."

Time said you had to take an $8,000 pay cut when you came to Detroit, the reason being salaries went down after the All-America Conference merged with the NFL.

"Not true. When I signed with the Bears, I got a bonus and signed for three years. In 1955, I walked into Nick Kerbawy's office and I felt in my own mind I had a horrible year. I think at that time I was making $22,500 or $25,000, right in there, because when I signed I got $77,000 for three years. It was with a bonus and $77,000 for three years. In '55 I had a bad year, so I went into Nick Kerbawy and I said, 'Nick, I had a bad year, so this is what I want to make.' I had to sign a new contract. So I said, 'Cut it $3,000 or something.' He'd never heard of this cuttin' my own salary. But I'd already figured out that it would cost me only about $400 in actual dollars.

"He appreciated it, so in '56 I had a real good year, led the league in scoring and then came back after that year and got me some on the other side. We hardly ever discussed contract. It took me three seconds to sign a contract. My ambition in football was to make more money than any other quarterback had made up to that time — which I did. Just for pride. We never had any jealousy over here about salaries. I guarantee you that."

Was there one game that stands out in your mind above all the others?

"Well, I'll tell you, the '52 championship game in Cleveland — nothing was ever as good after that. That was the happiest I ever was in football, winnin' the championship. I remember I drove all the way from Cleveland — got a new car over there, had it delivered from here — and I was so up in Cloud Nine. In a snowstorm, Carol and I got in the car and I drove all the way to Lubbock, Texas. Never got sleepy. The second title was never like the first one."

You broke your ankle in '57, then Tobin Rote took the team to the championship. When you came back in '58 and they had the two quarterback system, what was your reaction?

"I wasn't happy. I either had to play or not play, one of the two. That's the way I was. But I'd run out my time here. I was too well-known here. Believe me, one of the best times I ever had was when I first got to Pittsburgh. I didn't know a soul."

In '58, in your last game for Detroit, some reporters accused you of being jittery and lacking your old leadership after a 13-13 tie at Green Bay, the second game of the schedule.

"Yeah, I missed an extra point. But I never did want to kick, anyway. I inherited that. I wasn't a kicker. I was all they had left. Years before, we had three kickers hurt in one game — Pat Harder, Doak and Pat Summerall. Somebody had to kick. Hell, I even had to kick off. I kicked off for three years. I couldn't kick it. I could barely get it to the goal line. I'd kicked a little bit in college so I started kicking field goals and extra points. But it was time to leave."

According to stories at the time you learned the Lions traded you when you went to the airport to pick up your wife.

"That's when the new airport first opened. Carol was comin' in from Texas. That's the only thing that hurt me — the way they did it. Instead of calling me in the office and telling

me, they paged me. George Wilson paged me at the airport. And he said I'd been traded. So I was to get packed and get on a flight that night. I went to the Stadium Bar and told my good friends goodby. Then I showed up in Pittsburgh and went to practice Tuesday. I flew over there that night on a late flight."

Were you glad to be rejoining Parker?

"Oh, yeah. It was a pleasant setup. When I first got to Pittsburgh, I'd get these little letters from kids asking for autographs. The Pittsburgh players would take them and never open them, just throw them in the wastepaper basket. I walked in one day and said, 'Do you all have any pictures I can send to kids?' They never heard of that. These are important things you have to do. In Detroit, the club would get me a bunch of pictures. Well, over there I got my own.

"It was a strange team, I'll tell you. They had a little ol' bitty office in the Roosevelt Hotel. Mr. Rooney is a great man, but nothin' was first class. Their scouting system was somethin'. They subscribed to all the newspapers around the country. They'd read how the colleges came out on Saturday. That's how they drafted."

Looking back, do you have any regrets?

"Not really. We had a good time and we won some games. That's all that matters."

Buddy Parker

Position: Head Coach
Years: 1950-56
Height: 6-0
Weight: 195
College: Centenary

The history of professional football in Detroit is sharply punctuated along the way by incidents of turbulence.

The most turbulent incident in the history of the franchise occurred in the grand ballroom of the Statler Hotel in downtown Detroit. It was the evening of August 12, 1957 — and it was scheduled as a festive occasion. The annual Meet the Lions banquet always was. Every table in the ballroom was clogged with fathers and their sons, adoring fans of a viable football team. At the head table sat Raymond (Buddy) Parker.

As the usual banquet platitudes were spoken into a microphone on the dais, Buddy Parker listened. Inside, he simmered. At last he was introduced. The applause was thunderous. Parker rose and walked to the microphone.

"I'm getting out," he said. "I can't handle this team anymore. It is the worst team I've ever seen in training camp. They have no life, no go; just a completely dead team. The team got away from me, got beyond me.

"I've been in football a long time. I know the situation. I don't want to get into the middle of another losing season. Material-wise, it's a good team. Maybe somebody else can handle it better than I can."

The prebanquet behavior of his players had precipitated Parker's rash — and later regretted — decision to quit. Querulous factions of owner-directors had been squabbling for years. Parker was wedged in the middle. Before the banquet, when he entered a private party in one of the director's hotel suites, Parker discovered some of his players there, drinking. As he reflected about it while waiting his turn at the speaker's table Parker decided to quit. And so he did, in an announcement that stunned his players and the fans in the ballroom.

Parker had quit in a huff a number of times before in his stormy but successful six-year reign as head coach. Every time before he had recanted. This time nobody tried to induce him to change his mind. The next day George Wilson, an assistant, was appointed Parker's successor as head coach. In his rookie year, with a dramatic rally in the late season, Wilson coached the Lions to another world championship. Again the Browns were the Lions' victims, 59-14, on a frigid December Sunday at Briggs Stadium.

A couple of weeks after he quit, Parker was back in football as head coach of Art Rooney's Pittsburgh Steelers. The next year he acquired Bobby Layne to play quarterback for him again. But in Pittsburgh, they never could regain the championship magic together.

Parker had been the most successful of the Lions' coaches, winning two championships and a third conference title in six years. The men he coached were some of the finest in football — Layne, Joe Schmidt, Doak Walker, Cloyce Box, Pat Harder, Leon Hart, Jack Christiansen, Yale Lary, Vince Banonis, Lou Creekmur, Les Bingaman, Jim David, Charlie Ane, Thurman (Fum) McGraw, Darris McCord.

Two decades before, Parker played two seasons with the Lions. He scored a touchdown in the Lions' first championship game, the 1935 victory over the Giants. Dutch Clark traded him to the Chicago Cardinals in 1937. With the Cardinals, Parker learned the intricacies of football which enabled him to become a coach. For part of a season he was co-head coach of the Cardinals, sharing the job with Phil Handler. Then in 1950, he returned to Detroit as an assistant under Bo McMillin. When McMillin was fired three years into a five-year contract in 1951, Parker was elevated to head coach.

When you finished your college career at Centenary there was a story that Cal Hubbard, the Green Bay lineman and American League umpire, touted you to Detroit. Supposedly, Cal

told you "Detroit is an up-and-coming team."

"Cal was an assistant coach at Texas A&M under Homer Norton. We played A&M and at the end of the season I told Cal I wanted to play pro ball. That was before the draft and he could get me a contract with the Lions, Giants or Packers. I ended up with the Lions."

You played on a championship team your first year with the Lions, but two years later Dutch Clark became the coach and he traded you to the Cardinals. What was your reaction to that trade?

"I was disappointed. I was traded for Bob Reynolds, the Stanford All-American. They needed a tackle because George Christensen was supposed to retire. Later it turned out he didn't."

Later on, that put you under Jimmy Conzelman, one of the famous early pro coaches. What was the influence of Conzelman on your career?

"It turned out to be a good break for me. I learned a lot of things from Jimmy. He knew how to handle ballplayers, get the best out of them. When you're an assistant, there's always something to learn from a head coach."

Your superstitions became something of a legend. You'd never stay in a hotel room if the numbers added to 13 — such as 562 or 445. Supposedly you even made them change a room because it was 46C, four plus six make ten and C was the third letter. What was behind your superstition about 13?

"I don't know. It always seemed like something happened when I went into a hotel room that added up to 13. We'd blow the game or something."

After leaving the Cardinals in '49, you came back to Detroit as an assistant under Bo McMillin in '50 and then in '51 you became head coach. That first season the Lions had a winning record for the first time in six years.

What are your most vivid recollections of 1951?

"The biggest one was what happened at the end of '51. We beat the Rams and all we had to do was play the last game with San Francisco. We needed a tie or a win. Late in the game there were only about three or four minutes left — we were leading and Layne got knocked out. We put in another quarterback, named Fred Enke. All we had to do was move the ball to our own 40. All we had to do was make another first down and we could have run the clock out — which we didn't. We had to punt on fourth down and I believe it was Joe Arenas who ran the thing back about 55 yards to our 20. They scored on third-and-10. They had to have a touchdown to beat us as we were ahead 17-14, and Y. A. Tittle went on a rollout to get the ball in the end zone. Then they got an interception on us. They won 21-17. Otherwise, we'd have won our division. The Rams beat us out by half a game."

The next year you did win it. There were a lot of guys you acquired in trade your first two years who helped you a lot — Pat Harder, Jug Girard, Vince Banonis, Bill Swiacki, Jim Martin, Jim Hardy. What was the reason you made so many trades your first two years?

"Well, we had a good nucleus of a ballclub. But I started bringing in veteran ballplayers who had some years left."

Would you regard yourself as the George Allen of that time?

"Well, that was a good way to do it. I guess that's a way to say it. He trades for veterans, too."

What was your feeling going into the '52 season?

"Well, I thought we had a good chance, an excellent chance, to win it that year. We'd come close in '51. I thought we should have won in '51. We came back with a better ballclub in '52. The two best teams in our

Dutch Clark, coach of the Lions in 1937, traded Buddy Parker the player to the Chicago Cardinals. It was there that Parker came under the tutelage of Jimmy Conzelman (far left). The starting quarterback for the Detroit Lions before Bobby Layne, and the man called on in a critical game in 1951 after Layne was hurt, was Fred Enke (left). Paul Brown (right), coach of the Cleveland Browns, played Buddy Parker's Detroit teams eight times and lost seven of them.

division, of course, were the 49ers and Los Angeles. And we had to play them back-to-back. We started playing both of them the first two weeks on the Coast and then the next two weeks they both came to us in Detroit. In other words, we had four tough games. That wasn't a fair schedule."

Still you split the four, losing the two to the 49ers and beating the Rams, who were the world champs then, both times. You finished by winning eight of the last nine to get into the championship game for the first time since you were a player yourself in 1935.

"Yeah, then of course we had to beat Cleveland, another good team."

Your personal coaching record against Paul Brown was seven victories in eight games during the six years you were in Detroit. Could you explain the reason for this mastery over Paul?

"I think we got started good. In 1951 we played a preseason game with him and we beat Cleveland. Our ballplayers got up for this even though it was a preseason game. Cleveland had won our league the year before. I think that beating the Browns started it going for us. We knew that we could play the best of them."

You beat the Browns every time you had to play them except that '54 championship game. The Lions won the '52 and '53 championship games but the Browns were steaming in '54.

"They beat the devil out of us 56-10. We had to go over there and play the last game of the regular season with them. It was a rescheduled game. We were supposed to play them the second or third game of the year but due to the World Series we couldn't use Cleveland Stadium and they wouldn't transfer it to Briggs Stadium. So we had to play them the last game of the season and we beat them 14-10. Then we had to return to Cleveland the next week to play them for the championship. This had a heavy psychological effect on us. In other words, we

went into that game thinking we couldn't lose."

In '53, the Lions reached the championship game by winning their last six straight. Then you were behind 16-10 against the Browns in the championship game with just a couple of minutes left. Bobby went into the huddle near the Lions' goal line and made his famous speech: "Don't you all worry. Jest you block and Ole Bobby'll get you the championship." The coach wasn't worried on the sidelines then, was he?

"Well, I felt all along we were gonna win the ballgame. I thought we could put it in and there was a lot of time left. I had a lot of confidence in Layne. We had two minutes to go, I guess. We ended up with a third and about 10 at our 37 and he threw a pass to Jim Doran which got the first down. Then we came right back to Cloyce Box. He was at tight end because Doran had come in at wingback. Then Doran caught the ball down the sidelines for 33 yards for a touchdown. We won that one 17-16."

Before the offense left the bench for that drive, did you give Bobby any special instructions?

"No, nothin' special."

Did you ever give him any special instructions?

"Oh, yes, lots of times. Well, after he'd come out after a series I'd talk to him. We'd talk it over. I told him what to call, but I let him use his own judgment on what to call and when to call it. He'd pick the best time in the ballgame to use it."

What about Bobby's behavior? His lifestyle was different, his escapades were legend. Did you do anything to curb him?

"Yeah, but I don't think it (his behavior) was as much as what they like to make out of it. He was over 21 and I didn't see him do any of the things they say he did. All I asked was that he produce on Sunday. I never had to fine him. I

133

never knew what he was doing, and I didn't care."

What about Layne the player, the quarterback?

"He was the greatest quarterback the game has ever known. He was an incredible man. He was a good field general. He got the most out of his players. He was a passer and a runner. Most of all, he was a winner."

For several years after you succeeded Bo McMillin, you received nothing longer than a one-year contract from the Lions. It wasn't until 1957 that you got a two-year contract and that was the contract you had when you quit. Did the one-year contracts bother you?

"It bothered me some. But the reason for it all went back to the contract McMillin had which they had to pay off."

In '55 you started off 0-6 after losing the championship game so badly at Cleveland the previous December. What happened at the start of that season?

"Layne, or course, was injured during most if it. We had to go with Harry Gilmer at quarterback."

In 1956, the Lions went to Chicago for the final game with a half-game lead over the Bears. If you would have won, you would have been champions again. The Bears were in the same position. This was the game the Bears' Ed Meadows flattened Layne and knocked him from the game. There were all sorts of recriminations afterwards, accusations back and forth about dirty football. You even delivered a shot at the Chicago fans. What are your reflections about the game and the angry incident?

"Bobby had already made the pitchout and he was just standing there. Then he got hit. Meadows had a history of being that type of ballplayer. He hit Bobby right in the back of the head and knocked him out. I don't think there was any question about that incident

causing us to lose the game. The Bears lost to the Giants in the championship game, but I think we could have beaten the Giants."

It was your 43rd birthday that day.

"Yeah, heh, heh. The Bear fans sang Happy Birthday to me. That was really rubbing it in. They sang it when they were ahead — when we didn't have a chance to win."

While you were going through your succession of one-year contracts in Detroit, there were other clubs after you — Pittsburgh, Baltimore.

"The other clubs asked me after the '56 season."

Why did you turn them down, especially the Baltimore offer to replace Weeb Ewbank?

"I liked Detroit, that's the reason."

Before the '57 season you shocked everyone when you quit your job. Did you have regrets about it later?

"No question. I wish I'd stayed. I'm sorry I left Detroit. I've regretted it for a long time. If I had wanted to make a change I could have picked a better place to go than Pittsburgh. They weren't going all out in those days and it was a bad move on my part. I loved it in Detroit and I still think of myself as coach of the Lions. Not Pittsburgh. Detroit."

What prompted you to get up there and say what you did and quit?

"We'd just traded during the offseason for Tobin Rote. Some man saw me on the elevator and told me to come up to a social gathering before the banquet. I went up there and when I saw Tobin Rote and some other ballplayers in there drinking the night before a ball game, I just got teed off."

The party was in a suite belonging to Lyle Fife, one of the club's directors at the time. The incident revolved around a rift between two factions of directors.

"It's difficult working for 14 directors

Buddy Parker and Bobby Layne in 1953. "He was the greatest quarterback the game has ever known," Parker said of his field general. "He got the most out of his players. He was a passer and runner. Most of all, he was a winner."

instead of one owner. They all want to go different ways."

You mentioned the trade with Green Bay for Rote, a second quarterback. What was the reason behind that?

"When Layne was knocked out in '56, I didn't have anyone. I had a chance to get a first-string quarterback in Rote, so I made the trade."

Actually, that trade proved your theory correct, although by then you were gone to Pittsburgh. Rote was the Lions' quarterback when they beat Cleveland again for the '57 championship.

"Layne got hurt again that season and Rote came in to win it."

During your years in Detroit, Tom Fears of the Rams claimed the Lions played some roughhouse football. What about that incident with Jim David?

"That all goes back to one incident. We were playing against San Francisco in Detroit and Tittle was trying to score on a bootleg play from down about the 8 and David hit him. David's knees hit Tittle's body. It was a fair lick. David was a helluva defensive back. But they do the same thing today — they play the bump-and-run."

Tittle got a broken collarbone and it seems the whole West Coast became alarmed. David had some pretty rough matchups with Fears in Los Angeles, too. Wasn't there an incident in the Coliseum when the Rams' fans were so hot at David he had to put on another numbered jersey to get to the locker room safely?

"After Tittle's injury we had to go out there to play the Rams. And they had about 90,000 people there. If anything happened in the ballgame, they booed David. So to get him away from the crowd safely they put another jersey on him."

When you were in Pittsburgh you traded to

get Bobby in 1958. After the 1962 season, you suggested he retire.

"We played in the Playoff Bowl down in Miami after 1962. I told him then and I regretted it later. I think he could have played another year. If he had played, Pittsburgh would have gone to the championship game in '63. We went into the final game with the Giants with the winner winning the division. If I'd had Layne for that ballgame I think we'd have won it 'cause Ed Brown had receivers open all day but he couldn't hit them."

Among the contributions you made to football was the two-minute offense — or two-minute drill — the hectic drive against the expiring clock in hopes of turning defeat into dramatic victory. It was effective for Bobby and a lot of people are still using it. How did you originate that?

"Since a team gets three time outs, it should take advantage of them. There's a lot more time left to play than two minutes if you've got the timeouts. So I put that into the Lions' playbook."

Watching the game now, do you notice much difference in what the game was 20 years ago when you were coaching in Detroit?

"No, not particularly. The big difference today in the games I see is a lot of teams use a lot of bumping. A lot of the old AFL teams use what they call the bump-and-run on defense. We played that most of the time in Detroit."

And offensively?

"I don't see any change in the offense except that teams play their backs back deeper. But we always tried to do that. We had options on the holes we were supposed to hit. In other words, the offensive lineman was supposed to take the defensive lineman the way he wanted to be taken. And the backs would then pick the hole — and that's what they're doing today."

Joe Schmidt

Position: Middle linebacker
Years played: 1953-65
Height: 6-0
Weight: 220
College: Pittsburgh

Angry pale scars zipper down each of Joe Schmidt's shoulders. They are the result of making too many tackles on too many backs in too many places during 13 football seasons. Schmidt is not a giant of a man. He is stocky, unimposing. When he was a rookie with the Lions in 1953 he had blond hair. He wore it in a pompadour, the style of the '50s.

"Most of it went down the drain of the wash basin," said Schmidt when he became the 11th man to serve as head coach of the Lions in 1967.

Schmidt was not the first man to play middle linebacker. But he was the prototype of the men who would play the position years later — Dick Butkus, Willie Lanier, Tommy Nobis, Mike Curtis and Mike Lucci, who played for Schmidt when he coached.

Even as a boy, he had an authoritarian nature. He grew up in Pittsburgh. The neighborhood kids would use the side of the Schmidt house for ball playing. The sound of the ricocheting ball was a constant irritant to those inside.

"Joseph, have them stop," his mother would command.

Young Joe would go outside and mop up.

"But a little later they would be back there bouncing the ball off the side of the house," Schmidt recalled.

He played football and he was a fullback. Most high school fullbacks were converted to guard in college. Schmidt became a guard at the University of Pittsburgh. In 1952, his senior year, he was elected the team captain at Pitt. The game with Notre Dame was Pitt's biggest of the year. Pitt was a decided underdog.

"If you guys don't beat Notre Dame I'll beat up each and every one of you," Schmidt told his teammates on the train to South Bend.

The players got the message. They upset Notre Dame 22-19 in college football's shock of the year. Schmidt led the victors and was named

the outstanding defensive player of the game.

The next winter, the world champion Detroit Lions drafted Schmidt on the seventh round. Russ Thomas, who was to become the general manager years later, was a scout then. He went to Pittsburgh and signed Schmidt for $5,700.

Schmidt had his doubts about making the club. But Buddy Parker had him in the regular lineup when the season started. The Lions won their second successive championship in 1953 with Schmidt as the rookie left linebacker. When 350-pound Les Bingaman retired, Parker went to a four-man front, moving the middle guard position to linebacker. Schmidt became the most prominent middle linebacker in the new era of the 4-3 defense. He was the all-pro middle linebacker nine times in his 13 seasons before retirement in 1965. Ten times he played in the Pro Bowl. He was the Lions' team captain his last nine seasons.

His retirement was, perhaps, premature. He was 33 and he could have played longer. But the Lions were on the decline — and Schmidt could no longer play for Harry Gilmer. Instead, he was persuaded by Bill Ford to serve the final year of his contract as the linebacker coach on Gilmer's staff. Perhaps there was a promise or a hint of a future promotion. Schmidt accepted, but there was only scant, business-like dialogue with Gilmer during the year he was an assistant coach. It was a terrible season for the Lions . . . and at the end of 1965, Gilmer was fired with a year remaining on his three-year contract. His replacement was Joe Schmidt.

Ford gave Schmidt a five-year contract at $50,000 annually and a mandate to advance the Lions toward the Super Bowl. Just one week before his 35th birthday, Schmidt was a head coach.

Schmidt's first assignment was to restore order and discipline after the chaos of Gilmer's two-year regime. At times there was friction

A good showing in a preseason game against the Chicago Bears and two interceptions of Bobby Layne passes in a training camp scrimmage helped earn Schmidt his starting linebacker job as a rookie. When he was invited by Vince Banonis (left) to join the veterans after practice one day, he had progressed a step further — into the inner clique of Lions players ruled by Layne himself. Schmidt says the 1954 title game, when the Lions were blasted 56-10 by Cleveland, was a fluke. At right, Schmidt and Doak Walker tackle the Browns' Fred Morrison in that game.

between Schmidt and the front office, where Thomas had ascended to the general manager's desk, but four years into the five-year plan, in 1970, Schmidt's team reached the playoffs. It was a young team, a team that had to win its final five games to reach the playoffs as the best second-place club in the NFC. The Lions lost to the Cowboys 5-0, but it was the first time the Lions had qualified for any sort of championship playoff since 1957 — when Schmidt was the captain of the team and was carried off the field by frenzied fans after the 59-14 victory over the Browns in the NFL championship game.

Two years later, after 20 seasons' service with the Lions, Schmidt resigned. The Lions had gone into decline in 1971 and 1972. Schmidt became disillusioned at the plight of his ball club and he was the object of considerable criticism.

He said that he wanted to spend more time with his family, that he had lost some of the old gusto for the job. His resignation was made public on January 12, 1973. The next morning, at a regularly scheduled meeting of delegates before Super Bowl VII, Joe Schmidt was elected to Pro Football's Hall of Fame.

When you joined the Lions in 1953, they were already world champions — a team ruled by Bobby Layne, a team that played with gusto on and off the football field. Rookies were regarded as intruders. What was your welcome like?

"Gene Gedman, who lived in Duquesne, Pa., which wasn't far from where I lived, had a car. I was going to fly, but Gene called me. I got into Detroit around 3 o'clock Detroit time and we went into the Lions' office. Of course, prior to getting there I knew most of the players because I'd looked over their roster. I got into the lobby of the Lions' office and Bob Hoernschemeyer and Jug Girard and Dorne

Dibble were in there and evidently they were going out to play golf somewhere because they were dressed in golf clothes.

"I think at least two of them had been talking contract with Nick Kerbawy. Of course, they paid me no mind. They knew Gene because of his reputation, I guess. He was a second draft choice.

"Kerbawy came out of his office — Gene hadn't signed yet and Kerbawy was anxious to get him signed. So he took Gene into his office and I sat outside for an hour. I guess in the course of the conversation Kerbawy finally asked Gene who I was. And Gene said, 'He's one of your draft choices.' Kerbawy said, 'I thought he was a fraternity brother of yours.' With that Kerbawy came out and told me he thought Gene would be tied up for sometime and I should take the bus — which was right across the street on Michigan Avenue — and go out to Ypsilanti. I did that and that's how I got to training camp."

You'd already signed for the magnificent sum of what?

"$5,700. My college coach was John Michelosen, who had been a coach with the Steelers, and I asked him what he thought I could get. He said if I could get $6,000 it'd be a pretty good contract. That seemed like a lot of money. I can remember my father saying how anybody who made $10,000 was making a lot of money. Six wasn't too far away from 10, so I thought if I could get six I'd get a lot of money. I ended up signing for $5,700."

What kind of welcome did you get there in Ypsilanti?

"I remember seeing these people sitting on the front porch of the dormitory. I forget the name of the dormitory, but at that time, Eastern Michigan had only 500 or 600 students and had only one or two dormitories. Of course, I was very nervous like most rookies,

not knowing what they were expecting of me.

"I finally got into the dormitory and got squared away and I went outside and sat around with the other rookies, Pete Retzlaff and myself and a couple of guys who would be released, who would never get a chance to play. Lou Creekmur came by in his car and pulled up and had some of us unload his car and take his stuff up to his room. That was our first day as far as indoctrination was concerned. We had a meeting that night. It was in preparation for the All-Star game.

"It was just a regular training camp for a rookie. You didn't know what to expect. You were in the dark all the time, just wondering what your situation was or what would happen to you. Layne and Walker and Hoernschemeyer and Bingaman and all those people had a great story behind them in that they won the championship in '52. Hearing stories about all those people, you were taken aback, awed, and so forth, like any rookie. I was just happy to be there, really not knowing in my own mind when I left Pittsburgh what my situation would be."

When did you first meet Layne?

"I don't think I ever really had a formal introduction to him. The one thing I recall was after practice he'd take a bunch of rookies to a place called Hobbs, or Eddie's, and we'd drink a few beers. There was also a bar in Ypsilanti, and he'd always have to take four or five rookies with him and make them drink beer. I would try to escape those things as much as I possibly could because I felt drinking a lot of beer would take away from my conditioning.

"They'd drink prior to dinner and then come into dinner and make you sing. So I would try to get into the chow hall early so I didn't have to sing. I don't think Layne paid much attention to me, either, because at that time I didn't think they felt I had that much of a chance to

make the team because LaVern Torgeson and Dick Flanagan were around. As a result I didn't get much notice.

"Attention was paid to Harley Sewell — he was the No. 1 draft choice from Texas — and Layne more or less took him under his wing. Gene Gedman and Lew Carpenter were the other big names. I hung around with a little group of unknown people and unless we were really forced into it, we stayed pretty much away from Layne and the veterans."

How long was it before the team accepted you?

"I didn't play much in the first two or three games other than work on special teams. We went to Buffalo to play the Washington Redskins and that was maybe the third or fourth preseason game. Until then I hadn't played much at all. I felt I was going to be released. In fact, we played the Pittsburgh Steelers and I saw Bill McPeak on the field and I asked him if he would ask the Rooneys if they'd give me an opportunity to try out with the Steelers if I got released. That's where I wanted to play originally.

"We came to play the Washington Redskins up in Buffalo and Buster Ramsey came to me and said, 'You're going to sink or swim today. You're going to play the whole ball game.' So I had to do the best I could. For some reason we played a lot of 6-1 that day and I was the middle linebacker. I felt I could play professional football after that. As the weeks went on I could see that I was getting more of an opportunity to play and more of an opportunity to practice.

"One day I intercepted two passes off Layne, and George Wilson came across the field and said, 'Hey kid, that's the way to go, keep it up.' We finished training camp and we had a party at Bloomfield Country Club. They always had a party prior to opening the season. It was a fine

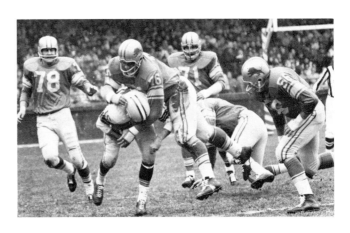

party for the players and their wives and everybody looked forward to it and I saw Parker talking to Flanagan that night at a table. The following morning I found out they had traded him to Pittsburgh. I was happy because of the trade, but also I realized I had replaced somebody who was well thought of as a team member. He had been on a championship team.

"So I just went about doing my job and really nobody talked to me or really took me under their wing until about the sixth league game. Then Vince Banonis said to me after a game, 'Why don't you come down to Kelly's?' That's where the players used to hang out. They would go down there and have a party after the game. From that time on I was more or less accepted."

Weren't you the first man to play middle backer in pro football?

"No, I think New York used a 4-3 defense before Detroit went to it. In '53 we played the 7-2 and in '54 we went to a 4-3. It was a blessing to me because in college I played a 5-3 in which I was a middle linebacker. So it was a natural thing for me being in the middle instead of outside. I think I had more ability to play inside rather than outside. And in short yardage situations — on the goal line — I'd always play middle anyway. The emergence of the 4-3 defense was a great thing for me because without it I wouldn't have got the notoriety and publicity."

What was it like playing for Buddy Parker?

"Well, I respected the man. I thought he was a fine football mind. He'd never say much to you. In fact, we would go out of our way to stay away from him. It was a little different in those days. You only had 12 football teams and you only had 33 ball players on each team and everybody was scared to death of losing their job.

"My rookie year I remember a guy named Blaine Earon had the next locker to me and after he had played six games he was cut. He was first string. No one picked him up, he didn't have any place to go — that was it. I remember we were sitting in a locker room — it was after a game on a Tuesday — and he was called into the coaches' room and when he came out I remember the look on his face. He was pretty pale and he sat down and he said, 'I've been cut. I don't know what I'm going to do. My wife's pregnant, I don't know what I'm going to do.' Nobody had a taxi squad at that time and they were only using 33 players. As a result, he was out of a job.

"That just made me realize then that this was not really a sport, but a business and you'd better do a job all the time. Otherwise you'd be facing the same thing. For years and years and years I always labored under that feeling if I didn't do my job someone else was going to take my job or I was going to be released. Even after I'd made all-pro three or four years in a row, I never had the feeling that I could just walk into training camp and make the team. I never approached the game that way because I always felt it could happen to me, too."

That philosophy carried over with you when you were coaching, didn't it?

"I think that you have to realize this is a business of bodies. It's a crude way to put it, really, but you're looking for the best bodies you can find that are able to do a job. In coaching, the guys who have the best people generally win more games than the guys who don't — even though the other guys might have a greater knowledge of the game. The character of a team will carry you a long way, too. This is why we always tried to get good people to play for us."

The Lions won the championship in '52 and repeated in '53 when you were a rookie. You have said that the Lions of those years could

have been the first of the modern teams to win three championships in a row.

"We won it in '52, '53 and in '54 we could have won it again. I think it was just a fluke that we got beat that championship game in '54. We had beaten Cleveland the week before. That was a game that had been postponed from early in the season because the Cleveland Indians were in the World Series. So when the game was made up, we beat the Browns 14-10 in a snowstorm. But we had to go back the next week to play the championship game. I think we all felt we were going to beat them.

"The game was turned around by a break. We went down and scored three points right off the bat and they got the ball and were ready to punt when Harley Sewell went in and bumped into the punter. The penalty gave them a first down and they took it in and scored. After that the whole damn thing just collapsed. But our team was good enough to win three championships in a row and it should have been the first team to do so. We had enough quality people to do it."

Then in '55 you lost the first six games and guys on the team said Parker failed as a coach.

"I'm not saying that. We just got off to a bad start and never recovered from it. We had some injuries. Parker was very upset about it and after being a coach, I can sympathize with him now. It was a bad season, but then we bounced back in 1956, only we got beat by the Bears in the last game."

In 1957, what was the players' reaction to Parker getting up at the preseason banquet and saying, "I quit, I can't handle this team"?

"At first I think we thought it was merely a joke and the next day everything would be resolved and he'd be back coaching. I'd heard he was disgruntled over the interference of the directors and owners. I can remember going back to camp that night with Bobby Layne. We tried to talk Buddy into taking the job back. But he wanted to get out. And of course, George Wilson took over and went on to win the championship. I don't think it was that Buddy couldn't handle the players. And it wasn't just that he was mad at the players. But he had seen players in the owners' suite and he felt let down."

Nevertheless, you had a great season.

"Yeah, we won the championship. Beat Cleveland bad when Tobie Rote came in after Layne was hurt and did a helluva job. We had to win a playoff game at San Francisco to make it to the title game, and we were losing at halftime 24-3 before we came back to win it 31-27."

What was the club's mood at halftime that day in San Francisco?

"I felt that we could recover and it wouldn't take that much to crank it up. The 49ers were selling tickets before the game and at halftime for the championship game and I think that this stimulated our club a little bit. We came back in and Tom Tracy scored on a long run and Jim Doran caught two for touchdowns and I intercepted a pass — a screen pass from Y. A. Tittle to Hugh McElhenny — and took it down to the 1- or 2-yard line. I think that set up the winning score. We went out in the second half and just blitzed the hell out of Tittle. And I think they were content to sit on that 21-point lead. After the half McElhenny took the ball in close, but we held them on the 10 and they kicked a field goal. It was 27-3 and the fact that they hadn't scored a touchdown really helped."

The next week you beat the Browns 59-14 for the championship as Rote threw four touchdowns. At the end of the game you were sitting on top of the crowd which had flowed onto the field at Briggs Stadium. You were bobbing like a cork on a sea of humanity. You must have been scared stiff.

"I wasn't scared. Matter of fact it was quite a thrill. The reason it happened was I had the ball as the game ended and I think people were going after the ball more than anything else. I remember I got the ball from the official and I started to get in the dugout and before I knew it I was up in the air. It took quite a time to get into the locker room."

That was a memorable victory. Of course, there are memorable losses, too — like that 9-7 defeat by Green Bay in 1962. The Lions led 7-6 with only seconds left but Milt Plum passed on third down and Herb Adderley intercepted. After the game, George Wilson had to rescue Plum in his own locker room.

"On the play, Wilson had talked to the people upstairs and they elected to throw a sideline pass. I think a sideline pass is a good call in that situation. But Terry Barr slipped and Herb Adderley intercepted. If Barr hadn't slipped, he may have caught the ball. A lot of people said we should have punted. Then they're deep in their own territory with one timeout left and they figure to have a helluva time going the rest of the way to win the game. That's hindsight, too. If we had made the sideline pass, they wouldn't have had a chance at all. But it's a game I'll never forget.

"The sad thing is no one will remember how good a defensive football team we were in those years because Green Bay was so dominant. After losing to Green Bay we went along and lost two games — 17-14 to the Giants and 3-0 to the Bears. Maybe we could have won one of those games, all of them maybe . . . maybe we could have been undefeated, I don't know."

Is it true that you went after Milt Plum after that loss to the Packers?

"No, that's wrong. People got that story all out of proportion. There was some screaming and hollering in the dressing room and everybody was disappointed. Some helmets were thrown around, but I made no attempt at all to go after Milt Plum and I think if you'd ask Milt today he'd tell you the same thing. No one went after Milt Plum. There were just some unpleasant things said at the time. That happens after ballgames, after a bitter loss when you've played so hard and you lose like that. Really, when you come right down to it, he was merely doing what he was told to do.

"Sitting back now and looking at it from a different viewpoint than I did at that time and having been both a ballplayer and a coach, I think that you really can't blame him at all. Maybe the pass should have been thrown out of bounds. But on a sideline pass it's largely timing and you can't wait to see what happens."

Five years later, in 1967, Joe Schmidt became the head coach — to restore discipline more than anything after the chaotic regime of Harry Gilmer. Were there any coaches in your past who influenced you with coaching philosophy?

"I think you have to look back at the way our team was run. I don't want to say whether it was right or wrong. Everybody I played had rules to a certain point. I always felt you should go according to rules. And this was the way I wanted to run the ballclub. I think maybe sometimes you can be too tough and sometimes too lenient. I tried to strike a balance in-between. I think that under Parker and under Wilson it was fairly loose and the majority of guys didn't take advantage of it. I'd say 90 per cent of the guys watched themselves. They would be in at bedcheck, they wouldn't go out during training camp. They'd make an honest effort to keep themselves in good shape. But the other 10 per cent didn't.

"When I took over, I felt we didn't have a good enough football team to let 10 per cent slide. I felt that if I could get that 10 per cent to be better football players by concentrating more and dedicating themselves to trying to

win, we'd have a much better team. I just don't feel you can run a football team any other way and this is my philosophy and I had to do what I felt was best."

You were a crony of Layne during the halcyon years. His reputation was that of a nocturnal being who could produce expertly on Sunday. What about Bobby's lifestyle?

"I think he got credit for a heckuva lot more than he really did. He was always ready to play. Wednesdays, Thursdays, Fridays – I'd been with him – he'd like to go out. He liked to be around people. He'd like to see the ballplayers out. He wanted a close-knit football team, which we had in the early '50s. It's hard to get this across to some young guys who never experienced this camaraderie of feeling among football players.

"He liked being around people, sitting around and drinking beer and telling stories and laughing and having a good time. Playing games and winning games and having good times, this is what promotes great team morale. This is why I think Parker overlooked a lot of these things because of the great team morale it promoted and the funny stories that came from it."

Did you recommend Layne's philosophies for your ballplayers when you were a coach?

"I liked to see them go out after the ball games and have a good time. I think Mondays and Tuesdays are a fine time for them to go out and have a good time. Again, some people can do it and some people can't. I was the kind of guy who couldn't do it. I couldn't go out and run around all week and expect to play a good football game. Psychologically it drained me.

"I remember my rookie year when Bobby and Les Bingaman took me out on a Friday night when I didn't want to go out. We went to a place where they played hillbilly music and we were out quite late. On Saturday we had a bad practice and then we were knocked off

severely by the Rams. I played very poorly. From that time I said I'd never go out on a Friday night prior to a football game and I never did. I think guys should go out and try to relax Mondays and Tuesdays. But I think from Wednesdays on in they should start thinking about football."

What caused you to lose your zest for a vocation which had dominated your adult life for two decades?

"It wasn't fun any more. My family was growing up and I wasn't spending much time with them. I owed it to my kids to spend a more normal life. It's gotten so there are things in life more important than winning football games. Maybe I don't want to sacrifice those things to win a Super Bowl. There are certain goals you want to reach in life, there are a lot of things you have to sacrifice. Maybe I'm not willing to do that. I started thinking about this in the summer of '72. Coaching got to be a chore. There are two ways to be in football – as a player and as an owner. I'm too old to be a player and I'm not rich enough to be an owner."

143

Wayne Walker

Position: Linebacker
Years: 1958-72
Height: 6-2
Weight: 228
College: Idaho

When Wayne Walker officially retired from the Lions he celebrated the melancholy event by hanging his bronzed jock in the rogue's gallery of the Lindell A. C. The pomp and ceremony over, Walker then tossed his own retirement party for friends, writers, teammates and assorted freeloading types.

"It was a different kind of retirement, wasn't it?" said Wayne Walker.

He came to the Lions as a sturdy athlete out of Idaho in 1958 and he became the last bridge between the eras of Bobby Layne and Greg Landry.

Walker played 15 years for the Lions, a club record. He played in 200 regular season games, more than anyone else has ever played for Detroit. In all, Walker played in 204 games, excluding preseason but including three Playoff Bowl games and one playoff game.

Each game was remembered as Walker sat in Lindell's that day of retirement in January 1973 after 15 years of excellent service. The Lindell itself is notorious in the history of the Lions. It is the place Alex Karras had part ownership of in 1963, when he admitted he had imprudently bet on some football games.

The bar was then a place of recreation for the Lions and other athletes, visiting and local. Walker was one of the habitues. Although the saloon has an unsavory reputation — more myth than fact — it remains a favored spot for athletes to congregate. There could be no other place where Wayne Walker could officially announce his retirement after 15 seasons and slip into tears of nostalgia.

Walker never played on a championship team in Detroit. He arrived as a No. 4 draftee in 1958, in a beat-up 1953 Chevy with Alex Karras as his passenger. The Lions were reigning world champions. But their dynasty of the 1950s was no longer in bloom. They would not win a championship again during the 15-year tenure of Wayne Walker at outside linebacker.

"Lots of guys have played on two or three championship teams who haven't had half the career I had," said Walker upon retirement.

Walker was all-pro in 1964 and 1965. He played in the Pro Bowl in '64, '65 and '66. He was one of the most famous of all Lions in the turbulent late 1950s and 1960s when the club sank, rose, sank and rose again.

Somewhere during that time a year managed to vanish from Walker's age. He arrived with the Lions in August of 1958 with a birthdate of September 30, 1936. One year, mysteriously, his date of birth appeared as September 30, 1937, in the Lions' annual guide. He would laugh about it — but would never confess.

There was considerable agony in his career. Ten losses in a row to the Minnesota Vikings in his late years and some unabashed tears in the locker rooms. Commissioner Pete Rozelle invited him to New York for conferences as an offshoot of the 1963 gambling investigation.

But nonetheless, there was ecstasy, too. Walker scored 345 points for the Lions, 331 of them as a placekicker.

The most delicious moment occurred on the afternoon of December 20, 1970. Six weeks before Walker had been red-eyed in the locker room at Minnesota. The Lions had just lost again to the Vikings. They were a doomed team in mid-November. But through a succession of bravura performances, the Lions won their final five games. They managed to squeeze into the playoffs as the NFC's best second-place team. A major reason was Walker overtaking John Gilliam in a 60-yard chase and preventing the Cardinals from scoring a touchdown in a critical game. Gilliam was one of the fastest runners in the NFL. And Walker was playing with a broken foot, numbed by painkiller.

Two weeks later the Lions reached the

playoffs. There was an emotional scene. The Detroit fans in their exuberance swelled onto the field. Some were just happy; some were souvenir seekers; others were vandals. A mob swept Walker up and joyously paraded him around.

Most men would fear a mob of victory-crazed people twisting steel goalposts into grotesque pretzels. Walker relished the moment. He rode the shoulders of the people, flailing his arms as though he were a cheerleader, exhorting the mob.

That was pure Wayne Walker — exuberant, emotional, egotistical, ecstatic . . . the man who played more football games for the Lions than anybody else. During the years Walker played, 1958-72, pro football proliferated from 12 franchises to 26.

He once said, "Anybody who says this game is beastly, brutal and nasty, he's right. You are out there to inflict punishment but not to take it. You want to be the hitter, not the hittee. It's a great personal satisfaction when you get a good hit on someone.

"You know you have done a good job. And you know that the other guy is wondering what the hell happened and who the hell you are and now he's got to respect you a little bit."

When you first joined the Lions you had just turned 21 and you were joining a world championship team. What was the atmosphere?

"It was a difficult year. We'd beaten the Lions in the College All-Star Game and Alex Karras and I drove up to Cranbrook, our training camp. They didn't make rookies too welcome. We lost the first game to Baltimore 28-15 and that wasn't too much of an upset because the Colts figured to be pretty good that year. Johnny Unitas was just getting started and the Colts eventually won the title. Then the second game was Green Bay. The Packers weren't too good then but we could only tie them 13-13. Bobby Layne missed an extra point, and on Monday they traded him to Pittsburgh. He was the veteran, the leader of the team and you could see how that trade upset the club. From there it went downhill.

"There were a lot of injuries and by the end of the season we had people like Tom Rychlec playing tight end and Perry Richards playing end . . . the kind of players you knew wouldn't play unless the team was decimated. It was a 4-7-1 season, not a good one. But it had some good things. It was the year Alex, Jim Gibbons and I came in."

What was a rookie's reaction to Layne, the tormentor of rookies?

"Well, I came in and heard stories about how the Lions were the toughest team for a rookie to join because of the hazing and the treatment. They told us stories about that at the College All-Star camp. I was apprehensive about it because I was concerned about making the team. Almost everyone had the same feeling. So you kind of lived in fear that he was going to single you out. You respected these guys so much, you had heard so much about them. For him to single you out and embarrass you, it was really hard to take.

"You never knew when they'd have you singing, chasing things down for them, shining shoes, bringing them coffee, running errands. The best thing you could do as a rookie was stay by yourself. That's not a very good existence or atmosphere to have on a ballclub. Even after you made the team and proved yourself, you were accepted a little bit more, but that thing still continued. Individually, I didn't care for it and I lived in fear of Layne a little bit and consequently, I didn't particularly care for him at the time. I've talked with him a few times since then and I don't hold the same feelings for him. But when I was a rookie I could have cared less about Bobby Layne."

Walker (far left) and Alex Karras were rookies together in 1958. They had been part of the College All-Star team which defeated the world's champions of 1957 – the Detroit Lions. At training camp, they endured the hardships of being rookies, like being awakened at night and having to go out to get pizza for Bobby Layne. Later, Walker had to scale a wire fence in Los Angeles to open the gate to a practice field. He made it over, but left his practice shorts on top of the fence, to the amusement of a crowd gathered to watch practice. One year at camp, Wayne and John Gordy (right) put pigeons in Joe Schmidt's dormitory room.

But he still found you and sent you out for pizza.

"Yeah, that's one of the things I was talking about. Late at night they'd get you up out of your bed. They'd have a card game going. They'd give you a short order for about 10 sandwiches and pizzas and things like that. I never thought it was a healthy situation. But by '62 and '63 we were completely done with it. The only thing that happened was guys would get up in the dining hall and sing."

What happened your first night in Cranbrook?

"Alex and I had driven all day from Chicago with a kid named Tom Schulte, a split end, and we got to Cranbrook in late afternoon. They assigned Alex and me as roommates. We went to bed pretty early and threw open our windows because it's so nice out at Cranbrook, all that fresh air, all that green grass, all those beautiful trees, all those cool breezes. But they also blew about 5,000 mosquitoes into our room and we had to spend the whole night fighting the damn things."

What were some other happenings in your rookie year?

"This is beautiful. We stayed at the Hollywood Roosevelt and practiced across the street at Hollywood High School before we played the Rams in '58. There was a fence around the field. I went out early with Tobin Rote, Charley Ane, Jim Martin, Jerry Perry and Bob Long. The gate was locked and I was the only rookie there. They said, 'You climb over and get the caretaker and have him let us in.' I said, 'Okay.' There were about 150 people waiting to watch practice because we were world champions that year. I had on blue shorts and a gray T-shirt and football shoes. I got up on top of the fence and it was a 10-foot drop. I leaped down and my shorts hooked and when I hit the ground I had nothing on but my jock. My

shorts were still on top of the fence. I ran under the grandstand. I thought for sure there'd be a Hollywood talent scout there and I'd get a contract."

There was a serious side to that story, too.

"I really sprained my ankle pretty badly in the fall from the fence. I was going to start that week for the second time. I knew I had sprained my ankle, but if you stay on it and run it won't swell up. I made it through practice not limping too noticeably. The minute practice was over I went back to the room and it started puffing up. I spent that evening with my foot in the bathtub running cold water on it and I didn't tell the coaches. In the game I wore hightop shoes for a little extra support. Things worked out fine. I intercepted a pass the next day against Billy Wade and ran it back 35 yards for my first touchdown."

Not playing on a championship team must have hurt you.

"I always thought that if I played 15 years for the same team that sooner or later I'd play on a championship team. I played on a lot of winning teams. But we got in the playoffs just one time. In my 15 years we were second seven times. I guess it just wasn't to be. I really thought we were the best team in 1962. We lost to Green Bay 9-7. We lost to the Giants 17-14 when they blocked a punt. We lost to the Bears 3-0 the last game of the year when it didn't mean anything.

"The 9-7 loss was probably the biggest disappointment of all my years here. We had the game won. They were the team we had to beat and we knew it. Now you can say we should have beaten Minnesota a couple of times, but, to be honest, we never proved we were better than Minnesota. I can say that now that I'm not playing. But I know that in 1962 we were better than Green Bay."

That 9-7 loss hung over you guys all year as

you waited for the rematch on Thanksgiving, the day the Lions got their revenge on the Packers in that memorable 26-14 victory. What was the feeling before the Thanksgiving rematch?

"Well, the Packers were undefeated at the time and we still had a chance. We'd also lost to the Giants, a helluva game, and the Giants went on to win the Eastern title. I had a chance to tie the Giants game at 17-17 with a 50-yard field goal in the last few seconds but it was blocked. That was a frustrating game for us because we also were a better team than they were

"So that set up the rematch. If we didn't beat the Packers on Thanksgiving we were really through. Added incentive was the fact they were undefeated. Added incentive was that 9-7 loss. We just got up for it like I've never ever seen a team get up for anything before. The Packers had been in *Life* magazine that year. That was when that whole Packer-Lombardi invincibility thing started and it really stuck in our throats. Everything we did that day was just perfect. If we blitzed, they didn't pick it up. If we looped linemen, they didn't pick it up. If we didn't blitz and played a zone, Bart Starr couldn't read it. We just killed them physically."

Isn't it true that the 9-7 loss influenced the Detroit football team for many years after that? Lots of people say so.

"That might be an excuse that you could use. Geez, if it did, why didn't the Thanksgiving Day rout that year influence the team the rest of the years? I think the 9-7 game hurt Milt Plum's career more than it influenced the thinking of the team. It was very hard for him to live that down. George Wilson came to his aid and said he called the play from the bench. I don't know whether that's true or not. Until this day I don't know who called the pass play that Adderley intercepted. But we lost it and

why single out one guy and say it's his fault?"

The following year Karras was involved in gambling and was suspended. And you were invited to New York to talk to Pete Rozelle.

"Five of us were implicated. Alex, of course, was suspended and I think Gary Lowe, John Gordy, Joe Schmidt, Sam Williams and myself were each fined $2,000 for betting on games. We bet on one game. I don't know how many games Alex bet on and I don't know how he was involved or what he'd been doing. I also don't know how Sam Williams became involved.

"The involvement with Gary Lowe, Joe Schmidt, John Gordy and myself was this: The four of us went to this house in Miami, the home of a friend of ours, to watch the championship game. We were down there playing in the Runnerup Bowl and there were lots of people at this party watching the game. Somebody was talking on the phone to a bookie. It seemed very innocent at the time.

"The guy was making this bet and somebody said, 'Who do you guys like?' And we said, 'Well, we like the Packers, they beat us, we like the Packers.' 'Do you like them enough to bet on them?' We all looked at each other and said, 'Yeah, let's do, let's place a little bet on this game. It'd be fun.'

"We didn't really think of the implications, we didn't think it was serious because we weren't playing in the game. We were spectating. So we all bet $100 on the game. It was the first time I'd ever bet on a game and I'm pretty sure it was the first time for the rest of those guys, too. It certainly was the last."

What about your hassles with Monty Stickles, especially the one in 1966 when you were tossed out of the game for punching him in San Francisco?

"He was the dirtiest guy in the league. He jumped on me while I was lying on the ground

and kicked me. I complained to Joe Muha, who was the umpire, and he said, 'Take care of it in your own way.' So I did. On the next play I punched him. I guess my way was the wrong way. I got thrown out for it. Stickles then scored the touchdown that beat us with six seconds left. But the funny thing is Stickles and I became friends and we go out together now."

The Lions always have been noted for their training camp high jinks. What about those pranks at Cranbrook?

"We had a lot of fun at training camp. Joe Schmidt and I used to dress up as Draculas. Joe would love to scare people. He had masks. He would lie under your bed or hide in your closet for 40 minutes just to jump out and scare you. One funny thing I don't think ever has been told is, Joe used to lock his door. He was afraid of retaliation. One night we were coming in a little bit late, John Gordy and myself, and Joe was already in bed. We got a pass key and opened up his door. There used to be a pigeon coop at Cranbrook and we got three or four pigeons and threw them in his room and Joe thought they were bats. They were all flying around his room trying to get out. That was funny.

"And of course Joe was great at making nicknames. He had one for everybody — from Vince Lombardi, whom he called Jap, to me whom he called Snoopy. But the best nickname of all was the one for Daryl Sanders when he played for the Lions. He had a premature gray streak through his hair.

"We were out at practice and Joe and I were trying to come up with some name. We went over Paint and Spot and they were no good. Daryl was Silver Fox at college, but we felt that had too much class for a rookie. Suddenly, I said 'Skunk' to Joe and that was it. Daryl was Skunk to all of us."

Of the 200 games you played can you think of one game you'd like to think of years from now as the highlight game of your career?

"After 200 there's a lot of them you like — and thank God there's more of them I like than I didn't like. I think 1960 Thanksgiving Day would be the first great game I ever played. It was against the Packers and I recall I got to the quarterback five times blitzing. This was two years before the great massacre. I also played great against the runs in that 1960 game.

"Don Shula, who was one of our defensive coaches then, told me it was one of the best games he'd ever seen an outside linebacker play. Don always told me that I just had to wait my turn and sooner or later I'd be the best outside linebacker in football. I think the game in which I probably had the most fun afterwards was when we got in the playoffs in 1970 and the crowd swept me up. That's something that doesn't happen to too many guys, especially in this town."

You had some memorable games against Gale Sayers when he was in his prime with the Bears.

"He liked to run around my side and I think one of the most memorable games I ever played was against him. It was Joe's second year as head coach, 1968. It was probably the best year I ever had in pro football. I think I got knocked off my feet one time on plays that were run at me all year long. That was the year I was voted most valuable player on defense. I played twice as good that year as I did in my all-pro years, but I didn't get a mention. But without a doubt it was the best year I ever had.

"I'll remember that whole year because everything I did turned out right. I'd give a guy a move with the ballcarrier behind him and the blocker would take my move and the ballcarrier would react right where I wanted him to and I'd get him for a loss. Sayers ran the ball about seven times at my side in the game over there in Chicago and I think I got him five times for no

gain. I think really that might have been my best game against a superior athlete. I felt like it was a man-to-man, head-to-head confrontation. The thing I'd like to be remembered for over the 15 years was the fact that I missed only four games. I like to think they gave me the job in 1958 and didn't have to worry about it for 15 years."

You talked during your career about the importance of ego.

"There's a very fine line between ego, vanity and pride. You've got to be vain enough to think you're good. That's vanity. But you've got to have enough pride in yourself not to downgrade yourself. And if you have pride and you have vanity you're going to have some ego. Everybody who's halfway successful has got it."

You were the placekicker several years. What about your placekicking frustrations?

"Placekicking was hard on me mentally. So much importance was laid on it because we weren't scoring many points at the time. It seemed we needed most of our kicks and my percentage was not good. I was always happy to see somebody else in there."

Yet your four field goals in one game was a club record until Garo Yepremian came in mid-1966 and a few weeks later set a pro record with six field goals in a 32-31 victory at Minnesota.

"When that happened I went into the office of Lyall Smith, our publicity man, and asked him to put an asterisk alongside Garo's record. I told him, 'I mean like Roger Maris when he hit 61 home runs. You should indicate the difference — left-footed Armenian-Cypriot soccer-style kicker instead of plain right-footed American.' "

What about the two dreary years when Harry Gilmer was coach in 1965 and 1966?

"They were lost years. One statistic that's lost from Harry's first year was the fact that we led the entire National Football League in defense. I remember it because it was one of my all-pro years."

But the players didn't really tune themselves to Gilmer during those two seasons. There was a near mutiny of players. He and Karras clashed and most of the players didn't relate to Harry.

"Harry really didn't have a very good staff, and he was a victim of circumstances, coming into a tough situation and following a great guy like George Wilson whom the guys liked."

But what about the players not getting along with Gilmer?

"I don't think that's important. I respected him because he knew a lot of football. He was a pretty good guy. He was so different from what everybody else was used to. I think if Harry had been the coach of the Dallas Cowboys or the old Houston Oilers, where there were a lot of guys from the South, he might have fared better. But our team was predominantly Big Ten and midwestern-type guys."

Was there a schism or a breach between the defense and the offense in those days when you didn't have much offense? There are lots of stories of Schmidt and Karras mumbling at Plum when the offense went onto the field.

"Heck, guys are going to gripe. Didn't the offense gripe about us on defense in '71 and '72? That's normal. But you still like each other. My best friends were John Gordy and Terry Barr and Jimmy Gibbons and other guys on offense. I never heard an argument over an offense and defense relationship. When you're playing bad you know it and nobody else has to tell you."

In 1970, you chased John Gilliam of the Cardinals more than half the field in St. Louis. One of the fastest men in the league had a tremendous head start. He was going for a touchdown and you caught him.

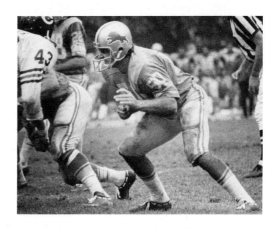

"Probably the most remarkable play I ever made. I really don't know how it happened. I actually gained on him. There was no way I should have. He was so far ahead, it was like you say, 'Oh man, I'll just run down here fairly fast and get ready for the extra point.' Maybe something down inside told me to get after him. I did and damn if he didn't start coming back to me. And it really shocked me when I was about five yards from him. Then I got to a point and I actually said to myself, 'My God I'm going to make this play.' I brought him down at the 7. And we held them for three downs. They got a penalty which moved them back and then Jim Bakken missed a field goal. At the time they were ahead 3-0. It would have been 10-0 if they had scored."

More amazing is you made it while playing on a broken foot.

"Yeah, that's right. I played eight or nine games with it."

After reaching a zenith in 1970, the Lions then dropped the next two years. What happened?

"We just ran out of defense. We didn't replace lost personnel. We lost three great veterans: Alex Karras, Darris McCord and Joe Robb. They were three good ballplayers. We just never plugged the holes. We were building offense, which was what our drafts were designed to do at the time. For a while we got away from drafting the best athlete. We were drafting for position. I think that cost us. The only real solid guy we got on defense during the late '60s was a surprise, Lem Barney."

You shed a lot of tears.

"I've cried when we won and I've cried when we lost. I don't sit down and bawl, but I do get emotional. If I have feelings I'm going to show them. I've always been that way."

A check of past press books shows you remained the same age for two seasons during the midpoint of your career. Now that you're retired, be honest.

"I did that when I was 28 years old. I had no idea I was going to play 15 years in Detroit. At the time I was having some contract difficulties and I knew there were some teams interested in me, Baltimore, Dallas. I thought if I could get a year lopped off my age it would never harm me if I was traded to another team. People always felt when you get to be 30 you're getting old. I fooled everybody. I got it changed on the records. Now I'm about to age one year faster. I really was born in 1936, not 1937."

The Other Years

It was a magnificent age. Babe Ruth was in his prime and Ty Cobb was in his twilight, still hitting .360 for Detroit and slicing infielders' shins open with his spikes. College football was the sport for autumn and the names were magic. Red Grange, the Galloping Ghost. The Four Horsemen – Elmer Layden, Harry Stuhldreher, Jim Crowley, Don Miller.

History states that the National Football League was founded in a Huppmobile garage in Canton, Ohio, in 1920. Detroit was a charter member of the NFL, with a team called the Heralds. The memory of the Detroit Heralds is vague. No record exists of their accomplishments – or lack of them. The NFL Record Manual says: "There was no planned schedule of games (and) formal standings were first compiled in 1921."

Meager mention is made of Detroit's first NFL franchise in the libraries of the city's newspapers. The late H.G. Salsinger, esteemed sports editor of the *Detroit News* for more than half a century, wrote briefly of the Heralds in a 1936 column:

"The Heralds passed out of existence when the old sandlot favorites got too old for the fall campaigns and the lineup became studded with imported college players."

In 1921, the second NFL season, the Heralds were defunct.

Detroit's second professional football team came four years later. Jimmy Conzelman got the franchise started in 1925. The team was called the Panthers. The franchise price, in what amounted to expansion in modern vernacular, was either $50 or $500. Both sums have been used in informal and sketchy histories of Detroit in pro football.

The Panthers were members of a league that included teams in Pottsville, Akron, Rock Island, Canton, Hammond, Duluth as well as Chicago, New York and Buffalo. The sport still was mostly a barnstorming affair. Conzelman gave this account of the establishment of the Detroit Panthers:

"In 1924, I was finishing my second year as coach of the Milwaukee Badgers, then a member of the National Football League. I ran into a group of Chicago theatrical agents after the season closed. They suggested I apply for a franchise at Detroit and said they would back the team. They felt we could get the Four Horsemen as the key stars around whom we could build the team. I was interested, so I applied for the franchise and got in for $500.

"We brought the Four Horsemen to Chicago and . . . made terms. As part of the deal, after they graduated in June, the four of them and myself were to go on a 15-week vaudeville tour before the season opened."

But the scheme flopped because of Elmer Layden's unavailability.

"Elmer had made a promise in his hometown of Davenport, Iowa, to oversee playground activities that summer for the Parks and Recreation Department," said Conzelman. "When Layden pulled out, the Four Horsemen part of the vaudeville and football deal fell through. With its collapse, the theatrical agents pulled the financial rug from under my feet. I had the Detroit franchise, but little else."

Conzelman was undaunted. He came up with some new backers and with the fresh money, the Panthers fielded a pro team for Detroit in the 20-team NFL. Frank Navin, president of the Tigers, rented Conzelman Navin Field (later Briggs Stadium and Tiger Stadium) for $10,000 for the season.

"We couldn't stand a rental of more than $1,000 a game, so I drafted a schedule of 10 home games," Conzelman said. "I had to get my money's worth."

The opening game was against the Columbus Tigers. Conzelman had recruited Gus Sonnen-

The 1935 NFL champions. Front row, L to R: Harry Ebding, Frank Christensen, Ace Gutowsky, owner G.A. Richards, captain Dutch Clark, coach Potsy Clark, George Christensen, Glenn Presnell and Ed Klewicki. Second row: trainer Dr. C.E. Joseph, Butch Morse, Clare Randolph, Red Stacy, Ernie Caddel, Jack Johnson, John Schneller, Jim Steen, Sam Knox, Ox Emerson and asst. trainer Abe Kushner. Third row: Bill Shepherd, Buddy Parker, Pug Vaughan, Bear Ward, Regis Monahan, Tony Kaska and Tom Hupke.

berg, Tillie Voss, John Lauer, Tom McNamara, Al Haddon, Al Crook and Phil Marion to play for the Panthers. Conzelman was the co-owner, business manager, coach — and also the quarterback.

The advent of the pro football Panthers made the sports sections on Page 4. Said one Detroit paper: "Manager Conzelman has worked unceasingly with the sole end in view of trying to erase the stigma upon professional football here." The Panthers beat the Tigers 7-0 in their debut.

"It rained the first seven Sundays we played at home," Conzelman said, "and with the rain, a fair amount of our investment went down the drain each time."

Late in the 1925 season Red Grange finished his intercollegiate career at Illinois. George Halas signed him for the Chicago Bears and turned him pro immediately.

"There had been scant interest in the Panthers," Conzelman said. "Our largest crowd was 3,500. But with Grange's fame, I figured we had a real selling point, so I booked an early December game with the Bears. We needed a big crowd to pull us out financially and I thought that if the fans saw our caliber of play they'd be converted to pro ball."

They lined up for tickets, and the advance sale hit $25,000. Then came disaster. Four days before the game a story came out of Boston that Grange was injured and probably would not play in Detroit.

Conzelman offered to refund the advance money. On game day, people lined up around the block outside the ballpark — to get their money back. Inside the Panthers beat the Bears 21-0.

"Those who saw us realized we had a good team," said Conzelman, "but there weren't enough of them." The Panthers, with an 8-2-2 record, finished third in the one-division league,

won by the Chicago Cardinals. The following year, 1926, the Panthers dropped off to 4-6-2 and Conzelman disbanded his franchise. He sold his best players to the Providence Steamrollers and went along as coach.

After a year's absence, Detroit entered the NFL again in 1928. Detroit's third pro football franchise was named the Wolverines. The club featured Benny Friedman, who had starred at Michigan. The Detroit Wolverines finished third with a 7-2-1 record in 1928, their only season. The league's champion was the Providence Steamrollers of Jimmy Conzelman.

After three failures, it was not until 1934 that anyone dared risk professional football again in Detroit. George A. (Dick) Richards, a Detroit and California radio mogul, was persuaded to invest $15,000 in the sport. He purchased a ready-made team, the Portsmouth Spartans. The Spartans, with George (Potsy) Clark as their coach and Dutch Clark as their superstar, had been one of the more formidable clubs in the NFL. Founded in 1930 in the southern Ohio community, the Spartans challenged the Green Bay Packers for the championship in 1931. They were 11-3 and finished second to 12-2 Green Bay. They finished third in 1932 at 6-2-4 and second in the West at 6-5 in 1933 when the NFL was divided into two divisions with the winners to play in an NFL championship game.

The transfer to Detroit was completed March 24, 1934 — and the old Spartans were renamed the Lions. The Lions took title to 26 players, among them some of pro football's brightest stars. Dutch Clark was one. He had sat out the 1933 season because he could make more money away from pro football. But he was induced to return and play for Detroit. Glenn Presnell, Ox Emerson, George Christensen, Frank Christensen, Ernie Caddel, Ace Gutowsky and Roy (Father) Lumpkin

were among those whose contract rights were included in the $15,000 transfer price. Potsy Clark, a wry, caustic man who wore a battered hat, moved along to become the first head coach of the Lions.

Tommy Emmet, who became the quasi-official historian of the Lions and one of the club's charter employees, credited sports editor Salsinger for serving as the catalyst in the relocation of the nearly bankrupt Portsmouth team.

In 1933, Salsinger went to cover the annual baseball meetings in December. There he encountered Joe Carr. Because of the economic climate of the day, Carr held employment in two jobs. He was vice president and general manager of the Columbus baseball team in the American Association. He also moonlighted as president of the National Football League.

Carr knew that pro football had failed in three trials in Detroit, but he still considered Detroit a likely landing spot for the impoverished Portsmouth club. So he sought Salsinger out during a break in the baseball meetings and commissioned him an agent.

Salsinger was receptive. He promised to help the NFL relocate the Spartans. He formed a committee of influential sportsmen in Detroit. They had prestige and clout — they still needed a donor.

One afternoon the group sat in the grill of the Detroit Athletic Club. They were about to concede defeat. Just then Leo J. Fitzpatrick, a high executive of WJR radio, walked in.

"There's our man," said E.J. Batchelor, a prominent journalist. "His boss has money and is a football buff."

Fitzpatrick listened to the proposition. He liked it and relayed the idea of to his boss, G.A. Richards. Richards had made his money in an auto franchise before he'd sold out to General Motors for $100,000. Within a month the deal was firmed. The franchise price was $15,000. Richards agreed to add $6,500 to bail the Portsmouth owners out of debt.

Thus, the Lions were born, their nickname adopted to fit into the jungle atmosphere created by the city's American League baseball club, the Tigers.

The Lions were spotted in the Western Division — with the Bears, Cardinals, Packers and Cincinnati Reds. They signed an agreement to play their home games at the 25,000-seat University of Detroit Stadium. The New York Giants were the Lions' first opponent.

The Giants had been in the 1933 championship game, the first under the NFL's new two-division format. The Bears won 23-21, but the Giants remained an attractive opponent. The apathy of Detroit's sports fans was disappointing, however, and only 12,000 showed up.

The new Lions won their first game 9-0 over the Giants on September 23, 1934, then shut out the Cardinals 6-0 the following week in New York.

The Lions went on to win the first 10 games, seven of them by shutouts.

Glenn Presnell, who alternated at tailback with Dutch Clark, won the Lions' third game with an incredible 54-yard field goal that beat the Packers 3-0 at Green Bay. Presnell's field goal kick was the NFL record for 19 seasons. Bert Rechichar broke Presnell's NFL record with a 56-yard field goal in 1956.

The new Lions continued onward. They beat the Eagles 10-0, then the Boston Redskins 24-0, then the Brooklyn Dodgers 28-0, then the Cincinnati-St. Louis combine 38-0.

They had played seven games and were unscored upon. Even so, there was little civic excitement in Detroit. Only 6,000 showed up for the next game, with the Pittsburgh Steelers of Art Rooney.

Pittsburgh became the first team to score against the Lions, but Detroit won its eighth straight, 40-7. The winning streak stretched to 10 games as the Lions beat the Cardinals and Cincinnati-St. Louis again.

The streak ended at the University of Detroit the Sunday before Thanksgiving. At 10-0, the Lions were winning in the West and seemed headed toward the championship game in their first season.

Only 12,000 fans were intrigued enough to watch the Lions play the Packers in the 11th game. The Packers avenged the earlier loss to the Lions on Presnell's record field goal. Clarke Hinkle's 47-yard field goal beat the Lions 3-0.

On the following Thursday, the Lions played the first of what would become a traditional Thanksgiving Day series. The game was the notion of clubowner Richards, who convinced George Halas, owner-coach of the Bears, to play the game on the holiday. Richards had another idea. As head of WJR, Richards had contacts in the radio industry. A friend was Deke Aylesworth, president of the National Broadcasting Company. Together they decided that a pro football game broadcast on a coast-to-coast hookup on Thanksgiving Day would be appealing. Richards felt it could give pro football excellent exposure. There were 94 stations plugged in for the holiday game between the Lions and Bears. Graham McNamee did the play-by-play and Don Wilson was the color announcer.

The game also caught the fancy of the Detroit fans. People lined up to buy tickets. All 26,000, standing room included, were sold out early.

The Bears were the world champions and they were unbeaten at 11-0. They had Bronko Nagurski and rookie Beattie Feathers, pro football's first 1,000-yard runner.

The Bears were ahead 19-16 in the fourth quarter. Led by Clark and Gutowsky's running,

the Lions marched the ball from their 20 to the Bears' 15. Presnell or Clark could have kicked a field goal to tie the score. The Lions went for the touchdown instead and the Bears held.

The Lions also lost the rematch by three points to the Bears 10-7 in Chicago just three days later. Detroit finished its first season at 10-3, second in the West behind the 13-0 Bears.

"I think we had a better team in 1934 than we did in 1935," said Dutch Clark.

But despite an ordinary start, the 1935 Lions were destined to win the championship for the first time.

The Lions were merely 2-2-1 after their first five games. They beat the Eagles in the opener, then tied the Cardinals. A loss to the Dodgers was followed by a victory over the Redskins and a loss to the Packers. They needed an about-face to move into contention.

Victories over the Redskins and the Cardinals provided flickering hope. Potsy Clark told the Lions they could win it all. Then they were crumbled by the Packers.

Im mid-November the Lions were 4-3-1 and last in the West, behind the Packers, the Cardinals and the Bears. They had just four games left to play.

On November 17 the Lions played the Packers for the third time in the season. Beaten by 24 points the week before at Green Bay, the Lions reversed the decision 20-10. The next Sunday they tied the Bears 20-20. Then on Thanksgiving Day in Detroit they beat the Bears for the first time, 14-2.

The Lions' final game was against the Dodgers at University of Detroit on December 1. The Cardinals were the only other contender. They had two games remaining, both with the Bears.

The Lions had to beat the Dodgers and hope the Cardinals would lose one of their games with the Bears. The Cardinals led the division with a 6-3-1 record. The Lions were 6-3-2.

Right halfback Ernie Caddel was one of the fastest players in the league. He was the first Detroit Lions' player to wear number one on his jersey. (Years later, it belonged to kicker Garo Yepremian.) At left, Caddel carries the ball against the Boston Redskins in a 1934 game. Blocking for him is Roy Lumpkin. Caddel's reverse to the weak side was one of the Lion's most devastating plays (diagram).

Lumpkin Blocking for
Caddel. Detroit_28
Boston-0. 1934...

The tension was enough to arouse 15,000 fans to watch the Lions in their finale.

"Keep running the ball," cautioned Potsy Clark before the game. "Don't go around throwing it. That goes for all three of you quarterbacks."

Dutch Clark, Presnell and Pug Vaughan all nodded. Potsy made one lineup change for the start. He reinstated Ace Gutowsky at fullback to replace Bill Shepherd.

When the game started, the quarterbacks ignored Potsy's careful orders not to pass. Gutowsky passed 45 yards to Presnell for a touchdown, and Vaughan threw 26 yards to Butch Morse for another touchdown. The Lions beat the Dodgers 28-0, thwarting the Brooklyn runners with minus 72 yards rushing.

In Chicago, the Cardinals were held to a 10-10 tie by the Bears. It meant the best the Cardinals could do now was tie the Lions for the Western title. To do that, they would have to beat the Bears at Wrigley Field in their last game. So the Lions were assured of an extra game in two weeks — either a divisional playoff with the Cardinals or the NFL championship game with the Giants.

On December 8, Potsy Clark watched the Giants play the Pirates, hoping to compile a scouting report. In Chicago, ignited by Keith Molesworth's punt-formation pass from his own end zone, the Bears pushed the Lions into the championship game with a 13-0 victory over the Cardinals.

Potsy's hoped-for scouting report for the Giants wasn't much use. Steve Owen, the Giants' coach, had used second-stringers against the Pirates to foil Clark. Still, Potsy knew the Giants' pass offense was to be feared against what he considered the weak pass defense of the Lions. He warned the Lions about the passing danger from Ed Danowski and Harry Newman and the receiving threat of Tod Goodwin. He also was concerned about the running of Ken Strong and Bo Molenda.

Potsy Clark's starting lineup, to play both ways, was listed as: ends Ed Klewicki and John Schneller, tackles Jack Johnson and George Christensen, guards Sam Knox and Ox Emerson, center Clare Randolph, backs Glenn Presnell, Frank Christensen, Ernie Caddel and Ace Gutowsky. Potsy said Dutch Clark and Bill Shepherd would replace Presnell and Gutowsky in the first quarter.

The weather was miserable — sleet and rain — but the Lions needed only six plays to score.

Presnell got the drive moving with a 26-yard pass to Frank Christensen to the Giants' 33. Then he passed again and the ball deflected off defender Danowski and into Klewicki's hands. It was another 26-yard gain to the 7. The Giants were surprised by the fact the Lions were passing with a wet ball, particularly since the Lions' strength was running. Now the Lions hit the Giants with their running. Presnell ran three yards. Then Gutowsky, the fullback, hit the Giants' line and went the final four yards for the first touchdown.

Danowski moved the Giants, but the drive was stopped when his pass was intercepted on Detroit's 26 by Frank Christensen. Christensen ran the ball back to the Giants' 46. Dutch Clark entered the game . . . and two plays later he cracked into the line, broke two tackles and was in the open. He streaked 42 yards for the Lions' second touchdown. The Lions were ahead 13-0 at the end of the first quarter.

The Lions' defense was immense — and it stopped the Giants three times near the goal line in the first half. The Giants scored in the third quarter on a pass — the only breakdown of the day in the Lions' suspect pass defense. Danowski connected with Ken Strong, on a 42-yard touchdown play. The Lions' lead had been sliced in half. It was now 13-7.

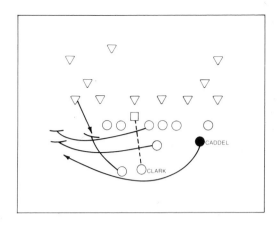

One of Potsy Clark's plans, prepared in secret, was to apply heavy pressure on the Giants' punts. Harry Ebding had blocked a punt by Danowski in the second quarter, but the Lions failed to turn it into points. Now, in the fourth quarter, Sam Knox and Butch Morse crashed in to block a quick kick by Danowski. George Christensen recovered the ball for Detroit at the Giants' 26-yard line.

The Lions stuck to the ground. Five running plays advanced the ball inside the Giants' 1. Then the Lions sent Gutowsky into the line. The Giants' defense, with Mel Hein in the lead, stacked up to stop Gutowsky. He was jolted back. But he didn't have the football. Ernie Caddel had it and he was far away from any tackler. Coming from wingback on a reverse, Caddel scored easily. Now the Lions led 19-7 and the Giants were desperate.

Harry Newman came in to pass the ball. In the defensive backfield, the Lions now had their best rookie, Raymond Parker. Young Parker, nicknamed Buddy, intercepted a pass by Newman and ran the ball back 23 yards to the Giants' 10. After a couple of cracks into the Giants' line, Parker scored the Lions' fourth touchdown.

The Lions won their first championship 26-7 and Detroit had its second major sporting championship in two months.

Dutch Clark was the game's offensive star. He gained 80 yards rushing, and his contributions nearly doubled with punt and kickoff returns included. Parker, running on spinner plays and straight plunges, gained 70 yards rushing. Caddel ran for 62 yards, mostly on reverses from wingback.

It was a notable triumph for the Lions in only their second season in Detroit. It would be another 17 years before they could win another National Football League championship — with Buddy Parker as their head coach.

The Lions sliced the leather covering off the championship game ball and cut it into 26 equal parts. The slices of leather were mounted on scrolls. Each player, Potsy, Dr. Carl A. Joseph, and club trainer-equipment man Abe Kushner were all awarded the scrolls as momentos.

Dutch Clark was all-pro the first four seasons in Detroit – 1934, 1935, 1936 and 1937. "He's like a rabbit in the brush," said Potsy of Dutch. At the summit of his career, the Detroit management sponsored a Dutch Clark Day.

After winning the championship in 1935, the Lions dropped to third place in the West in 1936. They were a streaky team. There was a three-game winning streak at the opening of the season, then they lost the next three. Then they won four in a row. The Lions finished 1936 at 8-4. Individually, Gutowsky's 827 yards for the season left him three yards shy of the league rushing championship won by the Giants' Tuffy Leemans.

At the end of the '36 season, Potsy Clark quit as head coach. He moved to Brooklyn to become head coach of the Dodgers.

Richards, now living in Los Angeles, hired Dutch Clark immediately to replace Potsy. Richards then stated publicly that Potsy had quit *before* the 1936 season and that Dutch had been named the new head coach then.

"I offered Dutch the job with the understanding that the post was still Potsy's if Potsy changed his mind," said Richards. "Dutch wanted the job, but he wasn't interested in it if Potsy wanted it. As things turned out, Potsy came around and said he would sign. Otherwise Dutch would have coached the Lions in the 1936 season."

Potsy's departure at the end of the 1936 season was punctuated by charges about a profit-sharing agreement in his contract. Richards was angered by Potsy's asserting the

owner should sell out his stock and get out of football.

"I'll pick Dutch Clark's Lions to beat Potsy Clark's Dodgers every time they meet," said Richards.

Dutch and Potsy were destined to meet only once as rival coaches the next two years. Richards' prophecy was accurate. Dutch's Lions beat Potsy's Dodgers 30-0 in the fourth game of the 1937 season. That season the Lions went 7-4 and tied for second in the West. The Lions were 7-4 again in 1938 and finished alone in second place.

By 1938, Dutch Clark was becoming more and more resentful of the alleged meddling by Richards.

Richards complained that the Lions' offense was dull, unimaginative and stereotyped. He felt Dutch could have made better use of Lloyd Cardwell in the backfield. The final estrangement between Clark and Richards was triggered by a disagreement whether to obtain Byron (Whizzer) White from Pittsburgh. White, a glamorous All-American at Colorado, had been made available.

"I don't need him," said Clark when approached by Richards about the possibility after a victory over the Bears. Two weeks later, after the Packers trounced the Lions, Richards openly second-guessed his coach.

At the end of the season, Dutch was told that Richards planned to fire him. With an opportunity to become coach of the Cleveland Rams, Clark quit the Lions. Two weeks later Richards appointed Elmer (Gus) Henderson, a former college and minor league pro coach, to be head coach of the Lions for 1939. Richards liked Henderson's offensive schemes — spread formations with a considerable amount of passing.

Thus started a five-year era of annual coaching turnover in Detroit.

Gus Henderson lasted one season with the Lions. His 1939 club won its first four games, but lost its last four. The season record was 6-5, third best in the West.

But it wasn't the third-place finish that cost Henderson his job. It was the furor over Clyde (Bulldog) Turner, the center from Hardin-Simmons.

Richards had learned about the attributes of Turner from the small college in Texas. There was an agreement — and payment of some money — that Turner would tell scouts from other NFL clubs he was not interested in playing professional football. The Lions believed they had Turner locked up when he became eligible for the 1940 draft. Turner answered the NFL's draft questionnaire: "I do not wish to play professional football."

It was an odd reply, because collegians who did not wish to play football normally tossed their questionnaires in the wastebasket. In Chicago, George Halas became suspicious.

At the draft, Henderson regarded the Lions' rights to Turner as certain. So he bypassed Turner on the first round and selected Doyle Nave, Southern California's Rose Bowl hero.

Halas then drafted Bulldog Turner, the man the Lions thought they had cinched. Richards was irate and blasted Henderson for his lack of judgment. The other NFL owners, who had taken a dislike to Richards years before because of his efforts to impeach Joe Carr, started an investigation. It showed that the Lions had given Turner $100 while he was still playing college ball at Hardin-Simmons.

The league discounted any claim the Lions had on Turner. The Lions were fined $5,000 for tampering. Within a month, Richards sold the Lions to Fred Mandel, a Chicago department store magnate. The sale price was $225,000 — a profit of more than $200,000 for Richards, who had paid less than $20,000 seven years earlier in the deal with Portsmouth. But

Dutch Clark, the ex-captain, now coach, squabbled with owner Richards over whether to trade for Pittsburgh's Whizzer White (left). Clark soon quit and became coach of the Cleveland Rams. After study as a Rhodes Scholar, White joined the Lions in 1940 and became the NFL's leading rusher – the only Lions' back ever to lead the league in rushing. Richards got into trouble when he paid Clyde Turner (right) while Turner was still in college at Hardin-Simmons. The star center was to inform other teams that he had no plans for pro football. George Halas crossed up the Lions, however, drafting Turner. The Lions were fined and within a month Richards sold out as owner.

the league withheld formal approval of the franchise sale to Mandel for 13 days until Richards paid the fine in the Turner case.

With the Bears, Turner became one of the Monsters of the Midway on the championship clubs of the 1940s. Doyle Nave never played for the Lions.

Mandel's first action as owner was to bring back Potsy Clark to coach the Lions. That year Whizzer White returned to the United States from his studies at Oxford as a Rhodes Scholar. He intended to enter Yale Law School. Nonetheless, the Lions paid $15,000 to Pittsburgh for his playing rights. They induced White to resume his pro football career. He teamed in an excellent backfield with Cardwell.

In 1940, Whizzer White, who would become a U.S. Supreme Court Justice two decades later, led the NFL in rushing, gaining 514 yards in 12 games. He scored five touchdowns. White remains the only Lion ever to lead the NFL in rushing.

A football historian of the age wrote:

"White was the running attack, the passing attack, the defense and the brains of the teams on which he played. He spent 40 to 60 minutes on the gridiron under conditions that any other player would have spent in a hospital bed. Although his performance never reflected it, the Whiz played several games literally taped from toe to neck with a few sponge rubber pads placed at strategic spots. For imagination and quick thinking it would be hard to beat the Whiz."

But even the omnipresence of Whizzer White for two years could not deter the slide of the Lions. They skidded first to mediocrity and eventually into the futility in which they were enmeshed for most of the 1940s.

After a 5-5-1 season in 1940, Potsy Clark left for the second time. He moved to the security of a college in Grand Rapids, Michigan, where

he began the relaxing life of an athletic director.

Bill Edwards, from Western Reserve, was hired to coach the Lions in 1941. He was the Lions' fourth head coach in four years. For the first time the Lions endured a losing season, 4-6-1.

Then World War II came. Whizzer White left to become a Naval officer and most of the other top Lions entered various branches of the service.

But the Lions managed to put a team – if that description is proper – on the field for the NFL season of 1942.

Edwards was a fundamentalist whose theories could not be used because he simply did not have talented ballplayers. His only standouts were Cardwell and lineman John Wiethe.

The Cardinals shut out the Lions in the opener, then the Rams did the same. At halftime of the next game the Dodgers were thumping the Lions and Mandel could take it no longer. He made up his mind to fire Edwards – on the spot. Mandel was waiting in the tunnel between the field and the locker room at Briggs Stadium as the Lions trooped through after their 28-7 licking by the Dodgers. It was a moral victory. At least the Lions had scored. But Mandel was determined. Edwards was fired, and John Karcis, an assistant coach, was named to replace him. Players Cardwell and Wiethe were named Karcis' assistants.

"I think he did the right thing," said Edwards. "I wish Bull Karcis all the luck in the world."

Edwards then joined the Marines. His assessment of the Lions' future had been generous.

At the end of the season, the Lions' record was 0-11. They had become the NFL's first winless club since the Dayton Triangles of 1933. The Lions were so punchless they managed only five touchdowns and one field goal all season. Never in any game did they

Alex Wojciechowicz (left), who had been one of the Seven Blocks of Granite at Fordham, began eight years as a star center and left linebacker for the Lions when coach Dutch Clark made him Detroit's first draft choice in 1938. Frank Sinkwich (far right), Heisman Trophy winner in 1942, tried valiantly to get into the war effort, but was turned down by the Marines because of high blood pressure and a heart murmur, and later by the merchant marines because of flat feet. In between, he was the NFL's outstanding rookie for the Lions in 1943. Detroit traded for the league's most valuable player, Bill Dudley of Pittsburgh (right), in 1947.

score more than seven points. They suffered the ignominy of five shutouts.

The firing of Bull Karcis at the end of the sad season was not a surprise. After lengthy negotiations, Mandel hired the noted Gus Dorais to coach the Lions with a five-year contract.

According to football legend, Charles (Gus) Dorais was responsible for making the forward pass a viable weapon of offense. He was the passer and Knute Rockne was the receiver when tiny Notre Dame upset Army in 1913 with footballs thrown through the air. Since 1925, Dorais had been head coach and athletic director at the University of Detroit. In 1938, he turned down Dick Richards' offer to become coach of the Lions. But in 1943, he accepted the guaranteed long-term offer from Mandel. Dorais was the Lions' sixth head coach in six seasons.

The Lions improved to 3-6-1 in Dorais' first season. It was good enough for a third-place finish. Dorais received a boost in September when Frank Sinkwich, the 1942 Heisman Trophy winner from Georgia, was released by the Marines because of physical disabilities. The Lions had drafted Sinkwich in the 1943 draft.

He was discharged because of high blood pressure and a heart murmur. They were disabling to the Marine Corps, but he still could play football. He could still run with verve and quickness, even though he also had flat feet. Sinkwich joined the Lions on September 15, 1943, four days after his medical discharge from the Marines. Four days later he played for the Lions in their opening game against the Cardinals.

Led by Sinkwich the Lions did in their first game what they failed to do in the entire 1942 season — they won 35-17. In one game they matched the five-touchdown output of the 11 losses in 1942. The next week the Lions won their second straight, 27-20 over the Dodgers.

The magic disappeared then . . . but it was a respectable season with three victories and third place. Sinkwich was the outstanding rookie in the NFL, contributing 1,000 yards to the Lions as a runner and passer. The 1943 Lions had some qualified pros other than Sinkwich — Chuck Fenenbock, all-pro center Alex Wojciechowicz, Augie Lio, Bill Callihan, Ned Mathews, Harry Hopp, Riley Matheson and Cardwell.

After the 1943 season, Frankie Sinkwich tried valiantly to go to war. He enlisted in the U.S. Maritime Service, the merchant marine. But his feet were flat and he was discharged again. He hoped he could get himself drafted. But he was found physically unfit. The Army announced that his feet were so flat they had to be bound in heavy tape when he played football. "I think I'll try to get a war job," Sinkwich said.

But late in training camp, Dorais induced him to rejoin the Lions for 1944. Flat feet and all, Sinkwich ran for 563 yards, third best in the league. His longest run was 72 yards from scrimmage. He was only a fair passer, but he threw 12 touchdown passes in 10 games. He was the leading punter and one of the leading punt return men in the war-deprived league. He did the placekicking and was responsible for 18 touchdowns. Scoring six touchdowns personally, 24 extra points and two field goals, Sinkwich was the No. 2 man in the league in scoring.

The Lions became winners again in 1944. Their 6-3-1 record placed them second in the West. And at the end of the season, Sinkwich was voted the NFL's most valuable player. He won the award over Don Hutson, the immortal receiver from Green Bay's champions.

Bob Westfall was an important backfield mate in 1944. And the defense was led by Wojciechowicz. As a linebacker on defense,

Wojie intercepted seven passes in 1944. He had been the middle member of the Seven Blocks of Granite at Fordham, the same fabled unit on which a guard named Vince Lombardi played. Wojciechowicz played nine seasons in Detroit, then finished his career on a championship team in Philadelphia.

The Army finally accepted Sinkwich in 1945 — and kept him when the war ended so he could play service football. Sinkwich would never rejoin the Lions.

The 1945 season was one of excellence and frustration for the Lions. With Westfall, Chuck Fenenbock and Andy Farkas in the backfield, the Lions were in contention for the Western title through most of the season. After a five-game winning streak, they were 6-1 in mid-November. Then they lost to the Giants. On Thanksgiving, the Rams edged the Lions 28-21. The victory gave the Rams their first Division title. Led by Bob Waterfield, the Cleveland club won the championship a few weeks later over the Redskins. At 7-3, the Lions finished second with their best record since the 1935 championship.

With the war ended, the All-America Conference was founded as competition for the NFL. A few days after his discharge, Sinkwich jumped leagues. He signed with the New York Yankees. The AAC had its first superstar drawing card.

The old soldiers returned to pro football in 1946. That year the Lions plummeted from the second-place finish of 1945 to the bottom again. They were an inept 1-10, the poorest record in the league. It was the beginning of the most futile period of the club's existence. Only two NFL clubs had losing records in 1946. The other loser was the Boston Yanks, a relatively new club. The Lions suffered the indignity of defeat by the Yanks in the battle for the NFL booby prize of 1946.

Some drastic action had to be taken to revive interest for 1947. The Lions took it in the form of a gamble trade for Bullet Bill Dudley. Back from the military in 1946, Dudley led the NFL in rushing with 696 yards for the Steelers. He was voted the NFL's most valuable player, performing for a weak club. But at the end of 1946, Dudley quit pro football to enter coaching at his old school, Virginia. "I know my limitations," Dudley said. "I'm just not big enough to take a beating in this league."

Dudley was 170 pounds — and he could take a beating. The Lions calculated that he merely wanted out of Pittsburgh. There were stories that he was not in sympathy with Jock Sutherland, the Steelers' coach. The Lions paid a high price for the privilege of talking to Dudley. They gave up Bob Cifers and Paul White from their roster. They also gave the Steelers their first draft choice for 1948, and the right to negotiate with Bob Chappuis, running star of Michigan's postwar juggernaut.

Mandel, who had worked on the deal for seven months, signed Dudley in a conference that lasted 35 minutes. His salary would be $20,000, the largest sum the Lions ever had paid one of their players.

Dudley had been the NFL's rushing leader twice in his two seasons for the Steelers, 1942 and 1946. But he was not a miracle worker for the Lions. He scored 11 touchdowns and intercepted five passes — they were still playing both ways — but Dudley did not even lead the Lions in rushing in 1947. He was second with 302 yards. Camp Wilson was the leader with 414. Dudley also was second best as a receiver. Johnny Greene, an adept man at getting into the open and underrated in his time, was best on the club. He caught 38 passes in the first T-formation year.

Dorais' first T-quarterback was Clyde LeForce with backing from Leroy Zimmerman,

who had been a star years earlier with the Philadelphia Eagles.

The transfusion of a streamlined passing-style formation resulted in only slight improvement in 1947 — a 3-9 record. But finishing last and losing more money terribly displeased Mandel.

The Lions had stability in their head coaching for five years — after the succession of annual firings and hirings. Dorais, so popular in the city, had served his five years. Mandel actually had given Dorais a new $25,000-per-year contract for five years in 1946. Now Mandel decided a change was necessary, even though Dorais' contract was four years from expiration. It was an odd contract. Mandel was obligated to pay off Dorais in full — $100,000 — if the coach was fired. But there was an escape clause. Dorais would be entitled to only six months' salary — $12,500 — should Mandel sell the franchise to a new owner.

"I have asked Dorais to resign," Mandel announced on December 17, 1947. "He has refused despite a substantial offer of settlement. That puts me in a position where either he goes or I will consider the advantages of selling the club."

Gus Dorais was a crusty man with a whimsical sense of humor. He knew the perils of coaching. He once said of his profession: "How would you like to have your kid's Christmas depend on whether some lunatic end caught a pass on a November afternoon. I wouldn't wish coaching off on anybody."

After Mandel's statement, Dorais charged the owner with attempting to shortchange him in the settlement. Then he wrote a public letter to Mandel:

"...I have been notified through Detroit's three daily newspapers that you have discharged me and have no further need for or desire of my services and consequently will abide by your wishes.

"I want to make this point clear, however, that I am not, directly or indirectly, waiving any of my rights under my contract..."

It took three weeks of haggling to solve the money issue. Dorais then received a reported settlement of $100,000 for the four remaining years on the contract.

A week later, even though Mandel had paid Dorais off, he sold the club to a syndicate of Detroit socialites and sportsmen. The sale price was $185,000 — a pittance. Eight years earlier Mandel had purchased the club from Richards for $225,000. He lost $40,000 in the sale plus another half million, according to a conservative estimate, in operating a moribund franchise for eight seasons.

The syndicate was headed by D. Lyle Fife, a Detroit electrical products magnate. Fife became president. Edwin J. Anderson, president of a Detroit brewery, was a vice president. The auto industry was in on the deal, with several prominent men investing money. Shares sold for $100. An investor could purchase a minimum of $1,000 worth of new stock and a maximum of $20,000. Their investment eventually would multiply to 15 times in value over the next 16 years — not including handsome dividends paid during the 1950s.

The new owners' first choice for a head coach was Frank Leahy of Notre Dame. Leahy wasn't interested. So they signed Alvin (Bo) McMillin of Indiana to a five-year contract as coach and general manager. McMillin had no background in pro football, but then neither did the new owners. McMillin had problems from the beginning. For one thing, the players had trouble relating to him. There was a communication problem. And the multitude of new owners became a cloying group. Directors clogged the locker rooms after ballgames. They pampered the players. The football team had become their toy. The intrusions created much

bitterness between the coach and the owners.

McMillin entered pro football with no illusions. The Lions had been a last-place club the previous two years, able to win a total of only four games in 20.

In 1948, McMillin had to go with a rookie, Fred Enke, as quarterback. There was sufficient offense with Enke and his backup, LeForce; runners Camp Wilson and Dudley; receivers Bob Mann, the Lions' first black player, and Johnny Greene and Joe Margucci.

But still the Lions were incapable of escaping last place in the West for the third season in a row. McMillin's first team finished with a 2-10 record. For the second time in three seasons, the Lions' record was the worst in the NFL.

McMillin shook up the club in 1949. Cloyce Box, John Prchlik, Don Doll, Bob Smith and Wally Triplett were among the newcomers. There was a front office shakeup, too. Fife and Anderson were not particularly harmonious. Anderson succeeded Fife as president. The aggressive young publicity man, W. Nicholas Kerbawy, was appointed assistant to the general manager.

For the first time since 1945, the Lions moved out of last place. They were fourth with a 4-8 record. In his last season in Detroit, Bill Dudley was the leading runner and scorer. Bob Mann, a brilliant receiver, caught 66 passes to rank second in the league behind Tom Fears of the Los Angeles Rams. McMillin had a season-long quarterback indecision though. He used three passers, Enke, LeForce and Frank Tripucka.

A major move was made early in 1950. McMillin traded for a young quarterback of great promise. The quarterback was Bobby Layne, who had spent a frustrating year trying to throw the football for the New York Bulldogs. The Lions gave up Camp Wilson for Layne. When Wilson refused to go, the Lions decided to send Bob Mann to the Bulldogs.

With Mann gone, McMillin converted Box from a halfback to receiver. McMillin also brought in a number of rookies with considerable promise in 1950 — Doak Walker, Leon Hart, Lou Creekmur, Thurman McGraw. Bob Hoernschemeyer, who had been with the Brooklyn Dodgers and Chicago Hornets in the All-America Conference, was picked in an allocation draft.

There was a massive personnel turnover in 1950. McMillin also made an addition to his coaching staff. Buddy Parker, a hero on the Lions' championship team of 1935, had quit as coach of the Cardinals. Parker became McMillin's backfield aide.

With their new players, the 1950 Lions were a vastly improved club. They had an explosive offense with Layne, Box and Walker. But they were not ready quite yet to challenge for a championship.

In one game against the Rams, Wally Triplett set a league record by accounting for 331 yards. His yardage was gained via rushing, pass receiving and returning kicks. But the Lions still lost 65-24.

Box caught 50 passes for the season, second only to Fears. Against the Baltimore Colts, who had come in from the AAC and would be disbanded at the season's end, Box caught 12 passes. In that game, Box caught four touchdown passes, three from Layne and one from Enke; his one-game yardage was 302, one short of the all-time one-game record.

The Lions finished with a 6-6 record and again placed fourth in their division. Doak Walker, with 128 points, became the NFL scoring champion as a rookie. He was the first Lion to lead the league in scoring since Dutch Clark in 1936.

Despite the optimism of the 1950 season, there was some player mutiny against coach

McMillin . . . and some of the owners sided with the players.

Typically, the change of command created a furor. The owners fired McMillin, buying up the remaining two years on his contract.

Buddy Parker was elevated to head coach in 1951. It was the first of the Great Years.

The departure of Bobby Layne from Detroit in October 1958 was preordained. "Tobin's the guy who won it for us," coach George Wilson had proclaimed after the Lions had won the 1957 championship.

Rote had his boosters but so did Layne. The trade was designed to solve the dilemma. The Lions were not doing well at the start of '58 with Layne — and Wilson thought Rote could lift them. But reaction of Layne's old team-mates was open resentment toward Rote. Eventually there would be accusations that the pass blockers were opening the gates on Rote, and intentionally allowing opponents to get to the quarterback.

Wilson had a scare the day after Layne was traded. Running in a practice session wind-sprint, Rote pulled a hamstring muscle. There was a crash indoctrination course for Earl Morrall, the new backup quarterback. But on Sunday Rote had recovered sufficiently to start against the Rams. He was ineffectual, and Wilson put Morrall in. The new quarterback almost won the game, but a fourth-quarter interception on a controversial call ruined the Lions. The Rams scored two touchdowns in the final 60 seconds to win 42-28.

Four games into the new season the reigning world champions were winless. They had three losses and a tie.

The Lions were out of contention quickly, but Wilson was encouraged by two new rookies on defense. A myopic tackle named Alex Karras excited Wilson with his pass rushing. In a victory in Los Angeles in the season's fifth week, a linebacker named Wayne Walker became a starter for the first time. Walker scored a touchdown with a pass interception.

But there were few hurrahs in 1958. The Lions finished with a 4-7-1 record, dropping to fifth place. Their only victory of consequence was over Cleveland. The Lions almost always could beat the Browns. They did again in 1958 with Rote throwing for three touchdowns in a 30-10 victory.

The Lions also lost a general manager in 1958. W. Nicholas Kerbawy, their erudite front-office leader, was hired away by the rival Detroit Pistons. Anderson, the club president, added Kerbawy's duties to his own.

In 1958, the Lions dipped further downward. They added only one prize rookie in the draft, Nick Pietrosante, to play fullback. Off the Browns' waiver list, the Lions also picked up Dick LeBeau, who would star for them for 14 years.

The record was 3-8-1 and the Lions finished fifth again. Rote became disenchanted with the Lions — and vice-versa. He played out his option in Detroit. His bargaining position was excellent. Toronto of the Canadian League bid against the Houston club of the American Football League which would start playing games in 1960. The Lions did not involve themselves deeply in the auction because Anderson did not care to accept some of Rote's demands for security. He wanted no-trade and no-release stipulations, and Anderson flatly refused. So Rote accepted the contract offered by the Toronto Argonauts and went to Canada.

Wilson wasn't terribly upset when Rote defected. Rote had thrown 19 interceptions — against five touchdown passes — in 1959. Morrall, who started five games and produced two of the three victories, had been the superior quarterback in 1959 anyway.

  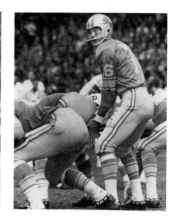

Wilson himself was in jeopardy during the 1959 season, but at the end of the year, he was given a one-year contract for 1960.

A vigorous rebuilding job was started by Wilson in 1960. Rote was gone. So were 10 other of his teammates. Wilson obtained Jim Ninowski from the Browns to compete with Morrall at quarterback. Bob Long and a No. 1 draft choice went to the Browns in the deal. Dick (Night Train) Lane was obtained from the Cardinals, who had forsaken Chicago for St. Louis. Gerry Perry was traded for Lane. Carl Brettschneider, a head-hunting linebacker, also was picked up from the Cardinals for Mike Rabold, a young guard. Sam Williams was obtained from the Rams when Jim David went to Los Angeles to start his career as an assistant coach. Years before the people of Los Angeles wanted to lynch David because of his aggressive play in the Lions' secondary. John Henry Johnson was traded to the Steelers. Jim Doran, Charley Ane and Gene Cronin were unprotected by the Lions in the draft to stock the expansion Dallas Cowboys. Lou Creekmur retired for the final time.

In the draft, the Lions' top pick was Johnny Robinson, an excellent prospect who had been overshadowed by Billy Cannon on Louisiana State's national champions. Cannon became a *cause célèbre* when he signed with both the NFL and AFL — and was awarded to the fledgling AFL to play for Houston. Robinson also spurned the NFL to go with the other league. He signed with Lamar Hunt's Dallas Texans.

The Lions lost Robinson — but they still drafted wisely. A fourth-round choice, a remnant of the deal for Bobby Layne, was Roger Brown, a huge defensive tackle. Gail Cogdill, a promising receiver, was a sixth-round choice.

There was great hope when the Lions broke

training camp at Cranbrook School to start their '60 schedule. "We are definitely back," Wilson said.

Even with rebuilt morale, an influx of new performers and unbridled optimism, the Lions lost their first three games, and the Colts, the champions, were the opponents in the fourth week.

The Lions rebounded against Baltimore, however. Jim Martin, the old Marine at age 36, kicked field goals of 52 yards, 51 yards and 40 yards. The 51-yard effort broke a 17-17 tie in the fourth quarter and the 40-yarder increased the lead to 23-17. Johnny Unitas rallied the Colts back but with two minutes remaining a pass intended for Alan Ameche was intercepted by Night Train Lane, who ran it back for 80 yards for a touchdown. The Lions beat the Colts 30-17.

At the season's midpoint, the Lions were 2-4 ... and glum. But in the second half, the Lions won all but one of their games to finish with a 7-5 record. The only loss in the last seven was to the Bears, and that was reversed in the last game.

Despite the late season rally, the Lions entered December with Wilson's position in peril. The Lions were going to Baltimore for the rematch with the Colts. It was said privately in Detroit that Wilson's job swung on this game. The Colts were 12 1/2-point favorites, leading the Western Division for the third season in a row.

Seven minutes into the final quarter, Morrall passed four yards to Hopalong Cassady to produce a 10-8 lead. With 79 seconds left, Martin kicked a 47-yard field goal. Detroit's lead was 13-8.

But Johnny Unitas was a master against the clock. He started the Colts from their 20. In the final 20 seconds, Unitas got the Colts to the Lions' 38. Then he dropped back and passed

for the ball game. In the end zone, Lenny Moore dived and skidded along the grass on his stomach. Then he reached for the football above him and, somehow, caught it. The Colts were ahead; they had pulled out the game in a lightning drive, scoring the winning touchdown on an astounding catch with 14 seconds left in the game. The Colts' fans poured onto the field. There was utter bedlam.

With 14 seconds, left, Steve Myhra kicked off to the Lions. Bruce Maher returned the kickoff to the 35. On the field fights broke out. The fans started out on the field again. They gathered around the Lions' bench. They flung insults and jeered.

"Please, please," beseeched the voice on the public address system. "There are 10 seconds left. This is one of Baltimore's finest days. Let's not spoil it."

The field was cleared and Morrall gathered the Lions. Gail Cogdill went out to the left. He broke from the line on his pattern. Three Colts' defenders tracked after him. From the right side, Jim Gibbons went straight downfield. Everybody watched Cogdill, the Lions' most dangerous deep receiver. Nobody paid much heed to Gibbons, a lumbering tight end. Nobody looked at him except Earl Morrall. Gibbons was wide open — and Morrall threw the football right at him at the Colts' 40. The catch was made and Gibbons turned around, tucked the ball under his arm and started off to run as far as he could before stepping out of bounds to stop the clock. But nobody was nearby and Gibbons ran for a touchdown. In 14 seconds, the Lions had reclaimed the victory 20-15. The Colts subsequently tumbled from first place and out of the race.

With a four-game winning streak at the end, the Lions finished second to the Packers in the West, and Wilson was given a two-year contract for 1961-62.

The runnerup finish qualified the Lions for an appearance in the first Playoff Bowl at Miami. The Lions won, beating the Browns 17-16 as Gary Lowe intercepted three passes.

While there was solidarity among the players, behind the scenes the owners were squabbling heatedly among themselves. D. Lyle Fife, who had been club president for two years in the late '40s, was feuding with Anderson, who had replaced him. There were 15 directors and 144 stockholders who owned the 12,600 outstanding shares. Anderson controlled one faction of shareholders; Fife led a group of dissidents aiming to gain command of the club. It was a nasty affair as each side campaigned and quarreled for proxy votes. The club's front office structure was virtually shredded by the intramural battle.

The only solution was a compromise and it was struck. Fife did not regain the presidency. Under pressure, Anderson abdicated his top office. The new president was William Clay Ford, a club stockholder, grandson of Henry Ford and brother of Henry Ford II. With the clout of a strong family name in the automobile industry, Ford was able to restore order soon after becoming club president. Anderson retained his title of general manager.

After their glorious 1960 finish and with the squabbling directors silenced, the Lions bubbled with optimism for 1961. Wilson had rebuilt quickly.

With four victories at the end of the year, Morrall was established as an NFL quarterback. Nick Pietrosante, who had broken Ace Gutowsky's club rushing record with 872 yards, was a workhorse runner. Danny Lewis was a capable running partner. Cogdill, Gibbons and Terry Barr were threatening receivers. The defense finally had been secured. Alex Karras was outstanding, perhaps the best pass-rushing tackle in the NFL. Roger Brown was poten-

Commissioner Pete Rozelle (far left) suspended Alex Karras (left) and Green Bay halfback Paul Hornung April 17, 1963, for placing bets on football games. Karras and Hornung rejoined their teams in 1964.

tially outstanding. Darris McCord, Bill Glass and Sam Williams were excellent outside rushmen. The linebacking corps of Joe Schmidt, Wayne Walker and Carl Brettschneider was the best in the league. The defensive backfield — the Four Ls — of Night Train Lane, Dick LeBeau, Yale Lary and Gary Lowe was an excellent secondary.

The draft was not productive in 1961. It was basically an unchanged ballclub.

The Lions started fast for a change. Their first opponent was the Packers, losers to the Eagles in the previous championship game. The Packers of Lombardi were the favorites for the championship in 1961.

The Lions knocked them off the first game of the season. Morrall's passing set up both touchdowns. Pietrosante scored them both and Jim Martin, still reliable at 37, kicked a field goal in a 17-13 victory.

The next Sunday the Lions beat the Colts 16-15 on Jim Martin's 49-yard field goal in the final four minutes. He had kicked two field goals earlier. He played with deep sorrow. Six days earlier his eight-month-old son had died of leukemia.

The Lions' third game was their home opener against the 49ers. In secret, during the week, Red Hickey, the 49ers' coach, had installed the shotgun formation operated by rotating quarterbacks. John Brodie, Billy Kilmer and Bobby Waters shuttled into the game one play at a time to run from the shotgun. The Lions' defense yielded seven touchdowns. The 49ers beat the previously undefeated Lions 49-0. "It looked like the Drake Relays," said Wayne Walker.

The next Sunday Pat Studstill ran a kickoff back 100 yards — but the Lions lost to the Bears 31-17. After a marvelous start, the Lions were faltering.

A major share of the problem was at quarter-

back. Wilson tried Morrall and benched him. He brought in Ninowski, then tried Morrall again. It was obvious the Lions had no dominant quarterback. They spent the autumn in pursuit of the Packers, who would win their first of five championships in the decade. The Lions won games in the final minute; and they lost them in the same manner. At 8-5-1, they had their best record since the championship year of 1957, but they placed second in the West again. That was worth only another journey to the Playoff Bowl and a week in Miami. There, the Lions beat the Eagles, 38-10.

With the war raging against the AFL, the NFL conducted its draft in November. The Lions drafted John Hadl, Eddie Wilson and Bobby Thompson one, two, three. Anderson went to see Hadl immediately, taking a contract along. Other emissaries contacted Wilson and Thompson. Hadl rebuffed the Lions and signed with the Chargers of the AFL. Wilson also went to the AFL, and Thompson chose the Montreal Alouettes of the Canadian Football League. The Lions had lost their first three draft choices.

The veterans, sensitive about the failure to overhaul the Packers, blamed the front office for its failure in the area of manpower replenishment. There had been a shortage of rookies in 1961. Now there would be another dearth in 1962. So without the top three drafted players to bolster the offense, Anderson dodged by saying: "We'll just have to make some trades."

In March 1962, the Lions completed their most important trade since the departure of Bobby Layne. Dissatisfied with the co-quarterbacking of Morrall and Ninowski, Wilson acquired Milt Plum from the Browns. Plum had been the NFL's most effective passer. The transaction involved six players. With Plum, the Lions obtained runner Tommy Watkins and linebacker Dave Lloyd. Ninowski returned to

Harry Gilmer (left) replaced George Wilson as head coach of the Lions in 1965. Gilmer made fullback Tom Nowatzke of Indiana (right) his No. 1 draft choice.

the Browns along with Bill Glass and Hopalong Cassady.

Plum was an introvert. Unwittingly, he soon would be responsible for irrevocably widening the division between offense and defense until it became insoluble. In 1962, the Lions resolutely believed they could overtake the Packers. They believed they could beat the Packers with their defense. They believed they would win the division, then the championship.

And for three weeks, Plum was the leader Wilson and the defense envisioned. The offense erupted. As though it had been dictated by fate, Plum's first game with the Lions was against Layne and the Steelers. Plum threw three touchdown passes as the Lions won 45-7. The next week the Lions erupted again. Plum threw four touchdown passes in a 45-24 rout of the 49ers.

The next Sunday the Lions beat the Colts 29-20. Plum turned the game with a 45-yard touchdown run on a quarterback draw on fourth down.

The Lions and the Packers were unbeaten at 3-0 and matched against each other in Green Bay on October 7, 1962. In an epic defensive struggle, the Lions led 7-6 as the clock wound down. The Lions had the ball and could waste most of the remaining time with it. They could protect their lead by running, then punt the Packers back to their own goal line.

But a third down play began a sequence of events which destroyed a season — perhaps several seasons — and eroded faith in a quarterback. For a reason never explained to anybody's satisfaction, Plum passed. It turned out to be an unwise call. Terry Barr, the intended receiver, fell down cutting in the muck. Herb Adderley intercepted and ran the ball back 40 yards. Paul Hornung's field goal with 27 seconds to go defeated the Lions 9-7. Whatever harmony that had been created between the

Lions' offense and defense was devastated on one play, by one interception.

The Lions were behind the Packers by one game, and two weeks later they trailed by two games when they lost 17-14 to the Giants.

The vow was made to beat the Packers in the rematch and avenge their loss at Green Bay. On Thanksgiving, with Plum throwing two touchdown passes to Cogdill and with the angry defense throwing Bart Starr 11 times, the Lions fulfilled their vow. With a magnificent display, they delivered a stunning 26-14 loss to the Packers. It merely deprived the Packers of an unbeaten season. Despite a seven-game winning streak, the Lions could never catch up. They finally lost their last game to the Bears 3-0.

The 11-3 record was the club's finest ever. The three losses had been by a total of eight points. But for the third straight year, the Lions were second. That meant they had to return to Miami again for the Playoff Bowl against the Steelers. It was a trip the Lions had no heart to make. But it was unavoidable. And in a remote, roundabout manner, the Packers would haunt them while they were in Miami.

It was in Miami on December 30, 1962, that several Lions congregated at a Sunday party. It was the day the Packers played the Giants in a championship game the Lions firmly believed they themselves should have participated in. A friend of Alex Karras had invited him to bring some of his teammates over.

In an ambience that was pure Miami — palms, a swimming pool, sharpies — the Lions settled down by the television set. Somebody asked which team they figured would win. They figured the Packers; after all, the Packers had beat them. Then they were asked if they might care to wager some money on the outcome. It all seemed quite innocent while the Packers beat the Giants 16-7.

A week later the Lions won their third

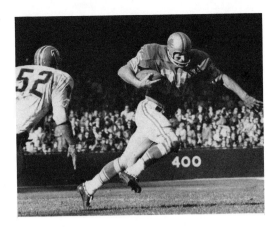

consecutive Playoff Bowl, 17-10 over the Pittsburgh Steelers.

The next day, January 7, 1963, all hell broke loose. Commissioner Pete Rozelle's probe of the Lions' gambling became public knowledge.

In Los Angeles for the Pro Bowl, Alex Karras appeared on the Huntley-Brinkley Report on NBC-TV. He admitted he had bet on football games. He inferred that betting on games was a practice indulged in by other players, and coaches and owners, too.

Interviewed by telecaster David Burk, Karras said: "I have bet on ballgames."

Burk: "Have you bet on a ballgame in which you were playing?"

Karras: "Yes, I have."

Burk: "You don't know of any case of point-shaving at all?"

Karras: "I know of none whatsoever in this league. I think the boys play too hard to be shaving points."

Another excerpt from the televised interview:

Burk: "I think you mentioned yesterday that coaches and managers and owners of teams and frequently players bet on games. Is that correct?"

Karras: "Well, I don't know if they do or not, but I assume that is going on. I enjoy betting. Naturally, I bet dogs in Miami. I bet an occasional horse race. I don't know how big a lot of them do bet, but I would assume there is betting going on in the league."

Rozelle ordered Karras to New York. "I thought I was being interviewed so they could help me clear myself and look how it turned out," said Karras, bewildered. "I haven't done anything wrong."

Karras was ordered to maintain silence during the investigation. The Lions tried to force Karras out of his part-ownership of the downtown Lindell A.C., a bar that catered to the sports set and people attracted by athletes.

Meanwhile, other Lions were interviewed by Rozelle, and the FBI entered the investigation. There were allegations of links between Lions and the underworld after surveillance of known racketeers by the Detroit police.

Rozelle examined every shred of evidence, and determined what the penalties should be. On April 17, he announced the suspension of Karras and Paul Hornung for a minimum of one year.

The Lions' management was fined $4,000. Five Lions who had bet down in Florida on the Packers' championship game with the Giants were fined $2,000 each. They were Joe Schmidt, Wayne Walker, John Gordy, Gary Low and Sam Williams.

Rozelle fined the Lions for failing to inform him of Detroit police investigations and for allowing unauthorized personnel to have sideline passes to sit on the bench during games.

Karras, Rozelle said, had made at least six bets of $50 to $100 since entering the league in 1958. Rozelle said there was no evidence that Karras had ever bet against the Lions.

From an 11-3 team that was the second strongest in pro football — some claim the strongest — the Lions plummeted pitifully in 1963. They obtained Floyd Peters in a deal with the Browns to replace Karras, and they managed to sign a No. 1 draft choice for a change, offensive tackle Daryl Sanders. Lucien Reeburg, another offensive tackle, became a rookie starter.

There were curfew violations and fines during the preseason in 1963. Wilson delivered tongue lashings.

The beleaguered Plum faltered. Wilson used Morrall frequently as a relief man, and sometimes as a starter. The pass rush fizzled without Karras. Wilson also was distressed because Roger Brown was not effective without Karras.

Early in the season, the Lions were thrashed

31-10 by the Packers. On the following week the champion-to-be Bears romped 37-21. That started the quarterback juggling. Wilson was in a quandary. In desperation, Wilson sought out the recently retired Bobby Layne.

"Would you be willing to make a comeback and rejoin the Lions?" Wilson asked.

"I would not," said Layne.

The defensive spark was gone with the loss of Karras. Joe Schmidt missed much of the year with a dislocated shoulder. The Lions' record was 5-8-1 and it could have been worse.

Late in the season club president William Clay Ford revealed his attempt to consolidate the ownership. He was buying out all stock from the 140 shareholders. The transaction was completed on January 10, 1964. The franchise the corporate stockholders had purchased for $180,000 in 1948 became Ford's property alone for $6.5 million.

One of Ford's first moves was to restructure the front office. Anderson's duties as general manager were modified. He was relieved of the responsibility for signing players — veterans and draft choices.

The job of signing players and of overseeing the draft was given to Russ Thomas, who was named director of player personnel. Thomas had been a player with the Lions in the 1940s and a scout and coach in the 1950s.

Ford announced that Wilson would be retained in 1964, but the coaching staff assignments were redefined and some of Wilson's authority was quietly removed.

But the Lions had miscalculated in the draft again. They chose Pete Beathard first and he was already committed to the AFL Dallas Texans, soon to become the Kansas City Chiefs. Matt Snorton, the second choice, and Gerry Philbin, the third choice, also were lured into the American Football League.

Then a tragedy struck the club when Lucien

Reeburg, who had been promising as a rookie starter, died.

Ford worked behind the scenes for the reinstatement of Karras. Karras finally said he would sell his interest in the Lindell A.C. On March 16, 1964, Rozelle reinstated Karras and Hornung.

The first of pro football's Fearsome Foursomes — so named by broadcaster Van Patrick — was reunited. Karras was back with Brown, Sam Williams and Darris McCord.

Plum won the opener with the 49ers 26-17 on his passing to Cogdill, but he was erratic the next week, and Morrall entered to salvage a 17-17 tie with the Rams.

It was that kind of spotty season for 14 weeks. There was a dilemma at quarterback, some decent running by Nick Pietrosante and new acquisition Hugh McElhenny and some excellent receiving by Cogdill. But it seldom meshed.

Victories in the final two games enabled the Lions to finish with a 7-5-2 record and a second consecutive fourth-place standing.

"There are going to be a lot of changes on the Detroit Lions after the season," Wilson said before the next-to-last game.

He was not aware how acutely accurate his prediction would be.

Days after the '64 season ended, Ford purged George Wilson's coaching staff. The Lions had been allowed to erode with age as a team while their draft mechanics failed to provide replenishment personnel. The loss of a succession of high draft choices to the AFL was starting to undermine the team.

The coaching staff took the blame when on December 20 Ford fired three of Wilson's assistants — Bob Nussbaumer, who also had been involved in the scouting, Les Bingaman and Don Doll.

A day later the other two assistants — Aldo

Faced with a team divided into factions favoring different quarterbacks, Milt Plum and Earl Morrall, Gilmer negotiated a three-way trade with Cleveland and New York. Morrall (left) wound up with the Giants, and linebacker Mike Lucci (right) was traded from Cleveland to Detroit and replaced Joe Schmidt as the team's middle linebacker.

Forte and Sonny Grandelius — were fired. Wilson was retained as a head coach for an indefinite period, according to a terse mimeographed press release. Wilson brooded overnight and decided he had been undermined when his aides were fired.

On December 23, Wilson submitted his resignation after eight seasons as head coach of the Detroit Lions.

On Christmas Eve, Ford revealed that Wilson had been stripped of some of his autonomy when the management had changed with the sale of the club the previous January. Wilson did not have the authority to make trades and draft rookies. That reduction of power figured greatly in Wilson's ultimate decision.

In the first week of January, columnist Pete Waldmeir wrote in the *News* that Sonny Grandelius would be the next head coach of the Lions. Grandelius had told friends around Detroit the job was his.

That night the Lions announced Harry Gilmer, former quarterback in Detroit and assistant coach with the Minnesota Vikings, as their new head coach.

Sonny Grandelius has testified often that Waldmeir's article was correct. But he charged that the newspaper piece had sabotaged his nomination because the Lions switched to Gilmer when it appeared.

The Lions denied the allegation.

The two years of Harry Gilmer's regime were fraught with dissension. They were the most turbulent years in the Lions' often tempestuous history. Almost immediately the players reacted to Gilmer's twang with aversion. He was a knowledgeable football man, but there was an ever-widening communications gap between him and his athletes. Player after player lashed out at Gilmer with vitriolic statements.

Wilson had been a players' coach, their friend. At times he partied with them.

"This is no reflection on George" said Gilmer, "but I don't want to be considered as a player's best friend."

Gilmer took the job with the restrictions that had been placed on Wilson his final year. Thomas would be in charge of dealing and drafting, in consort with the coach.

Harry Gilmer was a tobacco chewer with an affectation for western things. He was extremely accurate squirting a stream of ebony tobacco juice, sometimes into potted plants in hotel lobbies. He wore a wide-brimmed Stetson on the sidelines at games. He wore cowboy boots. At first his players were amused at such eccentricities. But before long they were talking behind his back, mocking him.

Gilmer turned the club roster over considerably in 1965. Tom Nowatzke, a fullback, was the club's first draft choice. They were not going to fail to sign their No. 1 draftee again. So they made sure he would sign with them before they drafted Nowatzke — though they had preference for other runners.

It was a boom draft year for the Lions. They also drafted Ed Flanagan, who became the starting center as a rookie and would later be all-pro. A lower draftee was Larry Hand, who made the club and eventually would become an outstanding defensive end. Tommy Vaughn, who would become a fine safety, also made the 1965 club as a rookie.

The training camp controversy swirled around the transactions involving veterans. It was here that the veterans started to undermine the new head coach. Gilmer coveted the line-busting abilities of Joe Don Looney, so the Lions ignored Looney's reputation — he had been booted off the squad at Oklahoma for slugging an assistant coach, he had passed through the Giants' camp and had been sent to the Colts as incorrigible, he had been in trouble for breaking down the door to a girl's apartment in Balti-

more. The Lions gave Dennis Gaubatz, a promising young middle linebacker, to the Colts for Looney.

The second deal irritated the veterans on defense. Gilmer believed he could remedy the factionalism between the pro-Morrall and pro-Plum groups by ridding himself of one. He watched the two men work early in camp and made up his mind. In a complicated three-club trade with the Giants and Browns, the Lions dealt away Morrall. He was freed to the Giants. The Lions gained a young middle linebacker who had been bench-ridden in Cleveland, Mike Lucci.

The players were furious over the departure of Morrall. And they stewed more about the special treatment given Looney at the Lions' camp at Cranbrook.

One night Looney stayed out after curfew and got himself into a restaurant disturbance in Royal Oak, a Detroit suburb near Cranbrook. The police were called, and the incident made front-page headlines. Looney got off with a reprimand from the coach.

Next, Looney went AWOL from practice, staying in his room because Gilmer had cut rookie John Flynn. Flynn had been a teammate of Looney's at Oklahoma and Joe Don was protesting. Gilmer dispatched team captain Joe Schmidt to persuade Looney to return.

"Joe Don, you really should come down to practice," Schmidt advised. "You should if you want to help the ballclub."

"Joe?" asked Looney, "how long you been here with this club?"

"Twelve years and I haven't missed practice yet," said Schmidt.

"Joe, you ought to take a day off every now and then," said Looney.

Gilmer let Looney off with only a reprimand.

Then the Lions proceeded to win their first three regular season games of 1965.

The Lions led in the West, but a collapse seemed inevitable. It was. The Lions lost the next three, won a couple and staggered to the end of a dissension-filled season with a 6-7-1 record. They were sixth in the seven-club West.

Looney was with the club all season, but he was inactive because he complained of chronic headaches.

Gilmer was reluctant to play him, although there were those who regarded the mysterious headaches with doubt.

In the locker room at Philadelphia, after the Lions ended the season with a 35-28 victory over the Eagles, there were a number of retirement announcements.

Joe Schmidt, one of football's greatest linebackers for 13 seasons, said he was through as a player. He hinted darkly that Gilmer was the reason, that he could no longer play for the coach. Sam Williams and Darris McCord, ends on the Fearsome Foursome, were more outspoken.

"I won't play another year for him," Williams and McCord said separately. Williams subsequently went to Atlanta. McCord recanted and played two more years for the Lions.

Terry Barr, before his knee injuries a peerless receiver, also retired.

In February 1966, Gail Cogdill went to Flint, Michigan, to speak to a women's group. A female reporter caught the speech. Among some of Cogdill's comments were:

"Gilmer doesn't know how to handle men and he's not ready for a coaching job . . . You can't talk to the guy. The men are afraid of him. How would you like to work for someone you can't trust . . . If Gilmer comes back at all, he might be the only one who does."

When Cogdill's quotes reached print in Detroit, he was immediately summoned to the Lions' offices. He denied making the critical statements in the quizzing session with Gilmer,

Kicker Garo Yepremian (far left, with holder Bruce Mahar) sent his first Lion's kickoff downfield, then turned to retrieve the tee – before the play had been whistled dead. Gilmer's cowboy hat (left) became the target for snowballs thrown from the Tiger Stadium seats. "At least they don't have rocks in them," Gilmer said. His replacement as head coach in January, 1967, was Joe Schmidt (right).

Ford and Thomas. Gilmer said he would conduct his own investigation of the Flint meeting. Within a week, a public apology had been evoked from Cogdill. Gilmer then placed Cogdill on indefinite suspension, a meaningless punishment because it was February in the offseason. Because of the estrangement between player and coach the Lions were not offered equal value in their efforts to trade Cogdill. The affair ended in May when Gilmer fined Cogdill $1,000 and reinstated him on the roster.

The 1966 training camp was no more serene than 1965. It provided ample foreshadowing of the season to come.

Ford had convinced Joe Schmidt to enter coaching if he wouldn't reconsider his retirement plans. Schmidt was placed on Gilmer's staff as the linebacker coach, working particularly with Mike Lucci.

Schmidt and Carl Brettschneider, the defensive line coach, worked for Gilmer all season but seldom communicated with the head coach. The cabal on the coaching staff was evident to the dissident players, and the atmosphere enveloped the club.

Seeking to create unity between defense and offense, Gilmer named Alex Karras team captain, replacing Schmidt. He'll be the strongest leader," said Gilmer.

The first time he was called to midfield to call heads or tails in the coinflip ritual, Karras looked at the referee and said coyly: "I am not allowed to gamble."

Just before the season opened, Nick Pietrosante was called in by Gilmer. Pietrosante had gained more yardage than any runner in the history of the Lions, 3,933 yards. He held the Lions' one-season ground gaining record, 872 yards in 1960. Gilmer told him he had been placed on irrevocable waivers. Pietrosante left the Lions in the fashion which had by now

become traditional -- with a rip at the coach.

The Lions were winless in the '66 preseason at 0-4-1, but somehow the Lions overcame their internal strife — the guerilla warfare in the locker room — to win their season opener, 14-3 over the Bears.

In the second week of the season, the offense stumbled and the Steelers, a struggling team at best, won 17-3. After the game, Gilmer confessed that he had erred a year before in deciding to keep Plum and trade Morrall. The coach also chastized the team for its "lack of mental discipline."

The furor continued during the week. The following Sunday the new Atlanta Falcons came to Detroit.

In the second quarter, Joe Don Looney entered the game to a tumultuous welcome from the fans at Tiger Stadium. He promptly slashed through tacklers 24 yards to a touchdown. Looney later got off another dazzling run. It was still the second quarter when Gilmer beckoned Looney. The coach gave Looney a play to take in to Plum. Looney balked.

"I'm not going to be a messenger boy," he said.

At halftime, Gilmer approached Looney. Looney told him his back had been stepped on and he was injured.

"Are you refusing to play?" said Gilmer.

"I'm not going in," said Looney.

"Stay here in the locker room," ordered Gilmer.

After the game Gilmer suspended Looney indefinitely. Looney then was sent to the Redskins.

The Lions lost their next five games, and the players became more and more mutinous. In a 45-14 loss to Baltimore, Milt Plum's knee was wrecked and he was lost for the season. Karl Sweetan, the rookie, was given Plum's job.

On the trip to San Francisco for the next

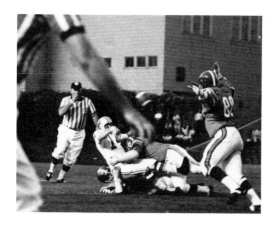

game, Ford disclosed that Gilmer twice had offered to give up his coaching job. "I tried to dissuade him from the notion," said Ford.

In San Francisco, the Lions lost 27-24 on a touchdown with three seconds left to play.

"I think this game clearly showed we aren't a team rife with dissension and morale problems," said Gilmer. It was an optimistic assessment.

In hopes of producing points, the Lions brought an applicant for a placekicking job in for a trial at midseason. Gilmer was so impressed, he suggested to Thomas the Lions sign the kicker immediately. The players had stood in a semicircle on the field at Tiger Stadium while the left-footed applicant had kicked ball after ball through the goal posts soccer-style.

The kicker's name was Garo Yepremian. In the locker room, Garo's enterprising brother, Krikor, negotiated quietly with Thomas. A writer approached Garo.

"I'd like to ask you some questions, if I may," he said.

"I don't speak English," he said in flawless English.

Later that afternoon he signed with the Lions, and his command of the language returned. The following Sunday he saw his first pro football game. He kicked off and as the ball sailed end over end downfield, he turned around. Garo bent over and picked up the kicking tee. His fortune was good, however; the return was stopped a distance away.

The Lions finished the year with a 4-9-1 record. After one loss, 31-7 to the Packers, the Detroit fans with anonymous voices sang a shameful dirge to Gilmer: "Goodbye Harry, goodbye Harry, we hate to see you go."

"The singin' was very poor," said Gilmer, retaining his sense of humor.

Yepremian was erratic. But at Minnesota he kicked six field goals, the most ever kicked at the time in a pro game, to beat the Vikings 32-31.

The victory merely interrupted the string of losses which caused the Lions to finish tied for last with the Vikings.

On a plane ride from league realignment meetings in New York late in the season, Ford indicated that Joe Schmidt would be elevated to head coach for 1967.

On January 5, 1967, it became public knowledge that Gilmer had been fired and Schmidt would be hired as head coach. Gilmer was paid off for the third year of his contract. He had suffered in Detroit, but he always had maintained his quaint sense of humor. At his final game, a 28-16 loss to the Vikings, the Detroit fans had pelted him with snowballs from the grandstands. Even his players were appalled. In a final gesture, they shielded him during the bombardment with their own bodies.

On January 11, 1967, Joe Schmidt, with 13 years as a player and one as an assistant coach, became head coach of the Lions. He was not quite 35. He was given a five-year contract at $50,000 a year.

His mandate was to restore discipline to a wild, uncontrolled ballclub – and to make it into a winner in the five-year period.

In a companion move, Ford gave Russ Thomas the title of general manager, although Thomas maintained the same duties he had performed as personnel director. Edwin J. Anderson, who had been titular general manager, remained as a vice-president. Carl Brettschneider was made director of player personnel.

"I'm going to make every effort to bring Detroit back to where we used to be," said Schmidt. "I feel we have 16 or 18 good football players here now I'd want on my ballclub. If there aren't people I feel are capable of making

us champions, then I want to get rid of them."

Schmidt's contract gave him the freedom to run the trading and drafting aspect. It was a freedom Gilmer didn't have. And George Wilson had quit partially because such latitude was removed. Schmidt negotiated his contract with Ford a week before he signed. Definition of duties was part of the reason for the drawn out negotiations.

Schmidt would coach the Lions through a six-year bittersweet regime. Through astute drafting in the early years, the Lions headed upwards from the bottom, reached the playoffs in four years – then faded again.

Schmidt assembled a staff from which there would be no defections for the duration of his regime. Bill McPeak and Chuck Knox were brought in and charged with building a viable offense. John North was the only holdover from Gilmer's staff as coach for the receivers. Schmidt hired old teammates Jim David and Jim Martin to coach the defense, the prominent strength of the club.

Two months after he became head coach, the NFL and AFL conducted its inaugural combined draft. It was March of 1967. The Lions drafted Mel Farr on the first round. Schmidt envisioned an explosive backfield of rookie runners, Farr and Nick Eddy, the 1966 future selection. Lem Barney, a defensive back from Jackson State, was picked on the second round. Paul Naumoff and Mike Weger were other draftees. Thomas prevailed on Chuck Walton, a previous draft choice who had gone to Canada four years earlier, to return to play in Detroit.

In training camp that year, Sweetan and Plum contested for the quarterback job. The old grudge between Schmidt and Plum made Sweetan the favorite.

The first Super Bowl had been played the previous January with the Packers winning for the NFL 35-10 over the Kansas City Chiefs of the AFL. Now in the summer of '67, the NFL and AFL clubs would be matched in preseason games for the first time. The Lions had the assignment of upholding the NFL's honor in the first interleague preseason game at Denver. The Broncos had been a bust in the AFL.

But history was made that day. For the first time, the AFL defeated the NFL on a football field. The Broncos won 13-7, with a rookie kicker, Errol Mann, providing the difference with two field goals. The Lions had the stigma attached of being the first NFL team to lose to the AFL in Joe Schmidt's first game as head coach.

Some of the pain was erased the following week against the Buffalo Bills. Mel Farr went 45 yards with a pass for a touchdown the first time he touched the ball as a pro. The Lions' hopes soared again.

But Eddy – who had signed with the Lions for a package estimated as high as $600,000 – soon incurred the first of a series of knee injuries. He would have an ill-starred career, wanting to contribute and not being able to. Schmidt's vision of a Farr-Eddy combo would be dashed.

Near the end of Schmidt's first preseason, he and Thomas negotiated a trade. They dispatched Roger Brown, who had not been a favorite of Schmidt's, to the Rams. In exchange, the Rams' George Allen gave the Lions a No. 1, a No. 2 and a No. 3 draft choice. The Los Angeles papers eulogized Allen's trading acumen. Brown did help Allen win a division title in Los Angeles. But the Lions used Allen's three draft choices to select invaluable young offensive talent – Earl McCullouch, Charlie Sanders, Jim Yarbrough – in the next draft. Jerry Rush replaced Brown as Alex Karras' defensive tackle partner.

At the end of training camp, Schmidt had to award the No. 1 quarterback designation to

Plum. The veteran had the experience and Schmidt had to lean toward him, despite their longtime enmity. Besides, Sweetan's off-the-field behavior made him a liability. Schmidt was stern in matters of discipline.

Lem Barney was the star pupil of training camp and won the left cornerback job as a rookie. Barney was a starter in his first regular-season game at Green Bay, against Vince Lombardi's Super Bowl I champions.

Early in the game, Bart Starr attempted a pass to Elijah Pitts in Barney's zone. Barney dived for the underthrown pass. He caught it on the grass, then somersaulted, jumped up and ran 24 yards to a touchdown with the intercepted ball. It was the first time he touched the ball as a pro. The Lions outplayed the champions and hung on to tie the Packers 17-17. In his first regular season game as coach, Schmidt had matched the imperious Lombardi. The following week, the Lions continued their mastery over the Browns 31-14.

But then, as had happened so often in years gone by, the Lions faded. Schmidt was a staunch one-quarterback coach, a philosophy developed as a young teammate of Bobby Layne. The new coach was a stubborn man and hung in with his starting quarterback. He remembered how a floundering Layne would suddenly become a heroic Layne and steal victories in the final seconds.

In his first year, though, Schmidt did not have the kind of quarterback he preferred. He switched to Sweetan as his starter, then back to Plum, then back to Sweetan. "The quarterbacks are driving me crazy," Schmidt confessed late in the season.

The Lions won their last game, 14-3 over the Vikings, when Barney intercepted three passes. It gave them a 5-7-2 record under their first-year coach. The Lions finished third in the realigned four-team Central Division, behind the Packers and Bears and ahead of the Vikings. The 14-3 victory in 1967 over the Vikings would become a piece of memorabilia for Schmidt. He never again would defeat them as head coach in Detroit, losing 10 straight in frustrating sequence.

There were honors in 1967. With 860 yards gained, Farr was chosen offensive NFL rookie of the year. With 10 interceptions (including a record-tying three for touchdowns), Barney was chosen defensive rookie of the year.

Another excellent draft could make the Lions competitive.

Before the draft, Schmidt wanted to obtain the vitally needed new veteran quarterback. He arranged a deal with the New Orleans Saints for Gary Cuozzo. Perhaps he was too presumptuous. Ford and Thomas didn't like the trade — and they refused to approve it.

At the 1968 draft, Schmidt, counseled by old ally and personnel director Brettschneider, wanted to select running back Mike Hull of Southern California on the first round. Ford and Thomas insisted the Lions draft Greg Landry, a young, obscure quarterback. Landry had been scouted at Massachusetts by Bobby Layne, who recommended him. When the Lions drafted Landry over Schmidt's objections, the coach put on his coat and stalked out of the draft room.

"I quit," he said, and he headed in the direction of his Bloomfield Hills home. Before he reached home, however, he reconciled himself to the fact that the absolute freedom he had expected was not to be his. He returned, subdued.

The draft turned out to be a bonanza, however. In addition to Landry, the Lions gained McCullouch and Sanders in the early rounds of the 1968 draft. Sanders soon would be the prototype of the tight end in pro football. Thomas also picked up Rockne

Three gifted young Lions of the offense for the 1970s: quarterback Greg Landry (far left), tight end Charlie Sanders and running back Steve Owens (right).

Freitas, a young tackle from the Steelers.

Three months later, Thomas made another trade with the Rams to obtain a veteran quarterback, Bill Munson, who had lost his job in Los Angeles to Roman Gabriel. To get Munson, the Lions gave the Rams a No. 1 draft choice, Milt Plum, Tommy Watkins and Pat Studstill.

But at the end of the 1968 preseason, Munson's shoulder was damaged, and Schmidt had to start the rookie, Landry, in the season opener at Dallas. Landry managed to complete his first six passes. One went to Farr for a touchdown that put the Lions in front. Then the youngster became totally confused. He threw four interceptions. The Cowboys trampled the Lions 59-13 in the season opener.

Any panic among the Lions' hierarchy was removed the next week. Munson returned to quarterback – and in his first start the Lions beat the Bears 42-0. The next week Munson talked Schmidt into trying for a touchdown pass instead of working for a field goal in the final minutes at Green Bay. The pass was good to Billy Gambrell – and the Lions beat the Super Bowl II champions 23-17.

In the October rematch with the Packers in Detroit, Munson fired two touchdown passes to McCullouch. The Lions led 14-0, but then they became conservative, and the Packers tied the score 14-14. In the final minute, Schmidt's strategy was to play to preserve the tie. The Lions ran out the clock while 57,302 fans booed the old Detroit folk hero.

Despite the boos, the tie had put the Lions into first place in the Central Division. The Lions were 3-1-1 . . . and happy.

But lofty aspirations soon vanished. The Lions managed only a single victory and a tie in their remaining eight games. They even lost 12-0 to the Eagles, a team that came to Detroit with a 0-11 record on Thanksgiving Day. The

4-8-2 record dropped the Lions into last place as the Vikings won the Central title. In one span the offense went 16 successive quarters without contributing a touchdown.

Schmidt's job appeared to be in jeopardy, but Ford stood behind him. "I think he's brought a great deal to this team," said Ford. "I'm satisfied with him."

But the coaching job was gnawing at Schmidt after only two years. "It's the hardest thing I ever had to do in my life," he said. "I can't even describe it. It's terrible."

Battling to save the jobs of some of his assistant coaches, Schmidt stayed. Like George Wilson, he was openly loyal to his colleagues on the staff.

Despite the absence of the No. 1 choice given to the Rams for Munson, the 1969 draft produced Altie Taylor, Yarbrough and flanker Larry Walton. Again the Lions were stressing the offense they needed so desperately – and neglecting the defense.

In the spring of 1969, the Lions' problems were in the front office. Brettschneider was considered the source for the polarized situation between the general manager and the coach. Schmidt and Brettschneider had been allied since they were linebackers together. They had led the anti-Gilmer faction on the coaching staff during the previous regime. So in March, 1969, Thomas fired Brettschneider as personnel director.

Brettschneider left with a volcanic tirade.

"Everyone in the NFL knows how screwed up this franchise is," Brettschneider said. "I don't want people to think it's my fault. I want them to know the truth about why Joe Schmidt isn't allowed to coach the team the way he sees fit."

The Lions called a press conference the same day to deny Brettschneider's charges. Unsmiling, Schmidt sat between Ford and

Thomas to offer a presentation of solidarity to a room full of reporters and television cameras.

"I feel like Robin Hood trying to run through Sherwood Forest without getting hit by an arrow," Schmidt said. "I believe the Lions can win . . . and we're no laughing stock. If any of you want to laugh at me, I'll meet you outside after this press conference and we'll straighten that out."

Thomas was even more adamant. "A bunch of damn lies," said the general manager. "No one ever tried to pressure Joe Schmidt into anything. Joe and I don't agree on everything. But we don't walk into a room with our fists up, either."

So with a united front, the Lions entered the 1969 campaign with the usual great expectations. Offense had been stressed in the rebuilding, and most of the players on the offense were young. The defense, while aging and somewhat ignored during the offensive buildup, remained viable.

Chuck Knox had reconstructed the offensive line, which two years earlier had been the club's biggest weakness. Young linemen such as Ed Flanagan, Chuck Walton, Frank Gallagher, Bob Kowalkowski, Rocky Freitas and Jim Yarbrough became early contributors.

A 5-1 record in the 1969 preseason sent the Lions soaring into their schedule. The season opened in Pittsburgh, where three years earlier Harry Gilmer had suffered a crushing loss. The Steelers, who would win only one game all season, made the Lions their ambush victim again. In an embarrassing performance, the Lions were dropped 16-13.

But the Lions rebounded to win their next two games, beating the Giants 24-0 and the Browns 28-21 with a comeback sparked by Farr and Eddy running together for the first time.

The next week, however, Bill Munson's hand was broken in a 28-17 loss to the Packers.

Landry, at 22, an apprentice quarterback with guts and confidence and a proclivity for running which concerned Schmidt, was asked to become leader of the offense.

"He runs so much, they ought to put a halfback's number on him," growled quarterback critic Alex Karras.

Landry recorded his first pro victory, 13-7 over the Bears, the next week. Then, in a courageous performance, he was smashed down by the Vikings, finishing the game with a badly sprained ankle. The Vikings beat the Lions 24-10.

The following week, Landry was unable to practice on his ankle. The shotgun formation was put in as an emergency measure. Greg Barton, the No. 3 quarterback, was the key man in the crash course. But on Sunday, Landry played from the T-formation against the 49ers. He managed a touchdown pass to Charlie Sanders which helped win the game 26-14. Immobile, Landry was buffeted around so often his passing net was minus one yard. But he was a winner, and the offense accepted him in the manner that the Lions' offense 17 years before accepted Bobby Layne.

Landry won three more games, for a four-game winning streak. The Lions were in the race against the Vikings – the rival that dominated them in the same way the Packers had in the early 1960s.

On Thanksgiving Day, with a four-game winning streak, the Lions played host to the Vikings. Landry had the Lions flying. The Vikings continued to be the superior marksmen, however. Minnesota destroyed the Lions 27-0, knocking them out of the race. And, to add insult, Landry suffered a shoulder injury that sidelined him for the year. Munson produced a 17-17 tie with Baltimore and victories over the Rams (28-0) and the Bears (20-3) to complete the season. It was a satisfying year.

The 9-4-1 record was the best since the 11-3 of 1962. It was the first winning record in five years. The Lions finished second.

The 1970 draft brought the Lions running back Steve Owens. Schmidt had stressed speed, but his running backs were getting hurt every year. Now he wanted a durable runner. Owens was the Heisman Trophy winner at Oklahoma. He had set college rushing records. But most of the scouts scoffed at him as a pro prospect because he was slow and had not been a pass catcher. Eighteen clubs passed him in the draft before the Lions took him, and they were ridiculed for their choice. Jim Mitchell, a defensive end, was another product of the draft in 1970.

Training camp was featured by a battle between Munson and Landry for the No. 1 quarterback job. Schmidt favored Landry, but in the final preseason game, Greg was indecisive and Munson was sharp. Schmidt awarded the job to Munson.

In the same game, Steve Owens' shoulder was crushed. He had already disproved general scouting reports by winning a starting assignment.

The 1970 schedule started at Green Bay. On the first play of the season, Munson connected with Chuck Hughes, a receiver who had been obtained from the Eagles, for a huge pass gain. The Lions were underway. They routed the Packers 40-0. Munson passed to Farr for two touchdowns. Barney intercepted a pass to score one. Errol Mann, who had beaten the Lions at Denver and then was picked up as a free agent after a $2.20 phone call, kicked four field goals. Landry ran 76 yards on a quarterback sneak.

The Lions followed with a 38-3 victory over Cincinnati, then beat the Bears 28-14. At 3-0, they were alone in first in the Central. They lost to the Redskins 31-10, but they beat the Browns 41-24 and the Bears 16-10.

They were 5-1, tied with the Vikings, their opponent in the seventh week. With touchdown passes to Farr and Larry Walton, Munson got the Lions ahead 14-7. And then the Vikings rallied to crush Detroit 30-17.

The next week the Lions were beaten 19-17 on Tom Dempsey's all-time record 63-yard field goal at New Orleans. At that point, Schmidt benched Munson and switched to Landry.

Landry started the next game at Minnesota. The Lions had to win to remain in contention for the title – and they held a 20-10 lead entering the fourth quarter. It seemed as if the Vikings' domination was about to end. Then the Lions' defense crumbled, and the Vikings scored twice to win 24-20, Detroit's sixth consecutive loss to the Vikings.

In 1970, the year of final NFL-AFL merger, the two teams with the best second-place records would qualify for the playoffs as "wild card" entrants. The Lions, who had been 5-1, were now 5-4. They had five games left, four of them against divisional leaders. Playoff dreams seemed optimistic.

With Landry prancing and passing, the Lions beat the 49ers 28-7.

Then in a classic game with a sensational comeback, they beat the Raiders 28-14 as Landry and Charlie Sanders collaborated on some unbelievable pass plays. The Lions beat the Cardinals 16-3 and the Rams 28-23 on Monday night television. Finally, with Lem Barney running kicks and passes back, the Lions finished with a 20-0 victory over the Packers.

The Lions had won the five games – and advanced into the NFC playoffs. They were going to Dallas, where Landry had been a 59-13 loser two years earlier in his first pro game.

After four seasons, the Lions had become winners and a playoff team under Joe Schmidt. The progress had been faster than anticipated.

The Lions, although they were second in the Central Division, had finished with a blazing streak. Some considered them the best team in pro football in December of 1970.

But their offense was still young, a little too young. In Dallas, fumbles and tightness cost them chances to score. The defense — with Karras, Walker and LeBeau in a meaningful playoff game for the first time — allowed only a field goal. Landry was trapped in the end zone for a safety. By a margin of 5-0 the Lions lost to the Cowboys. Dallas continued onward to the Super Bowl.

The Monday before the 1971 season opened, Alex Karras was released.

"He couldn't play anymore," said Schmidt. "He was a great player. But I told him he'd have to make the club this year like everybody else. It was the hardest thing I ever had to do."

George Allen claimed Karras for the Redskins, but Karras decided to leave football and go into show business fulltime.

An opening game defeat at the hands of Minnesota was the Lions' seventh loss in a row to the Vikings. But with Steve Owens starring, they beat the New England Patriots 34-7. After that, the defensive defects — the result of years of offense-oriented drafting — became apparent. They outscored the Falcons 41-38, then the Packers 31-28. A 31-7 rout of Houston was the Lions' fourth consecutive victory.

With a 4-1 record, Detroit was tied for first place with Minnesota. On October 24, 1971, the Lions were home against the Bears, whom they had defeated six times in a row. It was a wild game, featured by Ron Jessie's 102-yard kickoff return for a Detroit touchdown. Twice the Lions battled to take the lead. But the Bears went ahead 28-23 for a third time. Landry was guiding a march downfield. He fired a 32-yard pass to his reserve flanker,

Chuck Hughes, who made an excellent catch at the Bears' 32. Landry was working against the clock. On the next play, Hughes ran a post pattern downfield, cutting precisely. But Landry threw to Sanders, who was knocked away from the ball by Dick Butkus, the Bears' middle linebacker.

Hughes was returning to the huddle when he suddenly stopped, grabbed his chest and fell over. Butkus was the first to see him on the ground. He signaled frantically to the Lions' bench. Drs. Edwin Guise and Richard Thompson and trainers Kent Falb and Gary Tuthill worked feverishly over Hughes trying to revive him. But he was mortally stricken on the 15-yard line at Tiger Stadium. Chuck Hughes had died of a heart attack in a football game.

The Lions went to San Antonio, Texas, as a team to attend Chuck Hughes' funeral.

After their loss to the Bears, the Lions were out of first place — and they seemingly didn't care. Detroit's status in its final five games was the same as 1970. The Lions had to win all five to qualify for the playoffs as the wild card team. They won the first two, beating the Bears 28-3 and the Chiefs 32-21 on Thanksgiving as Sanders made some spectacular catches of passes by Landry.

But then they were upset 23-20 by the lowly Eagles. That loss was demoralizing. They lost to the Vikings for the eighth consecutive time, 29-10. The season ended with a 31-27 setback to San Francisco.

In the final game, Steve Owens, who had been considered an unlikely pro prospect by many scouts, became the Lions' first 1,000-yard runner. And Landry, the quarterback Schmidt had told not to run, set an NFL record with 530 yards rushing. Landry also was the NFC's top passer statistically and went to the Pro Bowl.

But it had been a discouraging season — a

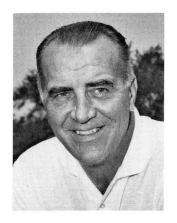

Don McCafferty (right) was named head coach of the Lions for the 1973 season.

7-6-1 record and the third second-place finish in a row.

The 1972 season opened with an impressive 30-16 victory over the Giants.

The next game was against the Vikings and there was no doubt now that the Lions had a phobia about Minnesota. The Lions had played well in most of the losses to Minnesota, but they always had endured heartbreak. This time they were terribly flat. They lost for the ninth time in a row to the Vikings, 34-10.

The Lions won three of the next four, losing only to the Packers 24-23 because of sloppy tackling on a kickoff return and a last-minute touchdown pass. Detroit had a 17-0 lead in the second quarter and blew it.

But the Vikings also were in trouble, losing close games. At last the Lions could win the division. They went to Minnesota with a 5-3 record. This time they played a strong game against the Vikings. They went ahead, but in the fourth quarter Minnesota rallied for a 16-14 lead. Landry slowly guided the Lions downfield. The aim was to get into field goal range and then go for the three points and the victory. It was an overcautious drive and the Lions played down the clock to the final six seconds. They were at the 25, a 32-yard attempt for Errol Mann. Flanagan's snap was slightly high. But Landry got the ball down and Mann kicked the ball squarely. He was accurate and sharp.

The ball didn't travel far. Bobby Bryant emerged from between two blockers and took the force of the kicked football on his face. The field goal attempt was blocked. For the 10th time in five years the Lions lost to the Vikings.

Even so, the Lions remained a formidable team in the race. They needed to win their final five, just as in the previous two years. They defeated the Saints 27-14 and the New York Jets 37-20. On Thanksgiving weekend, after the

Lions had won on Thursday, the Vikings and Packers both lost on Sunday.

"We're in the best shape we've ever been in," said Schmidt. "We win the title if we win our last three games."

The youthful Packers were the next opponent and the Lions were favored to handle them despite the one-point loss earlier in the year.

At Green Bay, with the title available for the taking, the Lions self-destructed against the Packers. They fumbled the ball away, and when they didn't do that, they threw it away. Again they failed, losing 33-7.

"Tension, pressure, crap . . . if you can't handle it, you shouldn't be in it," said Schmidt. "I guess I have to shoulder some of the blame. I'm the coach. Except in my days as a player, we'd be able to get ourselves up. If we weren't up I'd take care of it myself in the locker room. Today we don't have a player who can get all the other players up."

The Lions finished their 1972 season with a 34-17 victory over the Rams. They were 8-5-1, a disappointing year when they could have won their division. Instead they placed second for the fourth consecutive autumn, this time behind the Packers.

On January 12, 1973, after six bittersweet years, Joe Schmidt announced his resignation as head coach. He was gone after two decades, the final vestige of the Great Years of the '50s.

Before January had ended, Don McCafferty was hired as the Lions' new head coach. He had won a Super Bowl with Baltimore.

"I was with Baltimore 14 years as head coach and assistant coach," said McCafferty. "Front office personnel, coaches — we always worked together. It's my assumption that we'll be doing the same thing, working as a unit."

An age of sobriety, solidarity and silence seems almost out of character for the team of Layne, Parker, Schmidt and Karras.

The Names and Numbers

LIONS' ALL-TIME SCORES

1934
10–3–0, second place, Western Conference
Coach: George (Potsy) Clark

	Lions	Opp.
New York (H)	9	0
Cardinals (A)	6	0
Green Bay (A)	3	0
Philadelphia (A)	10	0
Boston (H)	24	0
Brooklyn (H)	28	0
Cin.–St. Louis (A)	38	0
Pittsburgh (H)	40	7
Cardinals (H)	17	13
Cin.–St. Louis (H)	40	7
Green Bay (H)	0	3
Chicago (H)	16	19
Chicago (A)	7	10
	238	59

1935
7–3–2, first place, National Football League
Coach: George (Potsy) Clark

	Lions	Opp.
Philadelphia (H)	35	0
Cardinals (H)	10	10
Brooklyn (A)	10	12
Boston (A)	17	7
Green Bay (A)	9	13
Boston (H)	14	0
Cardinals (H)	7	6
Green Bay (A)	7	31
Green Bay (H)	20	10
Chicago (H)	20	20
Chicago (H)	14	2
Brooklyn (H)	28	0
	191	111

NFL Championship

New York (H)	26	7

1936
8–4–0, third place, Western Conference
Coach: George (Potsy) Clark

	Lions	Opp.
Cardinals (H)	39	0
Philadelphia (A)	23	0
Brooklyn (A)	14	7
Green Bay (A)	18	20
Chicago (A)	10	12
New York (A)	7	14
Pittsburgh (H)	28	3
New York (H)	38	0
Cardinals (H)	14	7
Chicago (H)	13	7
Green Bay (H)	17	26
Brooklyn (H)	14	6
	235	102

1937
7–4–0, second place, Western Conference
Coach: Earl (Dutch) Clark

	Lions	Opps.
Cardinals (H)	16	7
Green Bay (A)	6	26
Pittsburgh (H)	7	3
Brooklyn (A)	30	0
Chicago (A)	20	28
Green Bay (H)	13	14
Cleveland (A)	28	0
New York (H)	17	0
Cardinals (A)	16	7
Chicago (H)	0	13
Cleveland (H)	27	7
	180	105

1938
7–4–0, second place, Western Conference
Coach: Earl (Dutch) Clark

	Lions	Opp.
Pittsburgh (H)	16	7
Cleveland (A)	17	21
Green Bay (A)	17	7
Washington (H)	5	7
Cardinals (A)	10	0
Chicago (H)	13	7
Cleveland (H)	6	0
Green Bay (H)	7	28
Cardinals (H)	7	3
Chicago (H)	14	7
Philadelphia (H)	7	21
	119	108

1939
6–5–0, third place, Western Conference
Coach: Gus Henderson

	Lions	Opp.
Cardinals (H)	21	13
Brooklyn (H)	27	7
Cardinals (A)	17	3
Cleveland (H)	15	7
Green Bay (A)	7	26
Chicago (A)	10	0
New York (H)	18	14
Chicago (H)	13	23
Cleveland (A)	3	14
Washington (A)	7	31
Green Bay (H)	7	12
	145	150

1940
5–5–1, third place, Western Conference
Coach: George (Potsy) Clark

	Lions	Opp.
Cardinals (A)	0	0
Pittsburgh (A)	7	10
Cleveland (H)	6	0
Cardinals (H)	43	14
Chicago (A)	0	7
Green Bay (A)	23	14
Washington (H)	14	20
Cleveland (A)	0	24
Chicago (H)	17	14
Philadelphia (A)	21	0
Green Bay (H)	7	50
	138	153

1941
4–6–1, third place, Western Conference
Coach: Bill Edwards

	Lions	Opp.
Green Bay (A)	0	23
Brooklyn (A)	7	14
Cardinals (A)	14	14
Cleveland (H)	17	7
Chicago (A)	0	49
Green Bay (H)	7	24
Cleveland (A)	14	0
New York (A)	13	20
Philadelphia (H)	21	17
Chicago (H)	7	24
Cardinals (H)	21	3
	121	195

1942
0–11–0, fifth place, Western Conference
Coach: Bill Edwards (3 games); John Karcis

	Lions	Opp.
Cardinals (A)	0	13
Cleveland (H)	0	14
Brooklyn (H)	7	28
Green Bay (H)	7	38
Cardinals (H)	0	7
Green Bay (A)	7	28
Chicago (A)	0	16
Pittsburgh (H)	7	35
Cleveland (A)	7	27
Chicago (H)	0	42
Washington (H)	3	15
	38	263

1943
3–6–1, third place, Western Conference
Coach: Charles (Gus) Dorais

	Lions	Opp.
Cardinals (H)	35	17
Brooklyn (H)	27	20
Chicago (A)	21	27
Green Bay (H)	14	35
Cardinals (A)	7	0
Green Bay (A)	6	27
Chicago (A)	14	35
New York (H)	0	0
Washington (H)	20	42
Phil-Pitt (A)	34	35
	178	238

1944
6–3–1, second place, Western Conference
Coach: Charles (Gus) Dorais

	Lions	Opp.
Green Bay (A)	6	27
Brooklyn (H)	19	14
Cleveland (H)	17	20
Chicago (A)	21	21
Green Bay (H)	0	14
Card-Pitt (A)	27	6
Card-Pitt (H)	21	7
Chicago (H)	41	21
Cleveland (A)	26	14
Boston (H)	38	7
	216	151

1945
7–3–0, second place, Western Conference
Coach: Charles (Gus) Dorais

	Lions	Opp.
Cardinals (A)	10	0
Green Bay (A)	21	57
Philadelphia (H)	28	24
Cardinals (H)	26	0
Chicago (H)	16	10
Boston (H)	10	9
Chicago (A)	35	28
New York (H)	14	35
Cleveland (H)	21	28
Green Bay (H)	14	3
	195	194

1946
1–10–0, fifth place, Western Conference
Coach: Charles (Gus) Dorais

	Lions	Opp.
Cardinals (A)	14	34
Washington (A)	16	17
Cardinals (A)	14	36
Los Angeles (A)	14	35
Green Bay (A)	7	10
Los Angeles (H)	20	41
Pittsburgh (H)	17	7
Green Bay (H)	0	9
Chicago (A)	6	42
Boston (H)	10	34
Chicago (H)	24	45
	142	310

1947
3–9–0, fifth place, Western Conference
Coach: Charles (Gus) Dorais

	Lions	Opp.
Pittsburgh (A)	10	17
Cardinals (A)	21	45
Boston (A)	21	7
Los Angeles (H)	13	27
Chicago (A)	24	33
Green Bay (A)	17	34
New York (H)	35	7
Cardinals (H)	7	17
Washington (H)	38	21
Los Angeles (A)	17	28
Chicago (H)	14	34
Green Bay (H)	14	35
	231	305

1948
2–10–0, fifth place, Western Conference
Coach: Alvin (Bo) McMillin

	Lions	Opp.
Los Angeles (A)	7	44
Green Bay (A)	21	33
Boston (H)	14	17
Chicago (A)	0	28
Los Angeles (H)	27	34
Green Bay (H)	24	20
Cardinals (A)	20	56
Washington (A)	21	46
Pittsburgh (H)	17	14
Cardinals (H)	14	28
Chicago (H)	14	42
Philadelphia (A)	21	45
	200	407

1949
4–8–0, fourth place, Western Conference
Coach: Alvin (Bo) McMillin

	Lions	Opp.
Los Angeles (A)	24	27
Philadelphia (H)	14	22
Pittsburgh (A)	7	14
Los Angeles (H)	10	21
Cardinals (A)	24	7
Green Bay (A)	14	16
Cardinals (H)	19	42
Chicago (A)	24	27
New York (A)	45	21
Chicago (H)	7	28
N.Y. Bulldogs (H)	28	27
Green Bay (H)	21	7
	237	259

1950
6–6–0, fourth place, National Conference
Coach: Alvin (Bo) McMillin

	Lions	Opp.
Green Bay (A)	45	7
Pittsburgh (H)	10	7
N.Y. Yanks (H)	21	44
San Francisco (H)	24	7
Los Angeles (H)	28	30
San Francisco (A)	27	28
Los Angeles (A)	24	65
Chicago (H)	21	35
Green Bay (H)	24	21
N.Y. Yanks (A)	49	14
Baltimore (A)	45	21
Chicago (A)	3	6
	321	285

1951
7–4–1, second place, National Conference

Coach: Raymond (Buddy) Parker	Lions	Opp.
Washington . . . . (H)	35	17
N.Y. Yanks . . . . (H)	37	10
Los Angeles . . . . (H)	21	27
N.Y. Yanks . . . . (H)	24	24
Chicago . . . . (H)	23	28
Green Bay . . . . (A)	24	17
Chicago . . . . (A)	41	28
Philadelphia . . . . (A)	28	10
Green Bay . . . . (H)	52	35
San Francisco . . . . . . (H)	10	20
Los Angeles . . . . (A)	24	22
San Francisco . . . . . . (A)	17	21
	336	259

1952
9–3–0, first place, National Conference

Coach: Raymond (Buddy) Parker	Lions	Opp.
San Francisco . . . . . . (A)	3	17
Los Angeles . . . . (A)	17	14
San Francisco . . . . . . (H)	0	28
Los Angeles . . . . (H)	24	16
Green Bay . . . . (A)	52	17
Cleveland . . . . (H)	17	6
Pittsburgh . . . . (A)	31	6
Dallas Texans . . . . . . (H)	43	13
Chicago . . . . (A)	23	24
Green Bay . . . . (H)	48	24
Chicago . . . . (H)	45	21
Dallas Texans . . . . . . (H)	41	6
	344	192

NFL Championship

Cleveland . . . . (A)	17	7

1953
10–2–0, first place, Western Conference

Coach: Raymond (Buddy) Parker	Lions	Opp.
Pittsburgh . . . . (H)	38	21
Baltimore . . . . (A)	27	17
San Francisco . . . . . . (H)	24	21
Los Angeles . . . . (H)	19	31
San Francisco . . . . . . (A)	14	10
Los Angeles . . . . (A)	24	37
Baltimore . . . . (H)	17	7
Green Bay . . . . (A)	14	7
Chicago . . . . (A)	20	16
Green Bay . . . . (H)	34	15
Chicago . . . . (H)	13	7
New York . . . . (A)	27	16
	271	205

NFL Championship

Cleveland . . . . (H)	17	16

1954
9–2–1, first place, Western Conference

Coach: Raymond (Buddy) Parker	Lions	Opp.
Chicago . . . . (H)	48	23
Los Angeles . . . . (H)	21	3
Baltimore . . . . (H)	35	0
San Francisco . . . . . . (A)	31	37
Los Angeles . . . . (A)	27	24
Baltimore . . . . (A)	27	3
San Francisco . . . . . . (H)	48	7
Green Bay . . . . (A)	21	17
Green Bay . . . . (H)	28	24
Philadelphia . . . . (H)	13	13
Chicago . . . . (A)	24	28
Cleveland . . . . (A)	14	10
	337	189

NFL Championship

Cleveland . . . . (H)	10	56

1955
3–9–0, sixth place, Western Conference

Coach: Raymond (Buddy) Parker	Lions	Opp.
Green Bay . . . . (A)	17	20
Baltimore . . . . (A)	13	28
Los Angeles . . . . (H)	10	17
San Francisco . . . . . . (H)	24	27
Los Angeles . . . . (A)	13	24
San Francisco . . . . . . (A)	21	38
Baltimore . . . . (H)	24	14
Pittsburgh . . . . (A)	31	28
Chicago . . . . (H)	14	24
Green Bay . . . . (H)	24	10
Chicago . . . . (A)	20	21
New York . . . . (H)	19	24
	230	275

1956
9–3–0, second place, Western Conference

Coach: Raymond (Buddy) Parker	Lions	Opp.
Green Bay . . . . (A)	20	16
Baltimore . . . . (A)	31	14
Los Angeles . . . . (H)	24	21
San Francisco . . . . . . (H)	20	17
Los Angeles . . . . (A)	16	7
San Francisco . . . . . . (A)	17	13
Washington . . . . (A)	17	18
Baltimore . . . . (H)	27	3
Green Bay . . . . (H)	20	24
Chicago . . . . (H)	42	10
Pittsburgh . . . . (H)	45	7
Chicago . . . . (A)	21	38
	300	188

1957
8–4–0, first place, National Football League

Coach: George Wilson	Lions	Opp.
Baltimore . . . . (A)	14	34
Green Bay . . . . (A)	24	14
Los Angeles . . . . (H)	10	7
Baltimore . . . . (H)	31	27
Los Angeles . . . . (A)	17	35
San Francisco . . . . . . (A)	31	25
Philadelphia . . . . (H)	27	16
San Francisco . . . . . . (H)	31	10
Chicago . . . . (H)	7	27
Green Bay . . . . (H)	18	6
Cleveland . . . . (H)	20	7
Chicago . . . . (A)	21	13
	251	231

NFL Championship

Cleveland . . . . (H)	59	14

1958
4–7–1, fifth place, Western Conference

Coach: George Wilson	Lions	Opp.
Baltimore . . . . (A)	15	28
Green Bay . . . . (A)	13	13
Los Angeles . . . . (H)	28	42
Baltimore . . . . (H)	14	40
Los Angeles . . . . (A)	41	24
San Francisco . . . . . . (A)	21	24
Cleveland . . . . (H)	30	10
San Francisco . . . . . . (H)	35	21
Chicago . . . . (H)	7	20
Green Bay . . . . (H)	24	14
New York . . . . (H)	17	19
Chicago . . . . (A)	16	21
	261	276

1959
3–8–1, fifth place, Western Conference

Coach: George Wilson	Lions	Opp.
Baltimore . . . . (A)	9	21
Green Bay . . . . (A)	10	28
Baltimore . . . . (H)	24	31
San Francisco . . . . . . (H)	13	34
Los Angeles . . . . (A)	17	7
San Francisco . . . . . . (A)	7	33
Pittsburgh . . . . (A)	10	10
Los Angeles . . . . (H)	23	17
Chicago . . . . (A)	14	24
Green Bay . . . . (H)	17	24
Cardinals . . . . (H)	45	21
Chicago . . . . (A)	14	25
	203	275

1960
7–5–0, second place, Western Conference

Coach: George Wilson	Lions	Opp.
Green Bay . . . . (A)	9	28
San Francisco . . . . . . (H)	10	14
Philadelphia . . . . (A)	10	28
Baltimore . . . . (H)	30	17
Los Angeles . . . . (A)	35	48
San Francisco . . . . . . (A)	24	0
Los Angeles . . . . (H)	12	10
Chicago . . . . (A)	7	28
Green Bay . . . . (H)	23	10
Baltimore . . . . (A)	20	15
Dallas . . . . (H)	23	14
Chicago . . . . (H)	36	0
	239	212

1961
8–5–1, second place, Western Conference

Coach: George Wilson	Lions	Opp.
Green Bay . . . . (A)	17	13
Baltimore . . . . (A)	16	15
San Francisco . . . . . . (H)	0	49
Chicago . . . . (H)	17	31
Los Angeles . . . . (H)	14	13
Baltimore . . . . (H)	14	17
Los Angeles . . . . (A)	28	10
San Francisco . . . . . . (A)	20	20
St. Louis . . . . (A)	45	14
Minnesota . . . . (A)	37	10
Green Bay . . . . (A)	9	17
Chicago . . . . (A)	16	15
Minnesota . . . . (H)	13	7
Philadelphia . . . . (H)	24	27
	270	258

1962
11–3–0, second place, Western Conference

Coach: George Wilson	Lions	Opp.
Pittsburgh . . . . (H)	45	7
San Francisco . . . . . . (H)	45	24
Baltimore . . . . (A)	29	20
Green Bay . . . . (A)	7	9
Los Angeles . . . . (H)	13	10
New York . . . . (A)	14	17
Chicago . . . . (A)	11	3
Los Angeles . . . . (A)	12	3
San Francisco . . . . . . (A)	38	24
Minnesota . . . . (A)	17	6
Green Bay . . . . (H)	26	14
Baltimore . . . . (H)	21	14
Minnesota . . . . (H)	37	23
Chicago . . . . (A)	0	3
	315	177

1963
5–8–1, fourth place, Western Conference

Coach: George Wilson	Lions	Opp.
Los Angeles . . . . (A)	23	2
Green Bay . . . . (A)	10	31
Chicago . . . . (H)	21	37
San Francisco . . . . . . (H)	26	3
Dallas . . . . (A)	14	17
Baltimore . . . . (H)	21	25
Minnesota . . . . (A)	28	10
San Francisco . . . . . . (A)	45	7
Baltimore . . . . (A)	21	24
Los Angeles . . . . (H)	21	28
Minnesota . . . . (H)	31	34
Green Bay . . . . (H)	13	13
Cleveland . . . . (H)	38	10
Chicago . . . . (A)	14	24
	326	265

1964
7–5–2, fourth place, Western Conference

Coach: George Wilson	Lions	Opp.
San Francisco . . . . . . (A)	26	17
Los Angeles . . . . (A)	17	17
Green Bay . . . . (H)	10	14
New York . . . . (H)	26	3
Minnesota . . . . (A)	24	20
Chicago . . . . (A)	10	0
Baltimore . . . . (H)	0	34
Los Angeles . . . . (H)	37	17
Green Bay . . . . (A)	7	30
Cleveland . . . . (A)	21	37
Minnesota . . . . (H)	23	23
Chicago . . . . (H)	24	27
Baltimore . . . . (H)	31	14
San Francisco . . . . . . (H)	24	7
	280	260

1965
6–7–1, sixth place, Western Conference

Coach: Harry Gilmer	Lions	Opp.
Los Angeles . . . . (H)	20	0
Minnesota . . . . (A)	31	29
Washington . . . . (H)	14	10
Baltimore . . . . (A)	7	31
Green Bay . . . . (H)	21	31
Chicago . . . . (A)	10	38
Los Angeles . . . . (A)	31	7
Green Bay . . . . (A)	12	7
San Francisco . . . . . . (H)	21	27
Chicago . . . . (H)	10	17
Baltimore . . . . (H)	24	24
San Francisco . . . . . . (A)	14	17
Minnesota . . . . (H)	7	29
Philadelphia . . . . (A)	35	28
	257	295

1966
4–9–1, sixth place, Western Conference

Coach: Harry Gilmer	Lions	Opp.
Chicago . . . . (H)	14	3
Pittsburgh . . . . (A)	3	17

Atlanta	(H)	28	10
Green Bay	(A)	14	23
Los Angeles	(H)	7	14
Baltimore	(A)	14	45
San Francisco	(A)	24	27
Green Bay	(H)	7	31
Chicago	(A)	10	10
Minnesota	(A)	32	31
Baltimore	(H)	20	14
San Francisco	(H)	14	41
Los Angeles	(A)	3	23
Minnesota	(H)	16	28
		206	317

1967
5—7—2, third place, Central Division

Coach: Joe Schmidt		Lions	Opp.
Green Bay	(A)	17	17
Cleveland	(H)	31	14
St. Louis	(A)	28	38
Green Bay	(H)	17	27
Chicago	(H)	3	14
Atlanta	(H)	24	3
San Francisco	(A)	45	3
Chicago	(A)	13	27
Minnesota	(H)	10	10
Baltimore	(A)	7	41
Los Angeles	(H)	7	31
Pittsburgh	(H)	14	24
New York	(A)	30	7
Minnesota	(H)	14	3
		260	259

1968
4—8—2, fourth place, Central Division

Coach: Joe Schmidt		Lions	Opp.
Dallas	(A)	13	59
Chicago	(H)	42	0
Green Bay	(A)	23	17
Minnesota	(H)	10	24
Chicago	(A)	28	10
Green Bay	(H)	14	14
San Francisco	(A)	7	14
Los Angeles	(A)	7	10
Baltimore	(H)	10	27
Minnesota	(H)	6	13
New Orleans	(H)	20	20
Philadelphia	(H)	0	12
Atlanta	(A)	24	7
Washington	(A)	3	14
		207	241

1969
9—4—1, second place, Central Division

Coach: Joe Schmidt		Lions	Opp.
Pittsburgh	(A)	13	16
New York	(H)	24	0
Cleveland	(A)	28	21
Green Bay	(H)	17	28
Chicago	(H)	13	7
Minnesota	(A)	10	24
San Francisco	(A)	26	14
Atlanta	(H)	27	21
St. Louis	(H)	20	0
Green Bay	(A)	16	10
Minnesota	(H)	0	27
Baltimore	(A)	17	17
Los Angeles	(H)	28	0
Chicago	(A)	20	3
		259	188

1970
10—4—0, second place, NFC Central Division

Coach: Joe Schmidt		Lions	Opp.
Green Bay	(A)	40	0
Cincinnati	(A)	38	3
Chicago	(H)	28	14
Washington	(A)	10	31
Cleveland	(H)	41	24
Chicago	(A)	16	10
Minnesota	(H)	17	30
New Orleans	(H)	17	19
Minnesota	(A)	20	24
San Francisco	(H)	28	7
Oakland	(H)	28	14
St. Louis	(H)	16	3
Los Angeles	(A)	28	23
Green Bay	(H)	20	0
		347	202

AFC First Round Playoff

Dallas	(A)	0	5

1971
7—6—1, second place, NFL Central Division

Coach: Joe Schmidt		Lions	Opp.
Minnesota	(H)	13	16

New England	(A)	34	7
Atlanta	(H)	41	38
Green Bay	(H)	31	28
Houston	(A)	31	7
Chicago	(H)	23	28
Green Bay	(A)	14	14
Denver	(A)	24	20
Los Angeles	(H)	13	21
Chicago	(A)	28	3
Kansas City	(H)	32	21
Philadelphia	(H)	20	23
Minnesota	(A)	10	29
San Francisco	(A)	27	31
		341	286

1972
8—5—1, second place, NFL Central Division

Coach: Joe Schmidt		Lions	Opp.
N. Y. Giants	(A)	30	16
Minnesota	(H)	10	34
Chicago	(A)	38	24
Atlanta	(A)	26	23
Green Bay	(H)	23	24
San Diego	(H)	34	20
Dallas	(A)	24	28
Chicago	(H)	14	0
Minnesota	(A)	14	16
New Orleans	(H)	27	14
N. Y. Jets	(H)	37	20
Green Bay	(A)	7	33
Buffalo	(A)	21	21
Los Angeles	(A)	34	17
		339	290

LIONS' RECORDS

SCORING
Most Points
Lifetime — 534, Doak Walker, 1950—55
Season — 128, Doak Walker, 1950
Game — 24, Cloyce Box vs. Baltimore, 1950
Most Touchdowns
Lifetime — 38, Terry Barr, 1957—65
Season — 15, Cloyce Box, 1952
Game — 4, Cloyce Box vs. Baltimore, 1950
Most Points After Touchdown Made
Lifetime — 183, Doak Walker, 1950—55
Season — 43, Doak Walker, 1951; 1954
Game — 8, Jim Martin vs. Cleveland, 1957 (title game)
Most Field Goals Made
Lifetime — 87, Errol Mann, 1969—72
Season — 25, Errol Mann, 1969
Game — 6, Garo Yepremian vs. Minnesota, 1966
Longest Field Goal — Glenn Presnell vs. Green Bay, 1934

RUSHING
Most Attempts
Lifetime — 938, Nick Pietrosante, 1959—65
Season — 246, Steve Owens, 1971
Game — 29, Mel Farr vs. Green Bay, 1968
Most Yards Gained
Lifetime — 3,933, Nick Pietrosante, 1959—65
Season — 1,035, Steve Owens, 1971
Game — 198, Bob Hoernschemeyer vs. N.Y. Yanks, 1950
Most Games, 100 or More Yards Rushing
Lifetime — 6, Nick Pietrosante, 1959—65
Season — 3, Nick Pietrosante, 1960
Longest Run From Scrimmage — 96, Bob Hoernschemeyer vs. N.Y. Yanks, 1950 (TD)

PASSING
Most Attempts
Lifetime — 2,193, Bobby Layne, 1950—58
Season — 336, Bobby Layne, 1950
Game — 49, Harry Gilmer vs. New York, 1955
Most Passes Completed
Lifetime — 1,074, Bobby Layne, 1950—58
Season — 181, Bill Munson, 1957
Game — 26, Bill Munson vs. Baltimore, 1968
26, Bobby Layne vs. Los Angeles, 1955
Most Yards Gained
Lifetime — 15,710, Bobby Layne, 1950—58
Season — 2,621, Earl Morrall, 1963
Game — 374, Bobby Layne vs. Chicago Bears, 1950
Most Touchdown Passes
Lifetime — 118, Bobby Layne, 1950—58

Season — 26, Bobby Layne, 1951
Game — 4, Bobby Layne (3 times); Greg Landry; Earl Morrall; Milt Plum, Tobin Rote and Frank Sinkwich
Most Passes Had Intercepted
Lifetime — 142, Bobby Layne, 1950—58
Season — 23, Bobby Layne, 1951
Game — 7, Frank Sinkwich vs. Green Bay, 1943
Longest Pass Completion — 99, Karl Sweetan to Pat Studstill vs. Baltimore, 1966 (TD)

PASS RECEIVING
Most Pass Receptions
Lifetime — 325, Gail Cogdill, 1960—68
Season — 67, Pat Studstill, 1966
Game — 12, Cloyce Box vs. Baltimore, 1950
Most Yards Gained Receiving
Lifetime — 5,220, Gail Cogdill, 1960—68
Season — 1,266, Pat Studstill, 1966
Game — 302, Cloyce Box vs. Baltimore, 1950

INTERCEPTIONS
Most Interceptions
Lifetime — 62, Dick LeBeau, 1959—72
Season — 12, Jack Christiansen, 1953
12, Don Doll, 1950
Game — 4, Don Doll vs. Chicago Cardinals, 1949
Most Yards Interceptions Returned
Lifetime — 787, Yale Lary, 1952—53, 1956—64
Season — 30, Don Doll, 1949
Game — 102, Bob Smith vs. Chicago Bears, 1949
Longest Interception Return — 102, Bob Smith vs. Chicago Bears, 1949

PUNTING
Most Punts
Lifetime — 503, Yale Lary, 1952—53, 1956—64
Season — 78, Pat Studstill, 1965
Game — 10, Lem Barney vs. Minnesota, 1969
10, Jerry DePoyster vs. Los Angeles, 1968
10, George Grimes vs. Chicago Bears, 1948
Best Average
Lifetime — 44.3, Yale Lary, 1952—53, 1956—64
Season — 48.9, Yale Lary, 1963
Longest Punt — 81, Bill DeCorrevont vs. Washington, 1946

PUNT RETURNS
Most Punt Returns
Lifetime — 126, Yale Lary, 1952—53, 1956—64
Season — 32, Tom Watkins, 1963
Game — 6, Lem Barney vs. San Francisco, 1968
6, Yale Lary vs. Pittsburgh, 1959
Most Yards Returned
Lifetime — 1,084, Jack Christiansen, 1951—68
Season — 457, Pat Studstill, 1962
Game — 184, Tom Watkins vs. San Francisco, 1963
Longest Punt Return — 90, Tom Watkins vs. San Francisco, 1963

KICKOFF RETURNS
Most Kickoff Returns
Lifetime — 91, Tom Watkins, 1962—67
Season — 29, Pat Studstill, 1964
Game — 7, Joe Watt vs. Chicago Cardinals, 1948
Most Yards Gained Kickoff Returns
Lifetime — 2,262, Tom Watkins, 1962—67
Season — 708, Pat Studstill, 1964
Game — 294, Wally Triplett vs. Los Angeles, 1950

SCORING
Most Points
Season — 347, 1970
Game — 52, vs. Green Bay, 1952
52, vs. Green Bay, 1951
Most Touchdowns
Season — 44, 1951
Game — 7, three times (1951 and 1952 vs. Green Bay; 1950 vs. N.Y. Yanks)

TOTAL OFFENSE
Most Yards Gained
Season — 4,577, 1971
Game — 582, vs. N.Y. Yanks, 1950
Most Offensive Plays
Game — 91 vs. Chicago Bears, 1953

RUSHING
Most Yards Gained
Season — 2,885, 1936
Game — 426 vs. Pittsburgh, 1934

Most Attempts
Season — 532, 1971
Game — 59 vs. Pittsburgh, 1952

PASSING
Most Yards Gained Passing
Season — 2,825, 1954
Game — 374, vs. Chicago Bears, 1950
Most Attempts
Season — 456, 1966
Most Completions
Season — 230, 1966

INTERCEPTIONS
Most Passes Intercepted
Season — 38, 1953
Game — 8, vs. Chicago Bears, 1968
Most Yards Gained Interception Returns
Season — 663, 1953
Game — 140, vs. Cleveland, 1970 (5 int.)

LIONS' ALL-TIME ROSTER

A

Addams, Abraham, E, Indiana	1949
Aiello, Anthony, B, Youngstown	1944
Alderman, Grady, G, Detroit	1960
Alford, Mike, C, Auburn	1966
Andersen, Stanley, E, Stanford	1941
Ane, Charles, T, So. California	1953-59
Arena, Anthony, C, Michigan State	1942-46
Ashcom, Richard, T, Oregon	1943
Atkins, George, G, Auburn	1955
Atty, Alexander, G, West Virginia	1941
Austin, James, E, St. Mary's	1939

B

Bailey, Byron, B, Washington State	1953-54
Baker, John, DE, N. Carolina College	1968
Banas, Stephen, B, Notre Dame	1935
Banjavic, Emil, B, Arizona	1942
Banonis, Vince, C, Detroit	1951-53
Barle, Louis, B, Duluth	1938
Barnes, Al, WR, New Mexico State	1971-72
Barney, Lem, DB, Jackson State	1967-72
Barr, Terry, B, Michigan	1957-65
Barton, Greg, AB, Tulsa	1969
Bass, Mike, DB, Michigan	1967
Batinski, Stanley, G, Temple	1941-47
Batten, Pat, FB, Hardin-Simmons	1964
Baumgartner, Maxie, E, Texas	1948
Behan, Charles, E, DeKalb	1942
Belicheck, Stephen, B, Western Reserve	1941
Bell, Bob, DT, Cincinnati	1971-72
Bernard, Charles, C, Michigan	1934
Berrang, Edward, E, Villanova	1951
Berry, Connie Mack, E, N. Carolina State	1939
Bingaman, Les, G, Illinois	1948-54
Blessing, Paul, E, Nebraska State Teachers	1944
Bodenger, Maurice, G, Tulane	1934
Booth, Richard, B, Western Reserve	1941,45
Bowman, William, B, William & Mary	1954, 56
Box, Cloyce, E, W. Texas State	1949-50, 52-54
Bradshaw, Charlie, T, Baylor	1967-68
Brettschneider, Carl, LB, Iowa State	1960-63
Briggs, Paul, T, Colorado	1948
Brill, Harold, B, Wichita	1939
Britt, Maurice, E, Arkansas	1941
Brown, Charlie, WR, N. Arizona	1970
Brown, Howard, G, Indiana	1948-50
Brown, Marvin, B, E. Texas State	1957
Brown, Roger, T, Maryland State	1960-66
Brumley, Robert, B, Rice	1945
Bulger, Chester, T, Auburn	1950
Bundra, Mike, T, So. California	1962-63
Busich, Samuel, E, Ohio State	1943

C

Caddel, Ernie, B, Stanford	1934-48
Cain, James, E, Alabama	1950-55
Callahan, J. R., B, Texas	1946
Callihan, William, B, Nebraska	1940-45
Calvelli, Anthony, C, Stanford	1939-40
Campbell, Stanley, G, Iowa State	1952, 55-58
Campbell, Mike, RB, Lenoir Rhyne	1968
Cardwell, Lloyd, B, Nebraska	1937-43
Carpenter, Lewis, B, Arkansas	1953-55

Cassady, Howard, B, Ohio State	1956-61, 63
Chantiles, Thomas, T, So. California	1942
Chase, Benjamin, G, Navy	1947
Christensen, George, T, Oregon	1934-38
Christensen, Frank, B, Utah	1934-37
Christiansen, Jack, B, Colorado A&M	1951-58
Cifelli, August, T, Notre Dame	1951-53
Cifers, Robert, B, Tennessee	1944-46
Clark, Al, DB, Eastern Michigan	1971
Clark, Earl (Dutch), B, Colorado Coll.	1934-38
Clark, Ernie, LB, Michigan State	1963-67
Clark, Wayne, E, Utah	1944-45
Clemons, Ray, G, Central Oklahoma State	1939
Cline, Ollie, B, Ohio State	1950-53
Clowes, John, T, William & Mary	1951
Cody, Bill, LB, Auburn	1966
Cogdill, Gail, E, Washington State	1960-68
Colella, Thomas, B, Canisius	1941-43
Conlee, Gerald, C, St. Mary's	1943
Compton, Dick, B, McMurry	1962-64
Cook, Gene, E, Toledo	1959
Cook, Ted, E, Alabama	1947
Cooper, Harold, G, Detroit	1937
Corgan, Michael, B, Notre Dame	1943
Cotton, Craig, TE, Youngstown	1969-72
Cottrell, Bill, T, Delaware Valley	1967
Crabtree, Clement, T, Wake Forest	1940-41
Creekmur, Lou, T, William & Mary	1950-59
Cremer, Theodore, E, Auburn	1946-48
Cronin, Gene, G, College of Pacific	1956-59
Cunningham, Leon, C, S. Carolina	1955

D

D'Alonzo, Peter, B, Villanova	1951-52
David, Jim, B, Colorado A&M	1952-59
Davis, Glenn, E, Ohio State	1960-61
Davis, Milt, HB, UCLA	1956
Dawley, Frederick, B, Michigan	1944
DeCorrevont, William, B, Northwestern	1946
DeFruiter, Robert, B, Nebraska	1947
DeMarco, Mario, G, Miami	1949
DePoyster, Jerry, K, Wyoming	1968
DeShane, Charles, B, Alabama	1945-49
Dibble, Dorne, E, Michigan State	1951, 1953-57
Diehl, David, E, Michigan State	1939-40, 1944-45
Doll, Donald, B, So. California	1949-52
Doran, Jim, E, Iowa State	1951-59
D'Orazio, Joseph, T, Ithaca	1944
Dove, Robert, E-G, Notre Dame	1953-54
Dublinski, Thomas, QB, Utah	1952-54
Dubzinski, Walter, G, Boston College	1941
Dudish, Andrew, C, Georgia	1948
Dudley, William, B, Virginia	1947-49
Dugger, John, E, Ohio State	1947-48
Duncan, James, E, Wake Forest	1950
Duncan, Rick, P, E. Montana State	1969

E

Earon, Blaine, E, Duke	1952-53
Ebding, Harry, E, St. Mary's	1934-37
Eddy, Nick, RB, Notre Dame	1968-72
Eiden, Edmund, B, Scranton	1944
Ellis, Lawrence, B, Syracuse	1948
Emerick, Robert, T, Miami (O.)	1934
Emerson, 'Ox', G, Texas	1934-37
Engebretson, Paul, T, Northwestern	1934
Enke, Fred, QB, Arizona	1948-51
Evans, Murray, B, Hardin-Simmons	1942-43
Evey, Dick, DT, Tennessee	1971
Flanagan, Richard, LB, Ohio State	1950-52
Forte, Aldo, G, Montana	1946
Freitas, Rockne, T, Oregon State	1968-72
French, Barry, G, Purdue	1948
Frutig, Edward, E, Michigan	1945-46
Fucci, Dominic, B, Kentucky	1955
Furst, Anthony, T, Dayton	1940-41, 44

G

Gagnon, Roy, G, Oregon	1935
Gallagher, Frank, G, North Carolina	1967-72
Gambrell, Bill, E, South Carolina	1968
Gandee, Sherwin, E, Ohio State	1952-57
Gatski, Frank, C, Marshall	1957
Gaubatz, Dennis, LB, LSU	1963-64
Gedman, Gene, B, Indiana	1953, 56-58
George, Ray, T, So. California	1939
Geremsky, Thad, E, Pitt	1951
Gibbons, James, E, Iowa	1958-68
Gibbs, Sonny, QB, TCU	1964
Gill, Sloko, G, Youngstown	1942

Gillette, Jim, B, Virginia	1948
Gilmer, Harry, QB, Alabama	1955-56
Gipson, Paul, RB, Houston	1971
Girard, Earl, B, Wisonscin	1952-56
Glass, William, G, Baylor	1958-61
Goich, Dan, DE, California	1969
Goldman, Samuel, E, Howard	1949
Gonzaga, John, T, No College	1961-65
Goodman, Henry, T, W. Va.	1942
Goovert, Ron, LB, Michigan State	1967
Gordon, Dan, DT, Hawaii	1972
Gordy, John, G, Tennessee	1957, 1959-67
Gore, Gordon, B, Okla. S.W. Teachers	1939
Graham, Lester, G, Tulsa	1938
Greene, John, E, Michigan	1944-50
Greer, Albert, E, Jackson State	1963
Grefe, Theodore, E, Notre Dame	1945
Grigonis, Frank, B, Chattanooga	1942
Grimes, George, B, Virginia	1948
Groomes, Melvin, B, Indiana	1948-49
Grossman, Rex, B, Indiana	1950
Grottkau, Robert, G, Oregon	1959-60
Gutowsky, Ace, B, Oklahoma City U.	1934-38

H

Hackenbruck, John, T, Oregon State	1940
Hackney, Elmer, B, Kansas State	1942-46
Kafen, Bernard, E, Utah	1949-50
Hall, John, B, TCU	1942
Hall, Tom, E, Minnesota	1962-63
Hamilton, Raymond, E, Arkansas	1939
Hamlin, Gene, C, Western Michigan	1972
Hand, Larry, DE, Appalachian State	1965-72
Hanneman, Chuck, E, Michigan Normal	1937-41
Hansen, Dale, T, Michigan State	1944, 1948-49
Harder, Pat, B, Wisconsin	1951-53
Harding, Roger, C, California	1948
Hardy, James, QB, So. California	1952
Harrison, Granville, E, Mississippi State	1942
Hart, Leon, E, Notre Dame	1950-57
Haverdick, Dave, DE, Morehead State	1970
Hekkers, George, T, Wisconsin	1947-49
Held, Paul, B, San Jose State	1955
Helms, John, E, Georgia Tech.	1946
Henderson, John, E, Michigan	1965-67
Heywood, Ralph, E, So. California	1947
Hightower, John, E, Sam Houston	1943
Hilgenberg, Wally, LB, Iowa	1964-66
Hill, Harlon, E, Florence State	1962
Hill, James, B, Tennessee	1951-52
Hill, Jimmy, DB, Sam Houston	1965
Hillman, Bill, B, Tennessee	1947
Hilton, John, TE, Richmond	1972
Hinchman, Hubert, B, Butler	1934
Hoernschemeyer, Bob, B, Indiana	1950-55
Hogland, Doug, G, Oregon State	1958
Hollar, John, B, Appalachian State	1949
Hopp, Harry, B, Nebraska	1940-43
Howard, William, B, So. California	1939
Huffman, Vernon, B, Indiana	1937-38
Hughes, Chuck, WR, Texas-El Paso	1970-71
Hupke, Thomas, G, Alabama	1934-37
Hutchison, Elvin, B, Whittier	1939

I

Isselhardt, Ralph, G, Franklin	1937
Ivory, Bob, G, Detroit	1947
Izo, George, QB, Notre Dame	1965

J

Jaszewski, Floyd, T, Minnesota	1950-51
Jefferson, William, B, Mississippi State	1941
Jenkins, Leon, DB, West Virginia	1972
Jenkins, Walter, E, Wayne	1955
Jessie, Ron, WR, Kansas	1971-72
Jett, John, E, Wake Forest	1941
Johnson, John (Jack), T, Utah	1934-40
Johnson, John Henry, B, Arizona State	1957-59
Jolley, Gordon, T, Utah	1972
Jones, Elmer, G, Wake Forest	1947-48
Jones, James, B, Union-Tenn.	1946
Jones, Ralph, E, Alabama	1946
Junker, Steve, E, Xavier	1957, 1959-61
Jurkiewicz, Walter, C, Indiana	1946

K

Kamanu, Lew, DE, Weber State	1967-68
Kaporch, Albert, T, St. Bonaventure	1943-45
Karilivacz, Carl, B, Syracuse	1953-57
Karras, Ted, G, Indiana	1965

189

Karstens, George, C, Indiana ... 1949
Kaska, Anton, B, Illinois Wesleyan ... 1935
Kearney, Jim, DB, Prairie View ... 1965-66
Keene, Robert, B, Detroit ... 1943-45
Kennedy, William, E, Michigan State ... 1942, 1944
Kent, Greg, DT, Utah ... 1968
Kercher, Richard, B, Tulsa ... 1954
Ketzko, Alexander, T, Michigan State ... 1943
Kipp, James, T, Montana State ... 1942
Kizzire, Lee, B, Wyoming ... 1937
Klewicki, Edward, E, Michigan State ... 1935-38
Kmetovic, Peter, B, Stanford ... 1947
Knorr, Lawrence, C, Dayton ... 1942, 45
Knox, Sam, G, New Hampshire ... 1934-36
Kopay, Dave, RB, Washington ... 1968
Kopcha, Joseph, G, Chattanooga ... 1936
Kostiuk, Michael, T, Detroit ... 1945
Kowalkowski, Bob, G, Virginia ... 1966-72
Krall, Gerald, B, Ohio State ... 1950
Kramer, Ron, E, Michigan ... 1965-67
Kring, Frank, B, TCU ... 1945
Krol, Joseph, B, W. Ontario ... 1945
Krouse, Raymond, T, Maryland ... 1956-57
Kuczinski, Bert, E, Pennsylvania ... 1943

L

LaLonde, Roger, DT, Muskingum ... 1964
Landry, Greg, QB, Massachusetts ... 1968-72
Lane, Dick, DB, Scottsbluff JC ... 1960-65
LaRose, Dan, T, Missouri ... 1961-63
Lary, Yale, DB, Texas A&M ... 1952-53, 56-64
Lay, Russell, G, Michigan State ... 1934
Layne, Bobby, QB, Texas ... 1950-58
Lear, Leslie, G, Manitoba ... 1947
LeBeau, Dick, DB, Ohio State ... 1959-72
Lee, Ken, LB, Washington ... 1971
Lee, Monte, LB, Texas ... 1963-64
LeForce, Clyde, QB, Tulsa ... 1947-49
Lewis, Dan, HB, Wisconsin ... 1958-64
Liles, Elvin, G, Oklahoma A&M ... 1943-45
Lindon, Luther, T, Kentucky ... 1944-45
Lininger, Jack, C, Ohio State ... 1950-51
Lio, Augustino, G, Georgetown ... 1941-43
Lloyd, Dave, C, Georgia ... 1962
Lomakoski, John, T, Western Michigan ... 1962
Long, Robert, E, UCLA ... 1955-59
Looney, Joe Don, HB, Oklahoma ... 1965-66
Lowe, Gary, B, Michigan State ... 1957-64
Lowther, Jackie, B, Detroit ... 1944
Lucci, Mike, LB, Tennessee ... 1965-72
Lumpkin, Roy, B, Georgia Tech. ... 1934
Lusk, Bob, C, William & Mary ... 1956

M

Mackenroth, John C, North Dakota ... 1938
Madarik, Elmer, B, Detroit ... 1945-47
Maggiolo, Chick, B, Illinois ... 1949
Magnani, Dante, B, St. Mary's ... 1950
Maher, Bruce, DB, Detroit ... 1960-67
Mains, Gilbert, T, Murray State ... 1954-61
Malinchak, Bill, E, Indiana ... 1966-69
Mann, Errol, K, North Dakota ... 1969-72
Mann, Robert, E, Michigan ... 1948-49
Manzo, Joseph, T, Boston College ... 1945
Margucci, Joseph, B, So. California ... 1947-48
Maronic, Stephen, T, North Carolina ... 1939-40
Marsh, Amos, FB, Oregon State ... 1965-67
Martin, James, G, Notre Dame ... 1951-61
Martinovich, Philip, G, College of Pacific ... 1939
Matheson, Jack, E, Western Michigan ... 1943-46
Matheson, Riley, G, Texas Mines ... 1943
Mathews, Ned, B, UCLA ... 1940-43
Mathewson, Morley, E, California ... 1941
Matisi, Tony, T, Pittsburgh ... 1938-39
Matson, Ollie, FB, San Francisco ... 1963
Mattiford, John, G, Marshall ... 1941
Maves, Earl, B, Wisconsin ... 1948
Maxwell, Bruce, RB, Arkansas ... 1970
Mazza, Vincent, E, No College ... 1945-46
Mazzanti, Jerry, DE, Arkansas ... 1966
McCambridge, John, DE, Northwestern ... 1967
McClung, Willie, T, Florida A&M ... 1960-61
McCord, Darris, DE, Tennessee ... 1955-67
McCoy, Joel, B, Alabama ... 1946
McCullouch, Earl, E, So. California ... 1968-72
McDermott, Lloyd, T, Kentucky ... 1950
McDonald, James, B, Ohio State ... 1938-40
McElhenny, Hugh, HB, Washington ... 1964
McGraw, Thurman, T, Colorado A&M ... 1950-54
McIlhenny, Donald, B, SMU ... 1956
McInnis, Hugh, C, Miss. Southern ... 1964
McKalip, William, E, Oregon State ... 1934, 36
McLenna, Bruce, HB, Hillsdale ... 1966
McWilliams, William, B, Jordan ... 1934
Melinkovich, Mike, DE, Gray Harbour JC ... 1967
Mello, James, B, Notre Dame ... 1949
Messner, Max, LB, Cincinnati ... 1960-63
Mesak, Richard, T, St. Mary's ... 1945
Middleton, David, E, Auburn ... 1955-60
Miketa, Andrew, C, North Carolina ... 1954-55
Miklich, William, B, Idaho ... 1948
Milano, Arch, E, St. Francis ... 1945
Miller, Robert, T, Virginia ... 1952-58
Miller, Terry, LB, Illinois ... 1970
Mills, Dick, G, Pittsburgh ... 1961-62
Mitchell, Granville, E, Davis-Elkins ... 1934
Mitchell, Jim, DE, Virginia State ... 1970-72
Mitrick, Frank, T, Oglethorpe ... 1945
Momsen, Robert, G, Ohio State ... 1951
Monahan, Regis, G, Ohio State ... 1935-38
Montgomery, James, T, Texas A&M ... 1946
Mooney, Ed, LB, Texas Tech ... 1968
Moore, Denis, T, So. California ... 1967-69
Moore, Paul, B, Presbyterian ... 1940-41
Moore, William, B, Loyola ... 1939
Morlock, John, B, Marshall ... 1940
Morrall, Earl, QB, Michigan State ... 1958-64
Morris, Glen, E, Colorado State ... 1940
Morse, Raymond, E, Oregon ... 1935-38, 40
Moscrip, James, E, Stanford ... 1938-39
Mote, Kelly, E, Duke ... 1947-49
Mugg, Garvin, T, N. Texas State ... 1945
Munson, Bill, QB, Utah State ... 1968-72
Murakowski, Art, B, Northwestern ... 1951
Myers, Tom, QB, Northwestern ... 1965-66

N

Nardi, Richard, B, Ohio State ... 1938
Naumoff, Paul, LB, Tennessee ... 1967-72
Nelson, Reed, C, Brigham Young ... 1947
Nelson, Robert, C, Baylor ... 1941, 45
Ninowski, Jim, QB, Michigan State ... 1960-61
Noppenberg, John, B, Miami ... 1941
Nori, Reino, B, No. ILlinois State ... 1937
Nott, Douglas, B, Detroit ... 1935
Nowatzke, Tom, FB, Indiana ... 1965-69

O

Obee, Duncan, C, Dayton ... 1941
O'Brien, William, B, NO College ... 1947
Odle, Phil, E, Brigham Young ... 1968
Ogle, Rich, LB, Colorado ... 1972
Olenski, Mitchell, T, Alabama ... 1947
Olszewski, John, FB, California ... 1961
Opalewski, Edward, T, Michigan Normal ... 1943-44
Orvis, Herb, DE, Colorado ... 1972
Owens, Steve, RB, Oklahoma ... 1970-72

P

Panciera, Donald, B, San Francisco ... 1950
Paolucci, Ben, T, Wayne State ... 1959
Panelli, John, B, Notre Dame ... 1949-50
Parker, Raymond (Buddy), B, Centenary ... 1935-36
Parson, Ray, T, Minnesota ... 1971
Parsons, Lloyd, B, Gustavus Adolphus ... 1941
Patt, Maurice, E, Carnegie Tech. ..., 1938
Pavelec, Theodore, G, Detroit ... 1941-43
Pearson, Lindell, B, Oklahoma ... 1950
Perry, Gerald, T, California ... 1954, 56-59
Peters, Floyd, T, San Francisco State ... 1963
Peterson, Ken, B, Gonzaga ... 1936
Piepul, Milton, B, Notre Dame ... 1941
Pietrosante, Nick, B, Notre Dame ... 1959-65
Pifferini, Robert, C, San Jose State ... 1949
Pingel, John, B, Michigan State ... 1939
Plum, Milt, QB, Penn State ... 1962-67
Polanski, John, B, Wake Forest ... 1942
Poole, Oliver, E, Mississippi ... 1949
Potts, Charles, S, Purdue ... 1972
Prchlik, John, T, Yale ... 1949-53
Pregulman, Mervin, G, Michigan ... 1947-48
Prescott, Harold, E, Hardin-Simmons ... 1949
Presnell, Glenn, B, Nebraska ... 1934-36
Price, Charles, B, Texas A&M ... 1940-41, 45

Q

Quinlan, Bill, DE, Michigan State ... 1964

R

Rabb, Warren, QB, LSU ... 1960
Rabold, Mike, G, Indiana ... 1959
Radovich, William, G, So. California ... 1938-41, 45
Randolph, Al, S, Iowa ... 1972
Randolph, Clare, C, Indiana ... 1934-36
Ranspot, Keith, E, SMU ... 1941
Rasley, Rocky, G, Oregon State ... 1969-72
Rasmussen, Wayne, DB, S. Dakota State ... 1964-72
Reckmack, Raymond, B, Syracuse ... 1937
Redmond, Rudy, CB, Pacific ... 1972
Reichow, Garet, QB, Iowa ... 1956-59
Reeberg, Lucien, T, Hampton Institute ... 1963
Reese, Lloyd, B, Tennessee ... 1947
Reynolds, Robert, T, Stanford ... 1937-38
Rexer, Freeman, E, Tulane ... 1944
Ricca, James, T, Georgetown ... 1955
Richards, Perry, E, Detroit ... 1958
Richards, Ray, G, Nebraska ... 1934
Richins, Aldo, B, Utah ... 1935
Rifenburg, Richard, E, Michigan ... 1950
Riley, Lee, B, Detroit ... 1955
Ritchhart, Delbert, C, Colorado ... 1936-37
Robb, Joe, DE, TCU ... 1968-71
Robertson, Lake, E, Mississippi ... 1945
Robinson, John, DB, Tennessee State ... 1966-67
Rockenbach, Lyle, G, Michigan State ... 1943
Rogas, Daniel, G, Tulane ... 1951
Rogers, William, T, Villanova ... 1938-40
Roskie, Kenneth, B, South Carolina ... 1948
Rosteck, Ernest, C, No College ... 1944
Rote, Tobin, QB, Rice ... 1957-59
Rouse, Stillman, E, Missouri ... 1940
Roussos, Michael, T, Pittsburgh ... 1949
Rowe, Robert, B, Colgate ... 1934
Rubino, Anthony, G, Wake Forest ... 1943, 46
Rush, Jerry, DT, Michigan State ... 1965
Russas, Albert, T, Tennessee ... 1949
Russell, Kenneth, T, Bowling Green ... 1957-59
Ryan, David, B, Hardin-Simmons ... 1945-46
Ryan, Kent, B, Utah State ... 1938-40
Rychlec, Tom, E, American Int'l ... 1958
Ryder, Nick, FB, Miami ... 1963-64

S

Salsbury, James, G, UCLA ... 1955-56
Sanchez, John, T, San Francisco ... 1947
Sanders, Charlie, TE, Minnesota ... 1968-72
Sanders, Daryl, T, Ohio State ... 1963-66
Sandifer, Daniel, B, LSU ... 1950
Sanzotta, Dominic, B, Western Reserve ... 1942, 46
Sarratt, Charles, B, Oklahoma ... 1948
Sarringhaus, Paul, B, Ohio State ... 1948
Sartori, Lawrence, G, Fordham ... 1942, 45
Saul, Bill, LB, Penn State ... 1970
Schibanoff, Alexander, T, Franklin-Marshall ... 1942
Schiechl, John, C, Santa Clara ... 1942
Schmidt, Joe, LB, Pittsburgh ... 1953-65
Schmiesing, Joe, ET, New Mexico State ... 1972
Schneller, John, E, Wisconsin ... 1934-36
Scholtz, Bob, C, Notre Dame ... 1960-64
Schottel, Ivan, B, NW Missouri State ... 1946, 48
Schroll, Charles, B, LSU ... 1950
Scott, Clyde, B, Arkansas ... 1952
Scott, Perry, E, Muhlenberg ... 1942
Self, Clarence, B, Wisconsin ... 1950-51
Seltzer, Harry, B, Morris-Harvey ... 1942
Sewell, Harley, G, Texas ... 1953-62
Shepherd, William, B, Western Maryland ... 1935-40
Shoals, Roger, T, Maryland ... 1965-70
Siegert, Wayne, T, Illinois ... 1951
Sieminski, Chuck, DT, Penn State ... 1968
Sigillo, Dominic, T, Xavier ... 1945
Simmons, John, C, Detroit ... 1949-50
Simon, Jim, G-T, Miami (Fla.) ... 1963-65
Sinkwich, Frank, B, Georgia ... 1943-44
Sirochman, George, G, Duquesne ... 1944
Slaby, Lou, LB, Pittsburgh ... 1966
Sloan, Dwight, B, Arkansas ... 1939-40
Smith, Bobby, DB, UCLA ... 1965-66
Smith, Harry, T, So. California ... 1940
Smith, J. D., T, Rice ... 1964, 66
Smith, J. Robert, Iowa ... 1949-54
Smith, Robert L., B, Texas A&M ... 1953-54
Sneddon, Robert, B, St. Mary's ... 1945
Soboleski, Joseph, T, Michigan ... 1950
Souders, Cecil, E, Ohio State ... 1947-49
Speelman, Harry, T, Michigan State ... 1940
Spencer, Oliver, T, Kansas ... 1953, 56, 59-61
Spangler, Eugene, B, Tulsa ... 1946
Speth, George, T, Murray State ... 1942
Stacco, Edward, T, Colgate ... 1947
Stacy, James, T, Oklahoma ... 1935-37
Stanfel, Richard, G, San Francisco ... 1952-55

Steen, James, T, Syracuse 1935-36
Steffen, Jim, B, UCLA 1959-60
Stits, William, B, UCLA 1954-56
Stokes, Lee, C, Centenary 1937-39
Stovall, Richard, C, Abilene Christian 1947-48
Stringfellow, Joseph, E, Mississippi Southern .. 1942
Stuart, Roy, T, Tulsa 1943
Studstill, Pat, FL, Houston 1961-67
Sucic, Stephen, B, Illinois 1947-48
Sugar, Leo, E, Purdue 1962
Summerall, George, E, Arkansas 1952
Swain, Bill, LB, Oregon 1968-69
Sweetan, Karl, QB, Wake Forest 1966-67
Swiacki, William, E, Columbia 1951-52
Szakash, Paul, B, Montana 1938-42
Szymanski, Frank, C, Notre Dame 1945-47

T

Tassos, Damon, G, Texas A&M 1945-46
Tatarek, Bob, DT, Miami 1972
Taylor, Altie, RB, Utah State 1969-72
Thomas, Calvin, G, Tulsa 1939-40
Thomas, Russell, T, Ohio State 1946-49
Thomason, James, B, Texas A&M 1945
Thompson, Bobby, DB, Arizona 1964-68
Thompson, Dave, C, Clemson 1971-72
Thuerk, Owen, E, St. Joseph (Ind.) 1941
Todd, Jim, HB, Ball State 1966
Tomasetti, Louis, B, Bucknell 1941
Tonelli, Anthony, C, So. California 1939
Topor, Ted, LB, Michigan 1955
Torgeson, La Vern, C, Washington State ... 1951-54
Tracy, Thomas, B, Tennessee 1956-57
Treadway, John, T, Hardin-Simmons 1949
Trebotich, Ivan, B, St. Mary's 1944-45
Tressa, Thomas, G, Davis-Elkins 1942
Triplett, Bill, RB, Miami, O. 1968-72
Triplett, Wallace, B, Penn State 1949-50
Tripson, John, T, Mississippi State 1941
Tripucka, Frank, QB, Notre Dame 1949
Tsoutsouvas, John, C, Stanford 1940
Tully, Darrell, B, E. Texas Teachers 1939
Turner, Harold, E, Tennessee State 1954

U

Uremovich, Emil, T, Indiana 1940-42, 45-46

V

Van Horn, Doug, G, Ohio State 1966
Van Tone, Arthur, B, Mississippi 1943-45
Vanzo, Frederick, B, Northwestern 1938-41
Vargo, Larry, E, Detroit 1963
Vaughn, Charles, B, Tennessee 1935
Vaughn, Tom, DB, Iowa State 1965
Vezmar, Walter, T, Michigan State 1946-47

W

Wagner, Sidney, G, Michigan State 1936-38
Walker, Doak, B, SMU 1950-55
Walker, Wayne, LB, Idaho 1958-72
Walker, Willie, FL, Tennessee State 1966
Walton, Chuck, G, Iowa State 1967-72
Walton, Larry, WR, Arizona State 1969-72
Ward, Elmer, C, Utah State 1935-36
Ward, Paul, T, Whitworth 1961-62
Ward, William, G, Washington State 1947-49
Watkins, Larry, RB, Alcorn A&M 1969
Watkins, Tom, HB, Iowa State 1962-67
Watson, Joseph, C, Rice 1950
Watt, Joseph, B, Syracuse 1947-48
Weatherall, Jim, T, Oklahoma 1959-60
Weaver, Charlie, LB, So. California 1971-72
Weaver, Herman, P, Tennessee 1970
Webb, Ken, HB, Presbyterian 1958-62
Seber, Richard, B, St. Louis 1945
Weger, Mike, DB, Bowling Green 1967-72
Weiss, Howard, B, Wisconsin 1939-40
Welch, Jim, RB, SMU 1968
Wells, Warren, E, Texas Southern 1964
Wetterlund, Chet, B, Illinois Wesleyan 1942
Westfall, Robert, B, Michigan 1944-47
White, Wilbur, HB, Colorado A&M 1936
White, Byron (Whizzer), B, Colorado 1940-41
Whitlow, Bob, G-C, Arizona 1961-65
Whitsell, Dave, DB, Indiana 1958-60
Wiatrak, John, C, Washington 1939
Wickett, Lloyd, T, Oregon State 1943, 46
Wiese, Robert, B, Michigan 1947-48
Wiethe, John, G, Xavier 1939-42

Williams, Bobby, DB, Central State 1969-71
Williams, Rex, C, Texas Tech 1945
Williams, Sam, DE, Michigan State 1960-65
Wilson, Camp, B, Tulsa 1946-49
Winkler, Randy, T, Tarleton State 1967
Winslow, Robert, E, So. California 1940
Wojciechowicz, Alex, C, Fordham 1938-46
Woit, Richard, B, Arkansas State 1955
Womack, Bruce, G, W. Texas State 1951
Woods, Larry, DT, Tennessee State 1971-72
Wright, John, WR, Illinois 1969

Y

Yarbrough, Jim, T, Florida 1969-72
Yepremian, Garo, K, No College 1966-67
Young, Adrian, LB, So. California 1972
Yowarsky, Walter, E, Kentucky 1955

Z

Zatkoff, Roger, G, Michigan 1957-58
Zawadzkas, Jerry, E, Columbia 1967
Zimmerman, Leroy, B, San Jose State 1947
Zofko, Mickey, RB, Auburn 1971-72
Zuzzio, Anthony, G, Muhlenberg 1942

Photography Credits

J. J. Abbate 23a, 37

Associated Press 39, 52

Vernon Biever 72-73, 74, 75, 76-77, 78, 79, 80-81, 140, 144, 166a

David Boss 56a, 102b, 133

Chance Brockway 149c, 167c, 174a, 177a

Cal-Pictures 148a

Cleveland Press Library 23b, 114

Merv Corning—Cover Illustration, 98a

Timothy Culek 19, 34, 139

Detroit Lions 14c, 32, 37, 68, 69a, 98d, 111, 115, 126, 143, 156, 159, 163b, 170

Malcolm Emmons 91, 93, 103, 177b

Bill Gallagher 143

George Gellatly 7, 18ac, 31, 48b, 50, 53, 58, 60, 98c, 99d, 129, 138, 150, 151, 164, 168b, 171, 175, 179, 181

Hall of Fame 11, 14a, 17ab, 29a, 46, 49, 97abcd, 98b, 99abcd, 128, 161, 162

Rod Hanna 178b

James F. Laughead 69c, 118b, 147, 148b, 170

Rob Meneilly 102c

Jack O'Grady 100-101

Hy Peshin 116

Russ Reed 84, 86, 87

Frank Rippon 66, 121b, 125

Russ Russell 178a

Herman Seid 114

Vic Stein 14d, 163a

Time, Inc 35, 116

Tony Tomsic 102ad, 104

Herb Weitman 149b

World Wide Photos 25, 33abc, 132a